Well Endowed

Also by Vivian Tu

Rich AF

Well Endowed

The Secrets to Strategic Spending, Building a Financial Foundation for You and Your Family, and Creating Lasting Generational Wealth

Vivian Tu

HARPER WAVE
An Imprint of HarperCollinsPublishers

This book is written as a source of information only. The information contained in this book should by no means be considered a substitute for the advice, decisions or judgment of the reader's financial or other professional advisor. All efforts have been made to ensure the accuracy of the information contained in this book as of the date published. The author and the publisher expressly disclaim responsibility for any adverse effects arising from the use or application of the information contained herein.

Without limiting the exclusive rights of any author, contributor or the publisher of this publication, any unauthorized use of this publication to train generative artificial intelligence (AI) technologies is expressly prohibited. HarperCollins also exercise their rights under Article 4(3) of the Digital Single Market Directive 2019/790 and expressly reserve this publication from the text and data mining exception.

WELL ENDOWED. Copyright © 2026 by Vivian Tu. All rights reserved. No part of this book may be used or reproduced in any manner whatsoever without written permission except in the case of brief quotations embodied in critical articles and reviews. For information, address HarperCollins Publishers, 195 Broadway, New York, NY 10007. In Europe, HarperCollins Publishers, Macken House, 39/40 Mayor Street Upper, Dublin 1, D01 C9W8, Ireland.

HarperCollins books may be purchased for educational, business, or sales promotional use. For information, please email the Special Markets Department at SPsales@harpercollins.com.

The ASK DOLLY™ trademark is used with the permission of Ask Dolly LLC. All rights reserved.

hc.com

FIRST EDITION

Designed by Chloe Foster

Library of Congress Cataloging-in-Publication Data has been applied for.

ISBN 978-0-06-345234-3

26 27 28 29 30 LBC 7 6 5 4 3

To my immigrant parents:

Thank you for leaving the only life you ever knew behind to give me a future you could only dream of. Your sacrifices became the foundation of the opportunities I was given, every story I tell, and every half-baked idea I dare to chase. This book, and all that I am, exists because you believed that your only child could carry the weight of two hearts' worth of ambition. I love you.

To my husband, aka Boo:

You are the greatest man I have ever met. You are my fiercest advocate and most trusted confidant, who sees greatness in me even when I cannot see it in myself. You push me to play bigger, dream louder, and never settle for anything less than extraordinary. Thank you for holding my hand in every triumph and through every challenge. Marrying you was the best decision I've ever made. I love you.

To my future kid(s):

I didn't have rich parents, but you will. I love you.

Contents

Introduction   1

Part One: Optimizing for Value

Chapter One: Deinfluencing Your Brain   11

Chapter Two: Investing in Yourself   35

Part Two: Building Your Financial House

Chapter Three: Buying a Car   57

Chapter Four: Buying a Home   78

Part Three: Growing Your ~~Family~~ Money Tree

Chapter Five: Marriage and Partnership   103

Chapter Six: Kids   131

Chapter Seven: Family and Friends   156

Part Four: Securing Your Legacy

Chapter Eight: Retirement	177
Chapter Nine: Inheritances and Windfalls	196
Chapter Ten: Insurance	210
Chapter Eleven: Estate Planning	235
Epilogue: Happily Ever After	253
Acknowledgments	257
Glossary	259
Notes	265
Index	271

Introduction

In the fifth grade, I got a part in the school play. We were putting on *Annie*, and young Vivian Tu was cast in the role of . . . Orphan Duffy.

And I was *pumped*.

Understand, this play was *the* hot ticket in town. Kids were desperate to get a part, to the point of crying and getting their parents to call the school and complain when they were cast as "random orphan number five" with no lines.

But not me. Because I, Vivian Tu, was lucky and talented enough to get a speaking role.

Ironically, I don't remember a single line of dialogue or any of the songs. But I *do* remember what happened after the show: Everybody's parents showed up with flowers, a camcorder, and a big Mom-and-Dad hug at the end.

Everyone's parents but mine, that is. Because they had to work.

For my parents, being Chinese immigrants, coming to this country (and not speaking the language at first) meant jumping into an environment where they felt that they were in *constant* survival mode. They had worked hard to get here, and they kept working, hard and often, to make ends meet and provide for our family.

Certainly, their prioritization of money bought me some creature comforts. They kept a roof over my head and food on the table—and eventually paid for my education. My parents did not spend money on *themselves*, but they did on me. They would buy me the newest Neopets game, Fruit Roll-Ups from the grocery store, and even an MP3 player when they first came out—whatever little things I wanted. Sometimes it seemed as though that might have been in exchange for feeling bad about missing the ballet recitals and the soccer matches. All because they had scrimped and saved and worked All. The. Time.

That was why they missed *Annie*. They missed my stage debut as Orphan Duffy. When the performance was over and all the other parents were mobbing the hallways and congratulating their kids, my parents were waiting outside in the car to pick me up and take me home.

In that moment, I made a mental note: I'll *never* do this to *my* kid.

Because to young Vivian Tu, nothing was more valuable than having that time with her parents.

Fast-forward to more recent times. I had just treated my parents to a luxury vacation overseas. And when I say luxury, I mean I spared no expense—we're talking first-class tickets from the United States to Asia, the baller suite at every hotel, prepaid Michelin star meals. For the final leg of their trip, I'd booked them flights to come visit me in New York on their way home. Their first morning here (after they took a li'l jet lag nap), we went out for dim sum. By the time we wrapped up, I still had another hour or so free before my next meeting.

And what did I do in that moment, as my parents—whom I rarely got to see now that I was an adult—were hanging out in my living room?

I opened my laptop to answer emails.

Thankfully, halfway through checking my inbox, I paused and had a little *What the hell am I doing?* moment. Yes, I'd spent all that money on gifting them a vacation—one I knew they'd enjoyed and had been thrilled to receive. And I'd *earned* that money by working hard—which was what I was about to pick right back up doing on my laptop. But I failed to realize that the most valuable part of the grand voyage probably wasn't the plane tickets, the eighteen-course tasting menu, or any of the other things I had leveraged my monetary wealth to obtain. It was my time. With them. The thing young Vivian Tu had been so desperate to have.

Now, you could choose to see this as a story about toxic hustle culture, but it's actually a story about *value*; not just *getting* or *having* money but *using* it to get what you really want out of life. It's about what it means to apply that wealth to something that actually matters: not fancy stuff (or a ton of zeroes in your bank account) but security, stability, and *time*, for us and for the people we care about.

The conclusion I came to in that moment was this: *I know the price of everything but the value of nothing.*

As someone who prides myself on being financially savvy, whose entire brand and business is built on expertise in that area, that was . . . kind of an alarming conclusion to reach.

As Your Rich BFF, I teach people how to be smart with money. I'm an ex–Wall Street trader and financial educator, after all. And I'm the bestie to a community of over 10 million people online and around the world who are helping one another get rich and stay rich. I firmly believe that not only *can* everyone learn the basics of financial literacy, they *should*.

In my first book, I laid out the essentials of how money—earning it, banking it, investing it, borrowing it, and (alas) paying taxes on it—works. I taught you how to maximize your income, grow your savings, wind down your debt, and more. I taught you basically everything I know about how to be *smart* with money.

And being smart with money is great—it's crucial, really. But to get the most out of your money, to put your money to work creating a life in which you and your loved ones are safe, secure, and stable, you need to be *wise* with money. You need to spend strategically.

That's what this book is all about. If *Rich AF* was about "how to maximize your money," *Well Endowed* is about "how to maximize your life *using* that money." It's the essential manual for how to spend your money in a way that builds wealth *and* aligns with your larger, long-term life goals. After all, it's not enough to have money; you need to leverage it. You need a strategy for how to use it wisely so that you can secure the life you want, spend time with those you want to, and pass down a financial legacy. You need to understand the value of your dollars, your time, and the people in your life.

If all that sounds intense, I get it. This stuff is important—but with me, it's not going to be boring or serious. (I mean, I made the title a dick joke. I'm basically a twelve-year-old boy.) So jokes about family jewels aside, I do want you to become well endowed. In this book, I'll give you the behind-the-scenes, inside-track intel on how to navigate big-ticket money decisions. Think of it not just as the insider's guide to things such as sharing finances with a partner, kicking the tires on major purchases (literally), and setting up retirement and end-of-life plans but also as a guide to optimizing your mindset.

Now, I am one of the *least* woo-woo people you will ever meet. I am not talking about manifesting wealth with your thoughts or cleansing your money aura or whatever. I'm talking about understanding what you want, why you want it, and what you're willing to do to get it—because ultimately, value is nothing more than a measure of how you feel about the money you spend. And no spreadsheet is going to be able to total that up for you. Yet even though money exists to bring us that value in life, strategically using that money is a basic life skill we tend to write off—or aren't taught in the first place.

I know that people can master the financial basics and still . . . struggle. Not struggle to pay their bills or make ends meet so much, but struggle with the bigger, life-ier decisions that can't necessarily be solved with a good budget or a better understanding of investing. It's these often overlooked decisions that are the key to obtaining true wealth in the physical and emotional senses. They have long-term repercussions—and almost no one talks about how important it is to get them right from the get-go:

Should I buy a house now, or should I wait for rates to drop?

Can I justify car payments? And should I lease, finance, or buy a vehicle outright?

How are we going to handle our finances if we get married?

Can we afford a kid? A dog?

What is a trust, and should I get one?

What will happen to the people I love most if I get sick and can't work?

These aren't questions of "How much will this *cost* me?" but questions of "Is this *worth it* to me?" And that's a much harder kind of question to answer.

Anyone can read a price tag and see how much something costs. Maybe there's a little fancy math involved if there's a loan, maybe there are some terms and conditions to pick apart, but at the end of the day, it's cold, hard numbers. Anyone can master the basics once they know the rules. But learning the rules to figure out the value something has to you? Where you can spend your money to get the *most* of what you want in the future and the *least* of what you don't? That's a lot trickier.

For one thing, a lot of us are living in very different environments from the ones we grew up in—but we're still holding on to the values we learned through osmosis in childhood. I don't mean values such as "Treat people with respect" and "Stand up for what you believe in"; I mean the value of a dollar *to you*. Unfortunately, very few of us have frank money conversations with our families; no one taught us things such as how and when it's "worth the money" to buy versus rent or have one, two, or no cars (or kids). If our parents did give us advice about "getting your money's worth," it might not be relevant to us by the time we need it; your parents may have been able to have two kids and a home by age twenty-five, but you might be thirty-five and struggling to make the rent. Conversely, you might have grown up in a paycheck-to-paycheck house and now pull in a healthy six figures. Even if you're still chilling in the same tax bracket you were raised in, odds are that your relationships, home, job, friend group, and/or general lifestyle don't exactly map to those of your family of origin. Bottom line: More often than not, we don't end up getting the guidance we need on how to use our dollars wisely.

For another, the odds are good that you've run into a life scenario that you just didn't know was a thing. For example, when it comes to strategic money-planning stuff such as trust funds, prenups, owning multiple properties, making an estate plan, and so on (things that, not coincidentally, have been low-key gatekept by rich people for years), you might straight-up not know what your options are. (And even if you've heard of them, they can be exhausting or intimidating to figure out.)

Finally, there are those big, life-y things you know are "worth it," that you might intellectually understand have value, but just . . . never get around to doing. You feel too _____ (fill in the blank: poor, old, unimportant, stupid) to _____ (fill in the blank: make a will, get a mortgage, plan your retirement). Or you feel as though you're too far down the road with whatever choices you already made and are too embarrassed to course correct. Or you're just plain avoiding the inescapable reality of death. (Sorry if I'm the one to break it to you, but you *will* die one day, RIP.)

My point is that it's no wonder most people don't have a real, meaningful understanding of how to leverage their money to get the most value. Leveraging those life decisions well can result in long-term growth of your assets, your money, your time, and your life. If we don't know how to spend strategically, we get in over our head (or stick our head into the sand), and when we don't know what to do, we default to what we learned while growing up. (In my case, that was "When in doubt, work.") We don't know about or fully understand the legal and financial tools at our disposal to safeguard the money we've earned.

The result? We end up spending money on the wrong things, *not* spending money on things that could really benefit us in the long run, and generally failing to get what we really want when it comes to our financial goals and our life.

Well, not anymore.

Here's how this book can help: I'll start off here with a little value system detox, breaking down how and why we got to this place of confusion, mixed messaging, and downright ignorance about what is actually worth our hard-earned money. Then I'll show you how to get the most value from yourself—by evaluating how and why you buy things, understanding how to calibrate your internal sense of time spent versus money spent, and more. After that, we'll dive into the big life decisions, from buying a car or a home to tying the knot and having some kiddos to planning for the future of yourself and your loved ones. I'll give you the strategic tools and tricks you need to make the best decision for *you and your future* every time. I'll show you how smart, value-based spending on almost every life decision can grow your money in a way that will enable you to have the time and the ability to secure your future and your legacy—which will allow you to secure the most valuable thing there is. And, spoiler alert, it's not a thing at all. It's people. The time to be with them. And the ability to take care of them.

That is the best and most critical way to deploy your dollars in life. Yes, the traditional markers of wealth—luxe vacations, VIP dining experiences, shopping sprees, and bottle services—are great (trust me, they are), but tell me that you wouldn't trade all of that in a heartbeat to get a few more good years with someone you lost too soon—or even just another few good years for yourself. I know it's hard (or morbid) to futurecast and think in those terms, especially when there's all that good stuff to spend on within reach right *now*. But I guarantee that before you realize it, one day will become now, and the diagnosis, the accident, the natural disaster will be real and right in front of you. And you don't want to wait until then to realize what's *truly* valuable, the one thing you can't get more of: time.

Young Vivian Tu knew that when she desperately wished her parents weren't so busy with work. Present-day Vivian Tu, I'm happy to report, got the memo and shut her laptop to spend some more quality time with her parents. Having the people you love together, healthy, happy, and secure; what else do you want from life, when it comes down to it? What else could be more worth your hard-earned cash?

That, besties, is value. That is ultimately what every dollar you spend should be working toward—that sense of security, stability, and time with the people you love. Because *that*? Is truly priceless.

Part One

Optimizing for Value

Real talk: The first step in securing true wealth is looking out for *you*. This starts with a value-based detox to help you change your mindset. Only then can you learn to optimize how you think and live in order to maximize your income, your savings, yourself, and your life—not because you can't rely on other people but because you are the only one who can know what *you* want, don't want, and care about deep down inside. (Not to mention that if you don't take care of yourself, your *self* will fall apart—and then how will you be able to get any enjoyment out of life?) Understanding what's worth your hard-earned money—why and how you buy things—requires reclaiming your mind from the con of consumerism and recalibrating it to recognize how to optimize the value of time spent versus money spent.

So let's drill deep on what it means to get right, think right, and do right by yourself so that you can tackle the rest of your life (social, financial, and otherwise) in the best possible shape and state of mind.

Chapter One

Deinfluencing Your Brain

While I was growing up, my parents and I very rarely went out to eat, but when we did, we would go to a Chinese buffet.

But that was not just dining out; it was a competitive sport.

I, as a child, always wanted to start with carbs, which anyone who competitively all-you-can-eats knows is not the correct strategy. So while I went right for the pizza and fried rice—which of course were right up front so as to lure you in—my parents would basically slap my hand away: "That's not how you eat at a Chinese buffet."

Instead, we had a system: We would stand next to the seafood section and wait for the server to bring out crabs, lobster, shrimp, and fish from the back. We would stock up on those, then eat our way through them before moving on to the meats. After that, we were allowed to have vegetables, but only the expensive ones such as snow peas—not salad. Finally, if we could still breathe or button our pants, we were allowed to have carbs. By the time we left the place, that buffet would have lost money on us; that was how ruthlessly efficient we were at eating.

Looking back, those buffets were probably $23.99 per person, which might not seem like a lot now but was a huge luxury for my parents back in the day. And while as a kid I never understood why I had to start with shrimp and work my way down to noodles, I now understand that my parents, given their financial situation, wanted to maximize the value for their money.

For me, because of the life lessons I was taught at a Chinese buffet, optimization feels like a birthright. The idea of maximizing value for money, no matter what temptations are trying to lead you astray, has been deeply ingrained in me. But it's important to acknowledge that most people don't receive an education on the difference between value and price or how to see (and ignore) the signals that are trying to derail you from your prudent financial path. And when you don't have a strong and grounded inner sense of what's worth your money, it is easy—nay, *trivially* so—for corporations and marketers to swoop in and try to convince you why *their* product is worth your money!

So here's the rewind: We didn't get to this point of misvaluing things out of nowhere. It wasn't an accident, but it also wasn't some kind of moral failing on our part. It has been a slow burn, and it's been a long time coming.

I'm going to unpack just why we tend to value the wrong shit, how consumerism became the bedrock of our modern society, and how marketing manipulates us into using our money in ways that don't actually get us the life we want. Before we go any further, I'm going to give you a little lesson that is part economic history, part media studies, and part sociology—as well as some inside intel from my time in ad sales. I'll tell you this not to scare or shame you but to lay the foundation for how you can optimize your money and find security and stability, even when *this* is the context you're operating in. Optimization is the bedrock of understanding how to get rich and *stay* rich—both in material items and in life. Without it, we cannot distinguish between needs, wants, and what will actually bring us value.

These days, I don't go to a ton of Chinese buffets, but the last time I was back home, I went to one with my parents. Without thinking or asking, I got my first plate of food and returned with eighteen oysters.

You would have thought I had won the Nobel Peace Prize the way my dad was beaming at me when I sat back down. I've really seen that kind of pride from him on only a few occasions, such as my college graduation and when I got my first job.

The point is, once you understand the forces in play around you, learn the rules of the game, and understand how to use them to get what *you* want, you'll make optimization second nature.

Consumerism Is a Long Con

You know how on historical TV shows, you often see the same character wearing the same outfit for the entire season? Like, even the rich-as-hell Crawleys on *Downton Abbey* had a limited wardrobe they'd rotate through.

The thing is, when you're watching those shows, it seems normal, right? You think, "Okay, this person is living their life in this one dress," not "Ew, look at this dirty loser wearing the same dress for six months."

Now compare those historical dramas to another television classic, *Lizzie McGuire*. Lizzie is cornered by mean girl Kate, who tells her, "Lizzie McGuire, you are an outfit repeater"—the most wounding thing possible. (Of course, Lizzie, by the end of that episode, is like, "I may be an outfit repeater, but you're an outfit rememberer, which is just as pathetic!" Touché, girl.)

But Kate's kind of right: However comical it is, there's an expectation that we need a new outfit for every event we attend. This isn't just expensive and isn't just terrible for the environment; it isn't really necessary: the average American woman owns at least a hundred items of clothing.[1] Do I genuinely think that if someone sees me in the same navy blue blazer twice, they'll assume I . . . what, don't wash my clothes? I have a washing machine. Dry cleaners exist.

So how did we get here? Why do we own, buy, and lust after so much more stuff than we need or even want?

Clothing's an easy place to see this play out, but the reality is that in every aspect of our lives, we live in a consumer culture in which, basically, you are what you buy. Consumerism is like the Matrix: It's everywhere, it shapes our reality, and we're not trained to see it for what it is. But once you *do* see it, you can dodge some serious bullets.

Seeing consumerism for what it is isn't easy. It's foundational to the way we live, baked into our society for generations now. To unsee it, we need to look back at history—and probably not history the way your textbook taught it.

Let's start with the Industrial Revolution, when the horse and buggy was still a thing but big factories were starting to open up shop. As mass manufacturing started to make goods faster and cheaper, there was more stuff available to buy and at drastically lower prices. At the same time, newfangled things called mail-order catalogs (the TikTok shops of their day) were bringing shopping to people's living rooms with Parcel Post and Rural Free Delivery (the Amazon Prime of their day) making it easy for even farm dwellers to have the latest goods.[2] Meanwhile, in cities, department stores such as Macy's and Gimbel's created an entirely new shopping experience—as in, they invented the idea of shopping *as* an experience, with elaborate displays, welcoming environments to linger in, and restaurants and tea rooms to keep shoppers' energy up.[3]

Suddenly, shopping wasn't a chore; it was a pastime. Prior to that, the idea that shopping was in and of itself a fun activity did not cross most people's minds.

Now, there's a little problem with shopping as a leisure activity: You can do it only if you, you know, have money to spend. Realizing that limiting factor, retailers debuted installment plans, which allowed people to buy now but pay later (with a little interest tacked on, of course), and Americans jumped at the chance, especially to finance a new category of consumer good, the automobile.[4]

So by the late 1920s, America was full of big stores crammed with shiny stuff to buy for no money down. What could go wrong?

The Great Depression, that's what, and also World War II. Times were tough, but that extended period of economic hardship ultimately created an even bigger pent-up desire to buy nice things again when the dust settled. And buy people did.

In the postwar period, Americans were prospering, thanks to government programs such as the GI Bill, and with that economic stability came a whole new way of life: new houses full of new appliances in new suburbs, where you needed a new car to drive around. Plus, because fewer and fewer families relied on their older kids for unpaid labor, young people between the ages of thirteen and eighteen suddenly had leisure time *and* pocket money, and marketers quickly cashed in on that "jackpot market" with a boom of teen culture–focused goods from saddle shoes to prom dresses.[5] And with almost 86 percent of American households owning a TV by 1959 (up from just 9 percent in 1950[6]), mass advertising could now find people in their own living rooms and show them all the latest and greatest goods they were missing out on.

The way we bought things got simpler, too. The layaway buying plans of the early twentieth century got a technological upgrade in the form of credit cards. Now, rather than having to maintain a line of credit at every individual store, consumers could carry a single American Express or Diner's Club card to charge all kinds of purchases simply and quickly.[7]

The late 1960s and 1970s saw the rise of more and more dual-income households in the middle class and above (whereas previously a home with two adult earners usually had two adult earners only if they were seriously strapped for cash). Add to that the increasing pressures of maintaining whatever the midcentury equivalent of a Pinterest-worthy home was while working a career, and a whole new market for convenience products emerged: cheap, designed to be disposable, but handy in a pinch.

By the 1980s, owning stuff as a status symbol was basically a given. The so-called yuppies (young urban professionals) dropped their paychecks on designer sportswear and fancy sushi dinners to show off, while teenagers flooded to shopping malls as their default hangout.

In the 1990s, big-box stores—Target, Walmart, Bed Bath & Beyond—became the new hotness,[8] not only promising shoppers that they could get everything they needed in one quick stop but also enticing them in with gimmicks (Kmart blue light special, anyone?) and limited-time sales (Black Friday officially became the busiest shopping day of the year). That was also the era of "it" toys such as Beanie Babies, Furbies, and Tickle Me Elmos that successfully created so much hype that people would pay four-figure sums (in nineties dollars, no less!) to own them—or really to be able to brag about owning them.

But obviously, the biggest game changer was the internet, which gets us to more or less where we are today. What started with the convenience of being able to buy or bid on something from the comfort of your own home has now become the default way to shop for pretty much anything, and from one-click buying to double-tap to Apple Pay, retailers and platforms are always looking for ways to make it easier for you to part with your money.

When companies realized that consumers were getting away with paying for software and hardware just once, they changed the game up; now everything from Photoshop to printer ink comes on a subscription service, we upgrade our phones every year even though it's pretty hard to see the leap from one version to the next, and we get roped into yet another hamster wheel of consumption. I'd call it all a big conspiracy, but let's be real: It's pretty obvious that they're doing this. And we play right along: Instead of replacing a dead laptop battery or getting a blouse repaired at the tailor's, we throw them out and just buy new ones—which is terrible for the environment *and* our finances.

That said—and with the history lesson over—being trapped on the consumerism hamster wheel is not a personal failing or flaw; it's not even in any one person's, or even one company's control. Ultimately, consumerism is driven by the simple fact that companies are for profit, and the goal of every for-profit company is to make money for its investors. That's it. It's not to create good products for you, it's not to change the world; it's to turn a profit. Companies are legally obligated to make decisions that will benefit their shareholders; they don't have to do anything to make *your* life better. When push comes to shove, they don't reeeeally care about you that much, except insofar as you represent money to spend. But they sure want you to think they do. They want you to think that their products are not just the best but something you *need*. And they have many ways of getting into your head. Let's first talk about consumerism brainworms: advertising.

The Psychological Aspects of Advertising and Consumerism

In *Rich AF*, I talked about how we don't learn basic financial literacy in schools. Well, guess what else we don't learn in schools? Basic *media* literacy, the ability to see the message *behind* the message: to read between the lines, be appropriately skeptical, and understand how the content (including and especially the ads) you scroll through influences your thoughts, choices, and even mood. Media literacy is crucial these days because advertising is everywhere, and it is fine-tuned to a scary degree to get you to buy stuff.

How do I know? Because that used to be my job.

When I worked in Ad Sales at BuzzFeed, I worked with brands that tried to tug at your heartstrings—because a vacation's not just a vacation but a chance to create priceless family memories. I worked with brands that embraced the hustle culture and appealed to corporate employees by emphasizing maximizing their efficiency and becoming better at work so they could earn more money. I worked with brands that promised that the sooner you buy its skin care products, the sooner your life will be good, *finally*. I worked with brands that promised "If you buy this mattress, you will never have a bad night's sleep again."

Basically, we used every marketing tactic in the book. And notice that most of them aren't just saying, "This product is the best at what it does; buy it." That's because advertising isn't supposed to prove that something's the best; it's supposed to create a need.

Here's the deal. Every single product has what's called a total addressable market, or TAM. Say you've got an eczema cream: There are only so many people on this planet with eczema, so that's the start of the TAM. But of those people, some people can't afford the product, some people's insurance companies won't pay for it, some people's doctors won't recommend it. The TAM is everyone who has a need that a product can fill *and* who is able and willing to pay for it.

When a company starts out, it can reach only a very small portion of the TAM organically—through word of mouth, basically. By using advertising and marketing, however, it can reach more of its TAM, spreading the product gospel. But not only that: By using psychological tactics, companies can actually bring people into a TAM and expand the available pool of potential buyers. Ultimately, the goal isn't just to tap into as much of the existing TAM as possible, it's to expand the TAM as much as possible.

This is where advertising tactics can be particularly powerful and persuasive. It's why Pedialyte started partnering with influencers to soft-promote its children's rehydration solution as a hangover cure. It's why Ozempic went from being an effective diabetes treatment to a weight loss solution to a way for skinny celebs to get even skinnier. The bigger the TAM, the bigger the potential profit.

If you don't know what those tactics are, it is so easy to get sucked in by them (I know I still do sometimes). So let's run down just how and why advertisers mess with our heads and get us to pay for goods and services we may not need.

Emotional Appeal

We spend money to feel good—or not to feel bad—and advertisers know it. That's why instead of just giving you the facts about how good a product is and letting you come to a rational conclusion, they tap into feelings: happiness, fear, nostalgia, empathy.

A luxury car ad uses fast-paced cuts to get your pulse racing. A charity ad shows you sad puppies in cages to make you feel compassionate. An ad for hard seltzer shows you hot young singles having fun at a pool.

The images, clips, colors, and music that come together to form even the blippiest of short-form ads do *not* arise by accident; they're tailored to a specific emotional vibe that you're supposed to associate with a product or service's producer.

Things to ask yourself:
- Do I want the product in the advertisement, or do I want to be a character in the advertisement?
- Am I projecting personal changes that may come as a "result" of purchasing this product? Do I realize that this is actually quite unlikely?

Beauty Standards and Gender Norms

So much of our existence as human beings has been deeply impacted by the marketing world, and the media in general. We've been fed an unattainable beauty standard based on celebrities who say, "Oh, I just gua sha!" when they've actually had a facelift.

If you ever partake in retail beauty and "hot girl" stuff, I probably don't have to explain the mentality. It's like "If I get lash extensions, I'll be hot." "If I get lipo, I'll be hot." "If I have this moisturizer, this serum, this mascara, this lip gloss, I'll be hot." You won't be any hotter than you are now, unless you're making massive plastic surgery changes, in which case more power to you, but it's not necessary.

It's not just our ideas about what it means to be attractive and successful that come into play. I'd argue that our modern concept of what it means to be "feminine" or "masculine" comes mostly from advertising, too. To wit: Men didn't start giving diamond engagement rings until De Beers launched a campaign that basically made doing so the expectation (and shamed you for being too cheap *not* to spend money on a diamond), and women started shaving their legs only because razor companies wanted to sell twice as many razors and *made up a gender norm around it.*

It gets to the point of absurdity: Take my husband's deodorant, which is called "sports drive." What does "sports drive" smell like, I ask you? Or the shaving cream I once bought in "cashmere rain" scent, which makes equally no sense because neither cashmere nor rain has a particularly distinct smell.

Bottom line: The human need to be accepted and admired is powerful, and by making their products the key to that magical land of perfection and ideal form, advertisers can squeeze juuuust a little more money out of you.

The reality is that of course you don't need one more product to be hot, beautiful, or pretty. You need to address the root concern: Why do you want those things? Is it to gain the attention of others—your peers, or potential or actual partners? Is it because you feel inadequate at something—work, life—and are trying to buy your way to confidence? The solution isn't to buy another *thing*; it's to buy therapy.

Of course, it's more than okay to want to make changes to be your most beautiful, confident self, but you need to know why you're doing it: Is it from a place of confidence or a place of insecurity and fear?

Things to ask yourself:
- Do I ever find myself trying to overcompensate for my perceived shortcomings by throwing money at a problem?
- Are there parts of me that I do not like? If so, before I use money to fix the issue, is there a way I could improve the situation that is already under my control and free of charge?

Social Proof

If you're contemplating making a major purchase, what's the first thing you do? Read reviews, right? Or otherwise just get trusted, unbiased opinions. Companies know this. They splash their home pages with everything from five-star reviews to real-time (well, "real-time") notifications that "Sara from New Jersey just bought the Odette Settee in Espresso!" to fabricate a sense of "Real people are really buying and liking this." Or they run ads featuring "real customers" (together with tiny disclaimers at the bottom stating that the people were paid for their time and not just, like, brand superfans). Especially for "disruptors" or relative up-and-comers in a given industry that don't yet have the name recognition and trust that Coca-Cola or Starbucks has, social proof can subconsciously make people *feel* as though that product and its maker are trustworthy (while maybe also engineering a little FOMO to boot).

Things to ask yourself:
- Do I know a real live human person who owns this product and likes it?
- Do the celebs and influencers promoting this product use it themselves, or does this feel like a onetime cash grab?

Anchoring Bias and the Decoy Effect

In a famous study from 1974, psychologists asked participants what percentage of African countries belonged to the United Nations. But beforehand, they gave people a random number. What they found was that people's answers varied depending on which random number they heard before hearing the question.

This is anchoring bias at work: the idea that when you're in a decision-making situation where you aren't fully sure what to do or what the "right" answer is, you *anchor* yourself to the first suggestion you're given. This typically shows up in a situation such as salary negotiation: If your interviewer throws out $70,000 as a starting salary, you might subconsciously anchor to that number and counter with $75,000—even if you were hoping for $85k minimum.

Manufacturers and retailers *love* this bias. It's why they slap those "original price" stickers on sale tags: to make you think that you're not *spending* $120 on a jacket, you're *saving* $80 on a jacket that *was* $200! (Never mind that it probably never *isn't* on sale.) They're selling you the illusion of a deal as much as they are the product.

The decoy effect is another principle that companies deploy to hinder our ability to compare factors such as price and size. For example, one of my favorite pastimes is watching a movie in theaters, and my favorite thing is obviously the snacks, but those snacks are famously priced using this trick. Say a small popcorn is $9, a medium is $12, and a large is $13. If you're the average person, you'd opt for the large, right? (I would.) This is the decoy effect in action: If the options were just small and large, you'd likely pick based on the amount of popcorn you wanted, but when there are three options, people rely on comparison. Since the "decoy" of the medium size is present and it's only a dollar less than the large, you're tricked into thinking that the large is the best value overall, and the theater gets more of your money.

Things to ask yourself:
- How often is this product or service on sale?
- Am I buying this thing because I need/want it or because it feels like a "good deal"?

Reciprocity

To see this one in action, look no further than Costco. You're strolling through, pushing a cart full of bulk-buy toilet paper and laundry detergent, when a friendly employee hands you a sample of fancy cheese.

You didn't even want cheese, but now you feel the urge to buy a block. Your social brain is wired to reciprocate, to give something back because someone gave you something for free. Before you know it, the cheese is in your cart.

The same thing happens with those "We're giving you 15 percent off!" emails; you weren't even thinking of buying a new pair of boots, but knowing that the company was generous enough to offer you a discount? You feel compelled to return the favor. Or "Try for fourteen days for free"—sure, you *could* return that pair of leggings, but the company was so nice to let you try them out and they're pretty nice even if they're a bit out of budget, so . . .

Things to ask yourself:
- Is the product or service something I'd buy if I hadn't been given a sample or discount?
- Even if I'm getting a good deal, will I actually use said purchase in my day-to-day life?

Gamification

Those "Buy ten, get one free" punch cards are so last century. Companies have turned buying their products into full-on minigames, complete with points, levels, challenges, and rewards, which turns our natural human instincts for achievement, competition, and gratification into forces for spending.

Take Starbucks, for example. You earn "stars" for each dollar you spend, which takes the cash amount you've forked over and turns it into a fun abstraction, divorcing it from feeling like "real" money. Making more purchases promotes you from basic-ass green tier to deluxe gold tier, which taps into your competitive side. And you're bombarded with limited-time "challenges" and power-ups that leverage the feeling of FOMO and get you to Act Now. Plus, the app's visual tracker taps into the feeling of being "almost there" and ordering just one more cold brew to hit the next level. It may feel like just fun and games, but it's real-life money flowing from you to the company, and it works: these days, 40 percent of Starbucks' total sales are due to its rewards program.[9]

Of course, Starbucks isn't the only culprit. Everyone from Chipotle to Sephora uses these tactics, and damned if they don't work.

Things to ask yourself:
- Do I find myself increasing my spending on certain brands or at certain times of the year based on extra incentives?
- If so, had those incentives not existed, would I frequent the business as often or purchase as much?

Diversity Sells

In recent years, there has been a huge shift in how companies present their products. Not only are the models and actors in the marketing campaigns looking less and less like the flawless white housewives of the 1950s, but some companies are going so far as to address and acknowledge social justice issues outright. Which is heartwarming, and also 100 percent money motivated.

Diversity sells. The reason that every birth control and yogurt ad features a range of beautiful women who look as though they've come from a meeting of the United Nations is not that drug companies or dairy producers are suddenly megawoke; it's because audiences beyond middle-class white people have gained considerable spending power, and they're trying to court their dollars.

That's not to say that these campaigns can't have positive effects if they serve a genuine need (makeup products for a wider range of skin types, products that are usable by people with physical impairments) or donate some funds to a nonprofit cause (though you best believe that the companies are getting tax write-offs for their donations), but don't be fooled into thinking that big corporations are doing this out of the goodness of their hearts.

Things to ask yourself:
- Does the business I am giving my hard-earned money to truly believe in the causes and social initiatives that matter to me, or has this been a more sudden or recent development?
- If a business does claim to support certain causes, has it put its money where its mouth is through charitable donations, community programming, or investment in those causes?

Targeting

I saved the biggest and most sinister tactic for last: targeting.

When I worked at BuzzFeed, advertisers would work with us not just to run ads on BuzzFeed itself but to pay for certain audiences. We would target by geography. We would target by age. We would target by gender. We would target by ethnicity (not directly but through aligning with content targeted at certain ethnicities). We would target by sort of made-up demographics such as "household CEO," "pet parent," and "tech enthusiast."

In other words, we weren't just promising sales volume. We weren't just saying to marketing agencies, "Hey, we can get your products on a website that gets 10 gazillion eyeballs a month." We were saying, "We can get you in front of 2 million Latino millennials living on the East Coast," or "We can get you access to 3.5 million stay-at-home moms with kids under five." We were *precise*. And we could do it because we had data. So much data. On everybody.

To be sure, companies have always targeted their advertising by demographic (we've all seen *Mad Men*). But back in the preinternet days, the data any company—any *stranger*—could get about you was limited. You could get a name and address from a phone book (remember those?), documents such as marriage certificates and home deeds from county records, maybe a person's political affiliation, and then you could always make some educated guesses based on those facts. If a person signed up for a store loyalty card, that was a big one, too: Yes, they'd get a discount on their weekly box of Cheerios, but in return, General Mills knew that they were a loyal customer.

Now, though? When you visit a website, there's a tiny tracker on the page called a *pixel*: it's literally that size, a 1 by 1 pixel, typically in the corner, and you can't see it. But that pixel sticks to you like a barnacle and follows you around even when you visit other websites. It links your clicking and browsing and searching activity to your social media accounts, then throws that all together with the demographic info you fed into Facebook and basically fills in all the little details into a paint-by-numbers picture of you, the consumer.

These tracking pixels are why when you browse a store website for a pair of shoes, those shoes then follow you around the internet. You read an article, and there in the middle of it are the shoes. You're scrolling Instagram, and *boom*: shoes. By the third or fourth time you see them, you might think that it's divine intervention, as though the cosmos wants you to have them—and so you buy them.

But no; it's the internet overlords who want you to buy the shoes. They want to sell them to you because when you buy the shoes, Google gets paid (for selling your search data), the affiliate marketer gets paid (for driving you to the shoe website), the shoe manufacturer gets paid (for selling you its product)—everyone is incentivized for you to spend money.

Even crazier is the fact that with the rise of social media, companies have found ways to weave together entire personas. So they don't have to assume, Don Draper style, that a Le Creuset pan should be advertised to upper-middle-class women. They can target foodies. They can target chefs. They can target couples who just got engaged and are probably looking to upgrade their stuff with a wedding registry. They can even target people who have searched for "le creuset pans." So not only are they targeting people who've already looked at a product and making that product stalk them like Joe Goldberg in *You*, they're also targeting anyone with a high likelihood of wanting the product before they even know they want it.

This stuff *works*. How could it not? Surprise, surprise, the girl whose boyfriend is googling "engagement ring sizing" might be in the market for a white dress very soon. Surprise, surprise, the eighteen-year-old whose best friend just bought a laptop for college might *also* want a laptop—and maybe some bedding and a minifridge for their dorm, too. Like a lot of other people, I knew that I was leaving some kind of breadcrumb trail behind me, but I didn't know the extent of it until I started working in digital media sales.

The thing is, even as someone who has seen the back end, who has helped set up campaigns to target people, I still fall for them. I tell myself, "Come to think of it, I really do need this For Love & Lemons dress that I've now seen eighteen times." Yeah, no shit—you saw it eighteen times because you lingered on the website for a full three minutes. Companies know they've got you hook, line, and sinker—one little nudge, and you'll pull the trigger. So if it feels as though marketing is getting into your head—well, it is.

Things to ask yourself:
- Have I cleared my browser cookies or cache in a minute?
- Do I really need this, or can I just not escape seeing it on the web?
- Have I tried putting the item into my cart, X'ing out of the tab, and seeing if I remember it seven days later?

How Social Media Makes Marketing Even Worse

I am not a social media doomer—obviously. This is not me being like "Internet bad" or moralizing about screen time. But I also recognize that social media has crafted a perfect environment for marketers' psychological tricks to multiply exponentially, like a petri dish for consumerism. So I want to highlight a few ways in which we as a generation of consumers are *uniquely* subjected to forces driving us to spend more money.

Social Media Warps What "Regular" Means

Back in our parents' generation, it was about keeping up with the Joneses. We looked across the street with binoculars at those in proximity to us, roughly people who did the same things, worked the same jobs, had the same amount of money, and we compared the little minutiae of life. We knew who had the flat-screen TV or who got the new station wagon, but only within our little geographical area.

Now it's a different ball game, because since social media has been introduced, suddenly we are able to look behind the curtain at the most intimate moments of other people's lives. We can see how they live, where they live, what they do, what they eat, even if they're wildly outside our peer group. Suddenly we're seeing a level of wealth that is unattainable for 99.9999 percent of the population, and keeping up with the Joneses has become keeping up with the Kardashians.

But it's not just the ultrawealthy who alter how we see our lives. Social media has an insidious middle ground of "relatable" influencers: MomTok vloggers with spotless suburban kitchens, travel Instagrammers taking lavish vacations despite being "normal girls." They're normal people in that they're not celebrities, but at the same time, they're not *normal* normal—and, unfortunately, that's making us think that a happy life is very different from the one we have.

Social Media Builds Up the Bandwagon Effect

This can lead directly to a psychological principle known as the bandwagon effect, which is hopping on the bandwagon and making decisions based on what everyone around us is doing. When you see everyone else in your neighborhood driving a Tesla, you start to think you need one, too. When you see girls on Instagram carrying a new designer bag every day, you may feel compelled to buy a few yourself. And when you see people going on vacation weekend after weekend, you might start to think that that is normal and you should be doing it, too. What we *don't* see is how many of those people have large amounts of credit card debt or that their lavish vacation might actually involve eight people staying in one room. Because you don't see the army of things going on behind them, the assistants and hired help and family money or whatever's underpinning their lifestyle, you think, "I guess I have to buy the KitchenAid mixer and the Ninja CREAMi because *she* did."

Social Media Is a Series of Highlight Reels

When you're near your neighbors, the literal Joneses, you see not just the fancy parts of their life; sure, you see their new SUV, but you also see that the husband and wife do not talk to each other and don't seem very happy or that they're both working twelve-hour days to be able to afford their lifestyle.

But on social media, you get to see only the car. You don't have to see the rest of a person's life because you don't live next door and it's artfully kept out of view. The highlight reel deprives you of that dose of reality and the effort it takes to get those things.

Social Media Is Trying to Make Money Off of You

Speaking of earning money: Your incentives and those of the people and brands you follow are probably *not* aligned. You don't realize that the reason your favorite influencer has an unlimited budget for cool knickknacks from Anthro and the Stanley cup with all the doodads that go on top is that she's making affiliate revenue when you purchase those items. The tiny text in their bio or on their site saying "Hey, just so you're aware, we may or may not make money from any of the links you click on," the one that most people ignore? That's why they promote the products they do: They're getting a cut. This is true even of "review" websites such as Wirecutter, the Strategist, and my alma mater BuzzFeed: from "best humidifiers" to "best travel credit cards" to every Christmas list roundup, you better bet they're making money when you click. Most companies' incentives are not there to help you be a smart shopper; they are there to make money for shareholders, to be a for-profit company, and to generate cash.

What to Do About It: Understand Why You Buy

Let me tell you a story that both is and isn't about ripped jeans. When I was in middle school, I went to the mall with my girlfriend, and we ended up each buying the same pair of ripped jeans. After I got home, my mom found the receipt in the bag, and it basically started World War III. My mom and I had the *biggest* fight. She chewed me out hard, saying that those stupid ripped jeans weren't practical, they were so expensive, and I didn't understand the value of a dollar. Now, as a child, I had only one argument, which was "But . . . but . . . Lindsay bought a pair, too!"

My mom wasn't having it. "Yeah, well, Lindsay's dad's a lawyer, and *your* parents are not millionaires."

I stormed up to my room, distraught and sobbing. I wanted those jeans so badly, and now I felt humiliated.

That was when I first realized, starkly, that money is different for different families. It was a really painful experience but one that shaped my worldview and path going forward. Because that was also when I made the decision never to be limited by a lack of money. While some kids wanted to chase their passion for being an art historian, I wanted to chase money because I deserved ripped jeans. That was truly the impetus; my mom told me that my family wasn't wealthy, and because of that, I felt I didn't deserve ripped jeans, even though my girlfriend had bought the exact same pair. That really hurt.

Obviously, those ripped jeans are not something I've kept and cherished forever. But as I said, this isn't really a story about ripped jeans; it's about the psychology of value.

There's a theory that says whatever you felt you lacked as a child is what you try to purchase as an adult. For example, when I think about my childhood—ripped jeans aside—at a certain point, there was enough discretionary income to satisfy my material wants. But at the same time, both my parents worked, so I didn't see them much. And because I didn't spend enough time with the people I loved and cared about while growing up, I now spend all my money on vacations and experiences to be with friends or my partner. I overdo it on those.

For other people, if their parents were bad cooks, they spend money on going out to eat or fancy kitchen gear. If they always felt bored at home or had risk-averse parents, they might become event people, going to concerts, skydiving, backpacking around the world. (Ironically, years later, my mom told me that while she was growing up, she hadn't had money for nice clothes and the kids at school had made fun of her—so now her impulse is to spend any extra money on beautiful outfits. Go figure.)

Regardless of that theory, the truth is that how we value things, and how we use money to obtain that value are ultimately driven by our psyche. Most of us can cover our material needs enough to keep our human body alive; we may not have the swankiest apartment or the fanciest clothes or the organic-est food, but we can keep the machine running for another twenty-four hours. For everything beyond that, our emotions more than our animal needs tend to take the wheel.

That's why understanding the consumerism soup we're all swimming in and the mind games advertisers and media use is only half the process. The other half is understanding *ourselves* and what it looks like for *us* to pursue security and stability.

Ultimately, we have only so many days on this planet, and it's up to each of us to make the most of them—to play along with the rules of the game and still get as much as we can out of them. On planet Earth and in our capitalist society, that means having money and spending it. And because we have only a certain number of hours in a day and during those hours we can garner only a finite number of dollars, we have to be mindful of how we're spending them. If we're not, we might spend them on the wrong stuff—stuff we might enjoy in the moment but come to regret spending money on in the long term.

Time is the only resource you can't buy more of. Every one of us is born with a finite amount of time, and it only gets smaller as we go on. You can be born poor and die rich or be born rich and die poor. You can be born middle class and die middle class. It doesn't matter; time is the thing you can't get more of. And the last thing you want to feel at the end of your limited time is buyer's remorse.

So let's close out this chapter with a little introspection. Ask yourself:

1. What am I trying to achieve with my money?
   I don't mean like "I want to have groceries in my house" or "I want to own a Lambo." Work backward from the material to the emotional: If you spend a lot on date nights, is it because you want to be closer to your partner? If you drop thousands of dollars on your work wardrobe, is it because you want to be better respected in your professional life?

2. What am I insecure about? What did I lack as a child, and what could I be compensating for now?
   I'm talking about deep-down kinds of insecurities—not just "I hate the way my teeth look when I smile" but "I never felt pretty growing up." Marketers are eager to prey on those feelings, so recognizing them in yourself (and thinking about how you can

really use your money to contend with them) is a huge step forward.

3. How am I spending money to gain time?
Whether that involves getting more time back in your day or creating more quality time with the people you care about, this is a key question. Lifestyle upgrades and material things are all well and good, and I'm not arguing for not spending on them. But it's terrifyingly easy to take the people around us for granted and assume that we'll have access to them forever, and if we don't consciously make a point of spending our money to safeguard ourselves and the people we care about, it can just not happen, and then it's too late.

Money Management To-Dos for Chapter 1

- Keep an eye out for psychological tricks in the wild: The next time you see an ad, be it as you're swiping on your phone or as you're waiting for a bus, see if you can identify which of the mind games described on pages 17 to 30 is at work.
- See what dirt advertisers have on you: For each of your social media accounts (the major ones, at least), navigate to your account settings and look for a section called "Ad preferences," "Personalize your ads experience," or something similar (it probably won't be easy to find, sorry to say). Poke around in it and see just what demographic attributes the site is using to target you—you might be surprised (or horrified). You can (and probably should) opt out of as many targeting categories as they'll let you, so go ahead and do that, too.
- While you're at it, the next time you find yourself refreshing your feeds for the millionth time that day, open your email and unsubscribe from all the marketing emails you see. Do this for

thirty seconds a day, and you will drastically cut down on the amount of marketing you're served.
- Ask yourself the three "Why do you buy?" questions starting on page 32, and think deeply about your answers. Write them down if you feel so moved.

Chapter Two

Investing in Yourself

My parents recently just got into lawn care. And by that, I mean my dad spent hundreds of dollars on equipment and DIY tools just to kill our entire lawn, and now my mom is mad at him. This is all to say that they now have a lawn care guy. Every two weeks, William comes by and cuts their grass, treats any bald spots, and weed whacks to perfection.

For my parents, who have been so frugal their entire lifetimes, outsourcing any sort of housework was just not on their radar. But these days, they're getting to the point (and age) where my dad's back is not backing the way it used to, so mowing the lawn is a literal pain. To have someone come mow their entire lawn means that for $50, they not only get a lawn that's looking fresh and A-OK by the HOA, they also get the benefit of my dad not throwing out his back.

In other words, they're not *really* paying for a freshly mowed lawn (not solely, anyway); they're paying to get time back—and to better enjoy the time they have.

I probably don't have to explain to you that taking care of your *self* in the long term is a smart investment. Sustaining physical wellness is probably the closest thing to "buying time" we can do, and it is well worth it to put your money and energy into it. But you can also spend your money on *getting back time*—by either being more efficient at doing what you're doing (especially earning money) or outsourcing some chore entirely, which can also be a huge way to invest in yourself, optimize your life, and leverage your money to provide serious value.

I fully recognize that this attitude is not without controversy. Spending money on yourself, on your health and sanity, even on time-saving services (especially in the app economy, where anything can be in your hand in thirty minutes or less without your even having to talk to a human) is low-hanging fruit for financial gurus. Old-school money experts love to come at us (by "us," I mean millennials and Gen Zers, because it's always justified when *boomers* do it) for "wasting" money on these things. At the same time, we're living in a society where health care is often treated—and priced—like a luxury instead of the basic necessity it is. Even with "good" health insurance (by US standards), the basic tune-ups your body needs don't necessarily come cheap or without a ton of red tape. So it can feel as though we end up screwed (or criticized) no matter what we do.

I humbly submit that spending money to keep your body feeling good and working well is the prime directive—and a very close second is spending money to do as few of the tasks that you hate (or that hurt your back) while maximizing your time for the things you don't hate (or that earn you more money). After all, what good is having all the cash in the world if you have to work twenty-five-hour days, get sick and tired, or just plain suffer to get it? You—your body, your time, your self—are the foundation of your life, and to get the most value out of life, you've got to start with the person in the mirror. *You* are your ultimate investment.

So building on the idea of deinfluencing your brain and the importance of optimization, let's focus on how you can use your money intelligently to get the best day-to-day life for your human self as possible. Of course, spending on ourselves and our lifestyle feels as though it makes us happier—and it does. But let's go into how you can optimize your health care, self-care, and joy.

Insurance Plans 101

Health coverage in the United States is (technical term here) a huge mess. And while I haven't taken a survey, I strongly suspect that, due to the messiness of the system, the vast majority of people are not picking the best plan for their bodies *or* their budgets. The good news is that if you have any kind of medical coverage—whether through your employer, your spouse, or the marketplace—you have *some* level of preventive care covered by default. Use it or don't use it, it's going to be paid for (whether by you or your employer) no matter what.

So let's break down how to get the best plan possible, how to make the most of what you do have, and how you can squeeze as much mileage out of that hot bod of yours as possible.

Let's start with some jargon. When you on-board at a new job (or are shopping the marketplace for a health plan—thanks, Affordable Care Act!) you're likely going to be handed a bunch of pamphlets or PDFs containing a bunch of terms and charts and abbreviations. Here's what some basic medical insurance terms mean.

Premiums are the payments you, the insured person, make. This is essentially money that you throw into a black pit every single month for the privilege of having insurance. If you're covered through your job, your employer will cover some of your premium, though how much it will pay depends on which plan you choose and your employment contract.

A **deductible** is a dollar threshold that you personally have to hit in medical costs before your insurance starts to pay. Yes, even with insurance that you're *paying for*, you're still going to have to pay some money out of pocket before you can *use* that insurance coverage. So if you have a $1,000 deductible, you'll have to spend $1,000 on medical expenses before your insurance will start chipping in. Depending on your plan, some basic medical costs (such as an annual checkup) might be exempt from the deductible, in which case you'd pay only the co-pay. Which, speaking of . . .

Co-payments, aka co-pays, are what you pay when you visit a doctor. They're called "co" payments because you're actually paying only a portion of what the doctor charges; your insurance covers the rest. Co-pays are charged either as a percentage of the cost or as a flat-fee amount, and they might be waived or reduced for certain kinds of visits (such as that annual physical exam).

This brings us to acronyms. A **PPO** is a preferred provider organization, meaning that your insurance company has a (usually) decent-sized "network" of doctors, hospitals, and specialists that it will cover and you can pretty much just make an appointment, show up, and have it covered. It's like casual dating: You're never committed to any one doctor, and there's no penalty for moving on.

With an **HMO**, or health maintenance organization, the commitment is higher. You're going to have to find a suitable match up front and pick a primary care physician (PCP), and they're going to be the one you will work with for everything else. If you want to see a specialist (such as a dermatologist or physical therapist), you'll have to ask your PCP for a referral.

An **HDHP**, or high-deductible health plan, is (duh) a plan with a high deductible and usually lower premiums as a result. It can also come with the added benefit of a health savings account, or **HSA** (which you may remember from *Rich AF*). An HDHP can operate as a PPO or an HMO; what matters is that the deductible is high enough to qualify.

When we stack up these plans against one another, you can see that premiums (the monthly payments you make) and deductibles (that spend threshold) are inversely related. Premiums are superhigh with PPOs, medium with HMOs, and low, if any, with HDHPs. For deductibles, it's reversed: With a PPO, your deductible is the lowest; with an HMO, it's at the middle level; and with a high-deductible health plan—I mean, it's in the name. It's high. (But an important caveat here: this is all *generally speaking*. Because our health insurance in the United States is largely tied to our employment, big companies have the ability to operate on economies of scale and therefore might offer a "cheap" plan that in fact provides more benefits and greater coverage than a smaller employer's "expensive" plan.)

Plan Type	Premium	Deductible
PPO	High	Low
HMO	Medium	Medium
HDHP	Low	High

Note: HDHPs (high-deductible health plans) can be structured as either PPOs or HMOs, but the defining feature is that high deductible.

With all that out of the way, which one should you pick? After you size up what you are eligible for (in all those pamphlets and PDFs from your employer or the marketplace), picking an insurance plan is kind of one big hedge, because no one knows for sure what kind of medical situations they'll find themselves in over the next twelve months. But broadly speaking, you can think of it this way:

If you're . . .	And your medical visits look like . . .	A good plan might be . . .
Healthy and/or young without any notable ongoing medical issues	An annual physical, plus maybe a specialist (such as a derm to check out a weird mole) once or twice a year	An HDHP (doc visits might cost more up front, but the lower premiums mean you'll save overall)
Medium healthy but have chronic conditions or take some prescription meds	Physicals, plus a few specialist visits or things such as physical therapy sessions	An HMO (will have to get referrals, but if your specialist visits are few enough, the lower costs might make it worth it)

Investing in Yourself

If you're...	And your medical visits look like...	A good plan might be...
Actively working on your health in a few areas or are anticipating a big medical event (including having a baby)	Physicals, plus routine specialist visits (including therapy) or treatments	A PPO (higher premiums, but the most comprehensive coverage for what you need)

> Besides not knowing what the plans actually include, the other reason I suspect that people don't pick the right plan is that they get overwhelmed and just choose what looks simplest. But your medical plan isn't something you are married to forever, even if you stay at the same job! You can change it every year, *and* you can change it after certain big life events (such as getting married, having a kid, etc.). So definitely reevaluate your plan every year when the open enrollment period comes around.

Once you have your insurance? USE IT. Seriously. I know no one likes going to the doctor, but the golden rule of money and health care? Preventive care is almost always going to be cheaper than an emergency patch-up.

Even if that care doesn't fully prevent a problem, it can intervene when it's easier (and less expensive!) to fix. For example, if you show up to your two dental cleanings every year, you will never, ever get to a point where a cavity is caught so late that the tooth has to be extracted. Even if you do turn up with a cavity, it'll have had only six months max to grow, so getting it filled will be way less expensive than eventually getting that tooth extracted, replaced with a peg, and covered with a crown. Side note: Dental and vision coverage are typically separate from medical insurance, but you can still think about it through the same lens. You can pay either more up front and less later on or less now and more later on. The decision will largely come down to your preexisting conditions and state of health.

So whether you're paying out of pocket or your insurance is footing the bill, the best way to get all the value out of your medical coverage is regular, routine maintenance. Get your annual physical, have that sprain looked at, go in for your twice-yearly teeth cleanings, and make sure your glasses are up to date. (If not for your health, do it for your bank account; you can save money just by not letting your body fall apart.)

But there's more to take advantage of than the bare minimum. First, don't sleep on opportunities to game the system. Remember that annual deductible? The flip side of having to pay for procedures until you hit it is that after you hit it, your costs will go way down. So if you meet your annual deductible with a few months to go, you should do your best to jam every doctor appointment, medical test, consultation, and procedure you humanly can into that calendar year. Seriously: The difference between you seeing your doctor on December 15 versus you seeing them January 3 could be thousands of dollars. Those are the rules, so it makes sense to play by them, right?

Second, your plan might come with a Flexible Spending Account (FSA). This is different from a Health Savings Account (HSA); it's not an investment account, meaning that your money doesn't grow if you don't spend it. In fact, it's "use it or lose it," meaning that if you don't spend your FSA money by the end of the year, it's gone forever (though you may be able to roll a certain amount over to the first part of the next year, depending on your plan). If your insurance offers an FSA, you'll have the chance to set aside a chunk of money for the year pretax that will be loaded onto a debit card, usually a few thousand dollars, which you can use for things such as co-pays and prescriptions—and a *lot* of other stuff. Band-Aids, massage guns, bougie sunscreen, medicated ChapSticks—you'd be surprised what kind of #selfcare stuff you might be able to use pretax dollars for.

Third, a lot of medical insurers offer wellness benefits beyond medical care—like, *surprisingly* beyond. It's not just their being nice, though; they want to help you stay healthy because sick people cost them more. Still, their looking out for the bottom line can be your way to score some sweet self-care and wellness stuff and services at a discount (or fo' free) that you might not have picked up otherwise.

You'll want to check out what your individual insurance plan covers and how exactly it works: Sometimes a treatment that you might consider to be aesthetic (hey, dermatology) is actually covered as specialist medical care; sometimes you will receive a discount or coupon; sometimes you will have to jump through a few hoops (such as documenting your gym visits) to cash in. Here's a starter list of things that medical insurers might help you pay for:

- Acupuncture
- Therapy (in person or virtual)
- Telehealth
- Home prescription delivery
- Massages
- Gym memberships or fitness classes
- Nutritionist appointments
- Emergency contraception (aka the morning-after pill)
- Prescription sunglasses
- Devices such as CPAP machines, breast pumps, and even teeth-whitening UV lights

Caring for things costs money, but doing so extends their life. Resole your boots, change the oil in your car, take your body to the doctor; it's all the same principle.

Glow-ups and Looksmaxxing: When Spending to Look Your Best Makes Sense

We all know that it's what's on the inside that counts. And we all know that our health matters. But let's be real: Looks matter, too. Appearance isn't everything, but it's also . . . not nothing.

Case in point: When I was in undergrad, as an aspiring baby Wall Streeter, I studied pretty hard. I didn't just want to earn good grades; I wanted to understand the concepts, to actually, dare I say, *learn the material*. I wanted to come out of that place with a head full of everything I could possibly need to succeed in my career.

In my senior year, I, along with my fellow prospective businesspeople, was invited to a dinner. It was held during lunchtime, but it was still a legit soup-to-nuts dinner. It was hosted by the UChicago Careers in Business group, and it was designed to show you how to behave.

And let me tell you, it was some real *Princess Diaries* shit. They literally had someone come through the room and walk you step by step through *buttering your bread* (did you know you're supposed to rip off a little piece, butter it with your knife, put the knife down, and then eat it, *mouth closed*?). They informed us of cultural nuances, such as how in the United Kingdom, it's considered rude to put your knife down while you chew, whereas in the United States, it's considered rude if you *don't* put your knife down as you chew.

That dinner made me realize how much perception matters. Sure, I'd learned all the business concepts and was good at what I did. But the fact that my college put some of my tuition money toward a pretend dinner to teach me table manners *as a career necessity* showed me that the make-or-break for my career success was just as likely to be someone else's judgment of how I presented myself as it was my competence and skills. Studies have shown that the way you and your appearance are perceived can influence everything from how much money you earn to how likely you are to be approved for a loan[1] (one study found that being hot in high school correlates with earning more money as late as your *fifties*[2] — tough news for all of us late bloomers).

In spite of this reality, spending money on the way you look can also feel . . . weird, for lack of a better word. Even if you know that Botox or Invisalign fits into your budget, you might be wondering whether it's "worth it." But I'd argue that spending money on how you look and feel isn't *always* self-indulgence or vanity; spending money on yourself in these areas can actually contribute to your security and stability in a number of ways. After all, the way you present yourself to the world and the more confidence you have and exude matter. Whether it's designer clothes or a personal trainer, a massage or a personal therapist, skin care products or plastic surgery, here's how to change your mindset about personal care and appearance so you can optimize your spending to give you the best chance at achieving success.

Suit up. "Dress for success" may be a cliché, but studies and statistics support it. This is especially true if you work in certain industries or roles: Short of another pandemic sending everyone virtual, you're not going to be able to practice law in sweatpants (and even then, you'd need business attire from the waist up at minimum). What you wear affects what people think of you to a surprisingly large degree; studies have even shown that you're more likely to be seen as confident, successful, and good at your job if you wear a bespoke suit versus one off the rack or a formal gown versus a nightclub dress.[3]

Is it ultimately stupid to think that "clothes maketh the man"? Sure. But are you shallow for playing along so you can maximize your career potential? I'd say no.

Treat your body as your instrument. Professional singers have a saying: "You are your instrument," the point being that in the same way that instrumentalists don't carry their instruments around in shopping totes, letting them bang into subway poles and get rained on outdoors, singers shouldn't subject their body to rough treatment such as lack of sleep, dehydration, or undernourishment. Granted, unless you're Ariana Grande (or LeBron James), your body might not be directly earning you a living, but it's still the machine that carries out whatever tasks your job *does* require. Spending money to make your body feel and look good can also make you better at whatever you do. Does working on your feet all day take a lot out of you? A foot massage can refresh you to show up and do better work than you would if you were feeling all achy and exhausted—and be well worth the cost.

Understand that how you feel is real. Getting your mental and emotional health into shape is the foundation for building the confidence you need to be a rock star, and if attending to something about your appearance will improve the way you feel, *go for it*. Maybe you were a carefree tanning salon girlie in your teens and now love getting facials that renew your skin and make you glow; maybe your smile's a little crooked and it bothers you, so you want to invest in orthodontic care; maybe you went through a period of bad mental health that left you worse for the wear and you now love your weekly therapy appointments. Spending money on a healthier, happier, more confident you is worth every cent. You're in charge of your money, and you can use it to help yourself! That, my friend, is a huge gift and one you should pat yourself on the back for giving yourself.

Time Is Money

Investing in yourself doesn't always mean your literal, physical self, however. Bold statement incoming: Sometimes, it's worth it to pay money *not* to have to do something. (Remember my parents and William the lawn guy?) As a resource, your time on Earth is finite, and there are many simple, satisfying ways that you can trade your dollars for—not more of it, exactly, but fewer things to occupy it. Yes: I mean paying for convenience.

Can this be a slippery slope? Absolutely. Does it always feel great to DoorDash lunch? No; I'll be the first to admit that sometimes the fees add up fast and it stings a little (or a lot) to see them coming out of your Apple Pay. But sometimes also? They are well worth the money because of the time you get back from *not* having to do something yourself.

The key is to understand when the trade-offs make sense for *you*. The key to getting value, in other words, is discernment: knowing what your time is worth to *you*.

So while I'm not going to endorse letting zombie subscriptions that you're not using linger on your credit card statement, I do believe that there's nuance—a lot of it—when it comes to paying for convenience. Here's how you can decide what is and isn't worth it.

Step 1: Determine if spending money to save time can *net* you money.

To do this, you need to figure out your delta. You might remember the delta from *Rich AF* (or middle school math): It's the difference between two rates of change. A positive delta is, generally speaking, good (because you're netting a profit despite spending money) while a negative one is not (because your spending is outpacing your earning).

In the context of time value, you can think of your delta as your earning potential during a given time period versus the money you would need to spend to get that time back. This can be calculated most directly if you work on an hourly wage or if you're self-employed and bill your own hours. Say you charge your clients $60 per hour and DoorDashing yourself lunch is $7 (on top of the cost of the lunch itself). If that delivery saves you a forty-five-minute round-trip (twenty minutes walking each way, plus waiting for your food and paying), then you have a positive delta, and it's worth it to order.

Step 2: If not, determine if the time you will save feels worth the cost to save it.

You don't *have* to be producing income to justify spending money to save time—because not all time is created equal.

If you work sixty-hour weeks and have only a sliver of your weekend to relax and enjoy, those precious Saturday hours might be worth their weight in gold to you. If you can, say, have your groceries delivered and get back maybe two hours from that limited pool of time off, those two hours might be well worth the Instacart fees and delivery charge.

Step 3: Understand what you're really buying.

If it's hard for you to reason through question 2, try this instead. Going back to the example of my parents and William, the lawn guy, yes, they are engaging his services technically to make the blades of grass on their lawn shorter. But what they're really buying for themselves is comfort—or rather the lack of *discomfort* that mowing it themselves would cause. They're buying time and peace of mind.

Similarly, if you're hiring someone to clean your house twice a month, yes, you could say that you're paying someone to scrub your tub and wipe down your counters. But what you're actually buying might be more time with your family, the confidence to have company over without worrying that your sink is gross, or just a higher-quality clean than you'd be able to do on your own.

Step 4: Consider how much of a pain in the ass the money-saving option is.

You may have seen the tip to get haircuts at beauty schools because students need to practice and so they charge way less than comparable salons do. (This is how I used to get a haircut and save money in college!) This is a great concept if your main focus is saving money, but have you ever had a beauty school haircut? It takes, like, three hours because they have to consult their instructor about every single snip. (And forget about getting color done—we're talking half a day.)

The point is that finally, you're allowed *not* to go for the cheapest option if it drains away more time than you're willing to commit, and you should weigh that as well. Money exists to make things easier, and sometimes that means not having to jump through a ton of hoops to save a buck or two.

By the same token, spending money not to save time but to save yourself from annoyance can be totally justified. For example, having TSA PreCheck or not having it doesn't change the end result of going through security, which is that you pass through it and go to your flight. But if you hate waiting in line (or always run kind of late, as I do), ponying up for the expedited option might be worth it to you, even if you eventually end up in boarding group six with the rest of us.

How to Buy What *You* Value

I'd be remiss if I didn't point out that investing in yourself does not always mean taking care of your body or getting time back. Sometimes, it just means . . . buying stuff. Whether it's a more comfortable mattress, a watch to track your workouts, a whole suite of smart devices that can make your breakfast for you as soon as you hit "snooze," or a cute little outfit that makes you walk, talk, and feel more confident, stuff can really make your life easier and better sometimes.

I've already covered how consumerism and marketing can drive us to value—and therefore buy—the wrong stuff. But that leaves a big question: How do you know what is the right stuff to buy?

While there are some solid strategies for picking apart the value versus price of some big-ticket items, such as cars and houses (which I'll get to in upcoming chapters), lifestyle upgrades can be a lot fuzzier and more subjective; there's less data to compare (there isn't a Kelley Blue Book value for mattresses), manufacturers' and stores' claims can be hard to verify (does the extract of rare purple Arctic blueberries actually improve the moisturizer?), and a product's efficacy can be highly user dependent (so you end up having to buy before you try—and buying a lot of things). Plus, designer labels and legacy "quality" brands mean less than they used to, and they may even be changing their manufacturing processes, so even tried-and-trues can pull a bait-and-switch.

Still, understanding what you value and how to judge the value of something you're looking at buying is possible, and it's a life skill that will serve you well whether you're buying a new refrigerator or a new lip balm. Ask yourself:

Would I still buy this if I couldn't tell anyone about it?

One of the best pieces of spending-related advice I've ever gotten was to ask myself this question. Sometimes when we invest in luxury items or upgrades, a big part of the appeal is being able to tell others we have them. This question cuts to the core of that: Would I want the BMW as much if everyone else thought I had a Kia? Would I truly value the driving stability, heated seats, and all the other features if I couldn't tell people I drove a BMW?

In my case, the answer is no because I'm not a car person. But if you're a car enthusiast and genuinely care about (and notice) a smoother drive (as my husband does), maybe you don't care if no one ever sees you behind the wheel, you just wanna *vroom vroom*.

On the other hand, there are plenty of things I couldn't GAF about bragging about and want to own regardless. For example, a really, really good moisturizer because how I feel when my skin is looking good is very different from how I feel when I'm breaking out, flaky, or oily, and I don't have to tell a soul to notice the difference in my mental state. A high-quality mattress because your back hurts; I would buy my dream mattress even if I had to take the brand name to my grave. Or even just good athletic undies with the rubber trim to help them stay in place so they don't budge, scrunch, and bunch when I'm halfway through a Pilates class. I don't need to tell anyone about these things to feel the difference myself.

This is especially important to ask because some luxury products have made "telling other people about it" one of the all but explicitly stated benefits of their brand. For example, I owned a pair of Louboutins, with their characteristic red soles, and I bought them basically so I could show people that I had a pair of Louboutins. And guess what? They were horribly painful to wear. Without the brand association, there's no way I'd have walked away in those.

This question works for experiences, too, in this age of social media; there are restaurants in New York City that I would pay for ten times out of ten because the food's so damn good, and there are restaurants I've been to just so I could take a photo of the spicy rigatoni. You can't feed yourself with ambiance!

So ask yourself the question, and listen to the answer.

Do I like it just 'cause it's pretty?

Look, we all love a good form factor, a good aesthetic bottle, or a luxury dust bag, but how much are you really willing to pay for . . . packaging? A glow-in-the-dark box with glittery letters doesn't make the deodorant inside work any better, and sometimes getting the best value means accepting that the most effective product might be kinda fugly. These items are basically the Crocs of their respective consumer category; we all basically agree that they're comfortable, and we all basically agree that they're hideous. Except unlike Crocs, there are plenty of less-than-aesthetic things that don't have to be publicly associated with you. For example, I will probably always keep a bottle of Head & Shoulders in my shower because no amount of expensive hair care products or trips to the salon is going to save my scalp the way that medicated shampoo does. Is a bottle that proudly proclaims "dandruff shampoo!" cute? Hell, no. But I'm not wearing it as an accessory; I'm storing it in my personal bathroom so I can dump it onto my head. Maybe it makes my shower experience a touch less aesthetic, but I can live with that—and I'm the only one who has to.

TL;DR: "Works but is ugly" will beat "doesn't really work but is pretty" nine times out of ten.

How long will I be stuck with this thing?

Let me tell you my tattoo story.

I was twenty-two, my frontal lobe was not fully developed, and I was leaving the University of Chicago in a few short weeks. So I thought, what better way to commemorate my last four years in Chicago than a tattoo? It was obviously an amazing idea that I would never regret. I told my best friend, Jenna, who wholeheartedly agreed. "That's a cool idea. If I were going to get a tattoo, I would get the four stars from the Chicago flag."

I told Jenna I liked her idea better than mine—I can't even remember what I was originally planning to get; that's how bad an idea it was—and she agreed to let me steal her idea *and* accompany me to the tattoo place.

Again, at the time, I was a broke college student, so we chose a place that was, let's say, affordable, which should have been my first concern. Jenna went first and got a double tragus piercing (one of which unfortunately got infected and to this day is uneven).

I went in next and asked the tattoo artist how much my four stars of the Chicago flag would cost, and he said, "A hundred bucks," which seemed perfect, because I happened to have exactly that much in cash with me. The tattoo, being four big stars, all filled in, took a while, but finally we were done, and after getting the tattoo, I asked for aftercare instructions. He said that there weren't any but to "just put Aquaphor on it and text this number if you have any issues." Naturally, I had an issue, and when I texted the number, he ghosted me.

Suffice it to say, thank God that the tattoo is in a location where no prospective employer can see it, because two of the stars are really pointy, one of them looks like Patrick Star from *SpongeBob SquarePants*, and none of them have the same shape or angles as the others.

The lesson I learned is obviously that cheaper is not always better. More than that, the lesson is that the longer you will be stuck with a decision, the more you should think it through—and seriously consider paying more for things that are permanent or semipermanent. A bad manicure can be soaked off. A bad haircut can grow out. A bad tattoo . . . well, you know.

Equally important, and along the same lines, is frequency of use. If you don't straighten your hair very often, but occasionally want to be able to tame your cowlick, you probably don't need to ball out with a diamond-plated Dyson supersonic hair dryer, because you're going to be spending only ten minutes with this thing every six months. But if you're a "I do my hair daily" gal? A Dyson Airwrap might be a worthy investment.

What is your minimum viable product?

In the tech world, the first version of an app, company, brand, or idea is called the minimum viable product, or MVP. The MVP is what results from founders and venture capital companies essentially sitting around a table and asking, "What is the minimum number of dollars we need to put into this to get a working product that will serve our needs?" A minimum viable product does not include marketing costs, it does not include branding, it does not include bells and whistles; it includes only the bare necessities. The MVP of a car would basically be "What can we make that has four wheels, will get people from point A to point B, and is street legal?"

When you're buying something new, ask yourself: What is the minimum viable product I can purchase? Maybe you look at the back of the sunscreens at Duane Reade and see that all of them have the same active ingredient, but some have glitter, a delicious banana scent, and a self-tanner tint—none of which matters to you because (in this case) SPF is SPF.

Your MVP may not necessarily be the cheapest option right off the bat. For example, if you're going for a job interview and need a suit, you wouldn't buy a $25 SHEIN suit that looks like shit, because it wouldn't meet the need of "making you look polished" or, more bluntly, "not drawing attention to your outfit." But go with something from the Ann Taylors, Banana Republics, or J.Crews of the world, and you'll be just fine—without having to shell out for Suitsupply, Theory, or Chanel.

You can also start with the cheapest option as your MVP, road test it, and discover that actually, this store-brand sunscreen is hard to rub in and leaves a nasty white cast on your skin, even with the same active ingredient. At that point, just bump up to the next cheapest option and try again. Yes, you had to pay for something that ultimately didn't work great, but the cost of the experiment might still be less than buying the premium product to start with.

Money Management To-Dos for Chapter 2

- Review your current medical insurance plan and determine if it's really working for you. Could you get away with a higher-

deductible, lower-premium plan such as an HMO or HDHP? Or are you chasing referrals for your doctor visits so often that a PPO might save you tons of time?
- Review what medical plans are likely to be on offer during the next open enrollment period; most employers make small updates to their offerings year over year, but you can consult last year's plan booklet for a baseline. If you buy through the marketplace, browse around to see what might be available to you.
- If you haven't had your yearly "freebie" health care done (we're talking a physical, a dental exam, an eye exam, new glasses or contacts if you have those), schedule those appointments now.
- Look into your other medical plan benefits to make sure you're not leaving anything good on the table, such as a discounted gym membership.
- Take inventory of your current work wardrobe and appearance-related expenses: What *one* change could you make that would appreciably boost your confidence and/or how you're perceived professionally? How much would that change cost? Could it fit into your budget?
- Identify one regular chore or task that you'd be happy to outsource. Look up what it would cost to have someone do that task for you, and use the steps in this chapter to determine whether it would be worth paying for.

Part Two

Building Your Financial House

Consider the snail. It's basically one part squishy stuff and one part shell, right? So assuming that everything's looking good in that little snail body, its survival depends on its shell. It's where snails live and what protects them when they're on the go.

Same goes for us (kinda). If your body and self are priority one—since if those aren't in good shape, doing anything else will be that much more of a struggle—the next layer when it comes to creating security and stability is what protects that body and self. Namely, it's what shields that self from the elements and gets that body from place to place safely. Yes, I'm talking houses and cars.

Cars and houses aren't just some of the biggest purchases that you're going to make in life, and they're not just the items with the biggest price tags. They're also the purchases that are likely to have the biggest impact on your overall quality of life—the shell that keeps you safe and sound as you navigate the world. So now that you've taken care of part one, you're going to tackle the next layer of optimizing your life: shelter and transportation. Understanding how to navigate these complex (both emotionally and financially) issues isn't just going to get you a better deal nine times out of ten; it's going to help you build a holistic financial life that will get you to where you want to be—safe, sound, and snug as a snail in a shell.

Chapter Three

Buying a Car

A while back, I posted a video to help people with car shopping: running the numbers, breaking down the basics, drawing some conclusions on what tends to make sense for most buyers. One person left a comment I will never forget.

> ur an idiot!!! by this math everyone should be driving a honda or toyota lol

Well . . . yes. In fact, this is what I am saying.

Let me back up. Cars occupy a weird place in our financial and cultural landscape. They're a tool with a purpose—and they're also a status symbol. You can't really argue that a car is a necessity the way a roof over your head or regular nourishment is, but you also can't really argue that it's not (at least for most Americans). In other words, they are complicated, and they tend to make people heated (like homeboy in the comment up there).

They can also act as a kind of canary in the coal mine when it comes to whether someone is trying to spend to get value—to maximize their sense of long-term security and stability.

Which brings me back to the Hondas and Toyotas. I first became a car owner at seventeen, and my car was a hand-me-down black Honda Accord with some paint missing off his roof. His name—yes, *his*—was Sheldon.

I ended up with Sheldon because he'd been my mom's car, and when she got a new (to her) galaxy blue Honda Accord, Sheldon became mine. My dad, meanwhile, drove a sandy Toyota Corolla. We were, in short, practical car people. Those cars didn't cost the most—not by a long shot—but they were safe and reliable and did what they needed to do. In giving me Sheldon, my parents knew that their teenage daughter would be able to get to high school in one piece without a hefty price tag.

But for that teenage daughter? Well, as much as Sheldon was my literal ride or die, as practical and functional as he was, he was also kind of . . . embarrassing.

It was embarrassing for me to pull up to the high school parking lot in that car with chipping paint—because Sheldon came from a batch that had been recalled due to paint chipping and it was too much effort to take him back to the dealer for the fix—and park next to the cars of the wealthier kids in my predominantly white, predominantly upper-middle-class school. In particular, I envied a girl I was in student government with. Her hand-me-down wasn't a ratty Accord with bad paint but a Mercedes-Benz SUV. It was an older model, passed down from her mom or grandparent—whatever, it was still hers to drive to school. I felt *such* envy because it was a beautiful car, big and cool, with the panache of being a Mercedes and having zero chipped paint.

One weekend, that girl was driving me home (carpooling is nice for saving on gas when you're a student) after a weekend student government event, and as we were enjoying the buttery smooth ride of her Mercedes and chatting about college and whatnot, she made some offhand comment about how "Oh, yeah, my family's up to our eyeballs in debt, so who knows how I'll pay for college."

I was genuinely confused. We were sitting in a luxury vehicle with a Kelley Blue Book value of five Sheldons, yet her family couldn't afford to send her to college? That sounded crazy. It did not compute. The girl *looked* rich, but . . . was my family actually better off than hers was? That was the moment I realized my family was not poor or broke—a moment that was borne to fruition when I was accepted to the University of Chicago and my parents basically said, "Don't worry, we got it." My family didn't run up credit card bills; the only debt we had was our mortgage, and we owned our cars outright, with no financing. It wasn't until later that I realized that the same mindset that had led my parents to buy dependable, unsexy cars with cash and drive them into the ground was the mindset that ultimately allowed them to help me fund a $250,000 education. This surgical penny-pinching on vehicles but balling out on my education spoke to how my parents wanted to get value out of their money, and while a fancy car may have been seen as a status symbol, upward social mobility through education was really what they were optimizing for.

So yes: When it comes to buying a car, I'm definitely team dependable. Sorry, commenter guy, and RIP, Sheldon.

If you want or need to buy a car, this chapter will teach you how, the Rich BFF way. But even if you're not planning to buy a car—you don't care about driving, you live in a city and will just metro it up until you die, whatever—I suggest that you stick around anyway. Knowing how to buy the best car for you isn't a nonnegotiable life skill, but you can still take away some serious lessons in decision making about emotional big-ticket items—which are going to be part of pretty much everyone's life, one way or another.

So to quote the immortal Regina George, get in, loser, we're going shopping—for a car.

Hooked on a Feeling: Why Smart People Make Dumb Car Decisions

Want to know what grinds my gears, pun intended? So many people—so many consumers—opt for the easiest solution to their problems. Not the best—the easiest.

I'll go ahead and throw my husband under the bus here as an example. Greg thinks, "You know, I want this pair of jeans," and he'll just . . . go to the brand's website and purchase them. Whereas *I* will search for these jeans on Google Shopping to see which place has them the cheapest. I compare prices on the brand's website, in department stores, and on the aggregator websites such as REVOLVE. Then I go onto Rakuten to make sure I'm getting cash back, and since I want to get those Amex points, I make sure I'm using the right credit card. Then, finally I fire up the Honey extension to ensure that I'm getting a discount code if there is one.

Should I be spending so much energy deciding where to buy a $150 pair of jeans? Probably not. It's not the best use of my time, and my max savings—if I somehow managed to get a 100 percent off coupon—could only ever be $150. But when it comes to bigger purchases, such as a car (or a home, as we'll see), doing painstaking research will help you get the best deal possible and avoid buyer's remorse.

Lots of people just . . . don't do it. But why? It's not that car buyers are dum-dums or saps wandering around car lots with hundred-dollar bills hanging out of their pockets, waiting for salespeople to prey on them. And it's not just that they opt for the easiest solution. It's that a car is an emotional purchase; it's not just a fun toy we get a measurable rush out of driving around in[1] but a status symbol that can literally make people see us as more attractive.[2] As a result, many people's first big car purchase is just "Ooh, shiny red car," and that often ends up biting them in the rear bumper, either as a monthly payment they can't afford month after month, a contract term they regret, or a model that's actually a lemon.

For example, take my friend Chris. When he was in high school, his parents helped him get a VW Jetta—not a Mercedes but not a Sheldon, either. Then, after college, he became a consultant, and his first car purchase? A BMW. Fast-forward to about a year ago, and he told me, "Yeah, that BMW? Huge mistake."

He admitted that he hadn't done enough research. He admitted that he had become enamored with the car and the perception it would give him—that he basically wanted to flex, do something flashy with his first big-boy salary. He didn't even really *need* a car, at least not compared to what else he could have spent the money on, such as a down payment on a home. Basically, he learned the lesson about being a thoughtful consumer the hard way, but *you* don't have to. Because car buying is an area in which the theory known as **hot and cold cognition** comes into play. And once you understand this theory, you can work it to your advantage.

Essentially, around the mid-1960s, researchers found that people do not in fact make decisions on a purely rational level but can be strongly influenced by emotionality. The "hotter" a person is emotionally, the more they make decisions in a reactive, automatic way, whereas the "colder" they're feeling (as in, chill aka Zen), the more they make decisions deliberately and analytically.

Car companies, especially car salespeople, might not know that there's a body of research into this psychological hypothesis, but they sure as hell know how to leverage it. Besides all the marketing tricks covered in chapter 1, the automotive industry has a huge cultural heft behind it, *especially* in America. From *Thunder Road* to *The Fast and the Furious* to Lightning McQueen, our media landscape is constantly telling us that cars—especially fast cars—equal swagger, confidence, and freedom. Add to that the fact that 92 percent of American households own at least one car[3] and that getting a driver's license often coincides with a tornado of teenage hormones, and we are basically preprogrammed to think of cars in a hot emotional state.

This is where car buying is not just about car buying. Because for Chris, was the pricey BMW a life-ending financial mistake? No. It won't cause him discomfort for the rest of his life; he's already bounced back. The dollars taken out of his account have more or less replenished themselves; it's just the regret that lingers.

What if we could avoid that kind of spending mistake, and the regret that comes with it, entirely? Why *wouldn't* we? All it takes is to build the muscle to think a little bit more coldly when it comes to making spending decisions. Once you learn to do it, you will be able to discern whether a given situation requires such effort (such as when you spend thirty minutes going onto various websites to save ten bucks on jeans, for example).

Too Hot: You test-drive a car before making a buying decision so you can get a sense of how it feels to drive it. By the time the test drive is over, you're imagining yourself cruising down the highway in that puppy, impressing all your friends and hot dates, and the monthly payment is just a technicality—so you'll agree to whatever the dealer offers.

V Chill: Before setting foot in a dealership, you find out how much car loan you're approved for—through a bank or credit union. Financing through a bank you have a relationship with is almost always going to get you a better deal than if you finance via the dealership, and once you're preapproved, you can use that preapproval as leverage with the salesperson (as in "I'm preapproved for this amount, so I need to negotiate if you want to sell me this car").

Too Hot: You focus so much on all the things you like about a car (stereo rules, color is cool, engine go *vroom vroom*) that you get serious rose-colored glasses about things that you're less into (everything from the price is higher than you'd like to the seats are mad uncomfortable).

V Chill: Remember in *The Blind Side* when Sandra Bullock says, "If you don't absolutely love it in the store, you won't wear it. The store is where you like it best." You took that as gospel truth. You know that you'll like the car best when test-driving it at the dealership, so if you're even a little iffy about it then, the iffiness is not going to fade with time. If the car isn't a perfect fit or at least one you can live with, it's out.

Too Hot: There's a limited-time deal, but only if you buy now! Steve at Legitimate Auto Sales says he'll reduce the dealer fee for you, but *only* because it's his birthday! You've gotta buy now to make it a December to Remember!

V Chill: Take. Your. Time. Be ready to walk away—not even as a hardball tactic to get a better price but to cool your emotions down and clear your head. (Though as a bonus, this is likely to make the salesperson sweat, because the next time they see you, they'll know you're serious, that you've already driven the car, and that you're not going to be a quick pushover of a sale.) Yes, there are "best times" to get deals on cars (usually the end of the month, quarter, and year), but that's historically proven to be more effective than it might be today; since the dawn of internet car listings and the ability for buyers to compare prices of cars hundreds of miles away, dealers have way less incentive to play dumb games.

Buy, Finance, Lease: Like Fuck, Marry, Kill but Less Fun

Okay, so you want to buy a car, you're prepared to keep cooler than a cucumber, and now it's time to figure out how you're going to pay for the thing. Before we actually get into the nitty-gritty math, let's quickly recap the main ways you can get your hands on your future set of wheels.

First up, you can buy the car outright, aka **pay cash**. Whether you buy from a dealer or a private party, used or new, this is simple enough: You show up, cash in hand, and pay in full on the spot.

> Note that paying "cash" for a car does not have to mean "literally with paper bills." More likely, you'll be using a check: You *can* write one from your checkbook, but most sellers will want a little more security in the form of either a cashier's check or a certified check. A cashier's check is the most secure form of check because the bank guarantees it (hence the name, because it may be signed by a cashier or teller at the branch), followed closely by a certified check, which, as the name suggests, is "certified" by the bank to confirm that the funds are in your account. You may also be able to put your car onto a credit card at a dealership—an excellent way to earn points if you're into that, but watch out for processing fees, which might wipe out your rewards!

This option gives you full ownership from day one, but it does mean a pretty hefty up-front payment. It's great if you plan to keep the car for the long haul. You won't have to worry about making monthly payments, and you can drive as many miles as you want without any restrictions. It may also be the *only* option if you're looking at a much older car, as most lenders offer loans only for cars up to a certain age. However, be prepared for higher upfront costs—as in, the whole purchase price—as well as to take responsibility for maintenance as the car ages, since you won't have any kind of dealer warranty to fall back on.

Paying cash is good if:

- You've got the cash.
- You plan on driving quite a bit.
- You don't want to be tied down to a loan or monthly payments.
- You're looking at an older (ten-plus years) model for which financing isn't an option.

Next, you can **finance** your car—that is, get a loan. You make a down payment to the dealer, borrow the rest of the purchase cost, and make monthly payments, including interest, over a set period. At the end of the term, you own the car. Think about it like taking on a home mortgage. Getting a loan gives you flexibility, especially cash-wise. With a lower initial cost and manageable monthly payments, you can drive a more expensive car than you could afford to buy outright. But remember, you'll be paying interest on that loan, so the total cost might be higher in the long run.

Financing is good if:

- You have limited cash on hand.
- You're going to drive a decent amount.
- You can handle a monthly payment (more on this in a sec).

> It's important to note that if you finance a large portion of your car's price, there may come a point in the first few years (when depreciation is rapid) when your car is actually worth *less* than what's left on your loan (also called being upside down or underwater on the loan). This doesn't mean that financing is always a bad idea; it just means that selling the car at that point would get you less than what you still owe the bank, so if you think that might happen, double-crunch the numbers before buying.

Last, you can **lease** your car, which is basically renting a car, but not in the way you do with Hertz and Enterprise. It's more like renting an apartment: you make monthly payments for a predetermined period, and at the end, you return the car.

Leasing might be the most controversial option, but I say, don't sleep on the lease, my friends. This way of paying has its merits, too—particularly if you love driving a new car every few years. With lower monthly payments and good warranty coverage, you can stay up to date with the latest models without having to worry about depreciation. However, you'll have mileage restrictions, and customizing the car might not be an option.

Leasing is good if:

- You don't plan to drive long distances.
- You value having a warranty.
- You want to drive something new (or newish) but not pay the full purchase price.
- You are uncertain about your future geographically (for example, you might be assigned to a new office in a foreign country for work in the future, you and your spouse may move to a new city, you anticipate going back to school in a different state, and so on).

Of course, we haven't talked numbers yet, so let's see how the math maths, shall we?

Let's say you're considering buying a car that costs $30,000 (which, for the record, is still way below the average cost of a car these days; the average new car in April 2025 costs over $48,000, according to Kelley Blue Book[4]).

Now imagine that you pay with cash and drive it for three years, at which point you sell it for $16,000. Your net cost over those three years would be $14,000. Not too shabby.

Now, imagine you finance instead. Say you make a $4,500 down payment and get an interest rate of approximately 11%. With monthly payments of $810, the total cost over three years would be around $34,000. That's higher than buying outright, but you do get full ownership, and if you were to sell it for that same $16,000, you'd have spent $18,000. So it would be more expensive over the long run by a few grand but involve paying considerably less money up front. (By the way, the dollars you didn't spend initially could've been working hard for you in other investments!)

Last, what if you lease? We'll assume the same $4,500 deposit and monthly payments of $345. Over three years, the total cost would be roughly $17,000—and you wouldn't have to deal with the hassle of selling it.

> You can math all this math easily with my premade car calculator spreadsheet; download it at yourrichbff.com/wellclub.

So there are clearly differences in the overall cost, but they're all within a range of a few thousand dollars. After you crunch the numbers and weigh the pros and cons, the best choice will depend on your individual needs, preferences, and financial situation. Because despite what your dad (or Dave Ramsey) may have told you, I do not think that taking out a car loan, or hell, even leasing a car, is universally the "bad" or "wrong" decision. A car is a depreciating asset, meaning that if you put it onto the market in a few years' time, you're likely *not* going to be able to sell it for more than you paid for it. So paying interest on a loan for something that loses value over time might not make sense "on paper"—but we do not live our lives on paper, do we?

First, consider **why you're getting a car**. Leasing can be sensible if you need a car temporarily, such as if you're living in a car-heavy city for a predetermined short term of time: for example, if your job transfers you from New York to Dallas for two years, leasing might be smarter than buying, since you won't need the car after you move back to a nondriving city. Likewise, financing is beneficial if you can get a low (or even just nonpredatory) interest rate and good terms that will allow you to pay off the car quickly without a large initial payment.

Furthermore, consider **your driving habits**. If you like keeping cars for the long term, buying outright or financing might be more suitable. On the other hand, if you enjoy driving the latest models and don't want to deal with maintenance, leasing could be your best bet.

You also need to consider **your opportunity cost**, or what *else* you could do with the money other than spend it on a car. If you have the money to buy a car outright, could you invest the money elsewhere and potentially earn a better return? The S&P 500 on average returns 8% to 10% annually, so if you pay cash for a $30,000 car, you could be missing out on $7,000 to $10,000 worth of investment returns versus buying a depreciating asset (in our three-year example timeline).

Finally, think about **your future financial situation**. If you anticipate changes in your income or expenses, leasing might provide more flexibility because you'll be on the hook for only a limited, fixed time, and you won't have to worry about selling the car afterward. Or, if you know you want to retain some cash on hand for another big purchase (a house down payment, say), financing might make more sense, rather than throwing all your available cash into buying outright.

Want a good rule of thumb for how much to pay for a car? Just remember four numbers: 35 and 20/4/10.

If you pay for your car in full, don't spend more than **35** percent of your annual income on it. So if you make $100,000 every year, buy a car that costs $35,000 or less.

If you're financing, plan to make a **20**-percent down payment on a car with a **4**-year loan without spending more than **10** percent of your monthly income on transportation expenses.

Ultimately, deciding how you will pay for the car is only part of the equation; you also need to know what kind of car you want to buy and *why*. New cars are great because they haven't been driven before, nor do they have any hidden damage, but they also depreciate in value quite quickly over the first five or so years. Used cars that are five years or older retain their value slightly better, but again, you are buying a car that someone else has driven, already has miles on it, and may have more maintenance issues that could crop up in the future.

What Car Should I Buy? Comparison Shopping like an Economist

Recently, I rode in the nicest car I've ever been in. I had a business meeting with a very successful man, a serial entrepreneur with many successful ventures, and when we were wrapping up, we got into his car, a metallic forest green Bentley convertible with gorgeous peanut butter–colored seats in the softest leather that, I swear to God, had a *massage* feature. Sitting in the front passenger seat, feeling the seat massaging me, I'm not going to lie: It was amazing.

However, at the end of the day, that Bentley still got me from Point A to Point B just as a black Toyota Camry Uber would have. Was the massage chair nice? Yes, of course. Was the riding experience much nicer? Yes. But is the incremental cost of buying a Bentley versus something else worth it? Eh, IDK. For some car enthusiasts, maybe the investment makes sense (though I hesitate to use the word *investment* because most cars are not investments; they are depreciating assets, with the exceptions of hyper-ultraluxury cars such as the limited-edition, we-make-just-twenty-per-year McLarens). But if you're that kind of car enthusiast with that kind of budget, you're . . . not reading this book.

The point is, when it comes to what you *can* spend on a car, to once again quote *Mean Girls*, the limit does not exist. What you *should* spend on a car is going to depend on a couple of factors, and to understand the optimal situation *for you*, you're going to have to be a bit of a Cady Heron and do some mathleting.

The Tipping Point: Finding Optimization Equilibrium

It might go without saying that you should choose a car based on your needs, but that principle gets you only so far. Let's say you know you want an SUV for whatever reason: You need the cargo space, you want something that'll handle dirt roads, whatever. Cool. So *which* SUV, of all the makes and models out there? It's like ordering DoorDash: You can't tell Chipotle to deliver you "a burrito"; you have to make decisions about what fillings and fixings will really hit the spot (and your budget)—because if you leave it up to Chipotle, the folks there will only be too happy to load you down with triple meat and double guac and upcharge accordingly.

This is especially important with cars because superficially, especially if you're not a car person, the options can *seem* the same. For example, my husband is an SUV guy. He grew up in an SUV family—as you do when you live in Cedar Rapids, Iowa, home of equipment-heavy sports and lots of snow—and he's driven SUVs his whole life. A while back, for some reason (it was a tax reason, lol, more to come), we became fascinated by the Mercedes G-Wagon. We thought it looked so cool, and we were a little jelly that it felt as though *everyone* else had one, so when we went to the Hamptons, we rented one to drive.

Immediately, Greg was like, "Actually, this car sucks." He explained that while it was visually stunning, the build of the car was lacking. The back row, where three people sit, was cramped, with passengers' knees up against the front seats because the trunk was so big. He also said it "handled like a tractor" (and he would know, as my Iowan boo has in fact driven a tractor).

On the flip side, when we took a weekend trip to Malibu, we rented a Range Rover, and that thing was amazing: cushy armrests, perfectly sized cup holders, and reclining leather seats. It felt *luxurious* in a way that the G-Wagon did not.

When it comes to optimizing your car buying, you're basically looking for something called **optimization equilibrium**. Basically, optimization equilibrium is achieved when all resources are allocated optimally and all benefits are maximized, i.e., no more changes can be made to improve an object without making some other part of it worse.

If this sounds complicated, it's actually something you've probably already figured out instinctively when deciding whether to buy a car at all: If you've concluded that yes, it makes more sense to pay for title insurance, car insurance, the monthly payment, gas, or charging stations than it does to use public transit or Uber everywhere, you've essentially felt out your personal tipping point and decided which side of it you're on.

When it comes to selecting the individual make and model of the car you're going to buy, you want to get the best fit of car for the least amount of money—boom, optimized to equilibrium. In my stories from earlier, the G-Wagon was *not* optimized because it was a lot of money for what I viewed as basically a ticky-tack build and shoddy handling, whereas the Range Rover was still pricey, but for me delivered an experience that better matched its cost. If both cars were in my budget and I was shopping for one, I'd probably opt for the Range Rover in the name of using my dollars in an optimal way.

Basically, figuring out the makes and models of cars you're interested in is all about making your life more efficient and allocating your limited resources (aka money) most effectively. But you don't have to test-drive a car or even be a "car person" to start learning about which models are known to be reliable and which ones are shady. Good old Google University can help you out here; I particularly recommend looking at forums for owners of the cars you're considering to see what their major gripes are (if any). You can also research your prospective car's potential resale value (if that matters to you—because maybe this is my Sheldon experience talking, but in my opinion, you should ideally plan to drive a car into the ground, barring major life changes) on Kelley Blue Book, an industry resource for data-backed car pricing.

> ### New or Used?
>
> People have been debating whether to buy a used or new car practically since the days of the Model T. While conventional wisdom says that new cars instantly lose value when they roll off the lot, the reality is that *all* cars are depreciating assets. I don't want to say that you should *never* buy a new car, because sometimes a new car is cheaper than a used car based on delivery date and other factors—a car in the hand is worth two in the bush or whatever—and dealerships typically offer bonuses, cash-back offers, warranties, or free service for a certain period on new cars. At the same time, the price of a car tends to stabilize three to five years after its first sale, so you can find some of the best deals on used cars in that sweet spot—without the new-car perks but perhaps at a tempting price that makes it worth it to you.

Enter the Matrix: Comparing Options

The second part of buying a car is not just what make and model you might want but which specific car you're going to buy off the lot (or from a private seller) and how much you want to pay for it. This is where the comparison is less apples to apples and more apples to oranges and kiwis and dragon fruits. Because you're not just making a little pros-and-cons list as though you're a sitcom character; some cars or dealers will have pros that outweigh their cons, or some perks and features might not matter to you as much if you can get a simpler car at a lower price. Plus, price—and how you're paying that price, aka the cash, finance, or lease question—is its own separate set of options.

To solve these kinds of multivariable conundrums, I like to bust out a **decision matrix**, an analytical tool used to compare options in complex decisions. Decision matrices (plural of matrix, and yes, it's spelled correctly) are used a lot in various economic and financial contexts, but personally, I learned about them when shopping for bras.

If you've ever shopped for a bra, you'll know that there are two main things to consider: band size (the part that goes around your ribs) and cup size (the part that holds the boobs). Unfortunately, I am the president of the Itty Bitty Titty Committee, so my cup size is on the small end of the spectrum, but I *also* have a relatively athletic build, so I can't wear a supertight band. This means that the typical sizing waterfall, where small cups go with small bands and bigger bands go with bigger cups, leaves me out in the cold. After years of wearing bras that didn't fit one way or the other, I finally found a matrix that let me line up my cup size on one axis and my band size on the other, then scan to the middle where they meet to find the bra size combo that actually fits me.

A decision matrix is basically that same chart of cross-referenced options, except in this case, you're evaluating the individual aspects of a given car and comparing its scores in those areas to how other cars stack up. You consider factors such as price, features, mileage (if buying used), and payment options, weight those categories based on how much each matters to you, score the cars in each category, and math out the math.

Let's break this down. Say I'm in the market for a nice family vehicle. I have $18,000 in cash that I could dedicate to this purchase (whether down payment or buying outright), and I've optimization equilibriumed myself down to a few models of crossover SUVs. After some online searching to find out what's for sale near me, I've narrowed the options down to three:

| Option 1: | Option 2: | Option 3: |
| New Toyota RAV4 | Used Honda CR-V | Used Mazda CX-5 |

Price: $31,000 · Price: $23,000 · Price: $18,000

Mileage: 0 · Mileage: 32,000 · Mileage: 120,000

Age: brand new, baby · Age: 3 years · Age: 6 years

Fuel: gas · Fuel: hybrid · Fuel: gas

Features: blue exterior, leather interior · Features: white exterior, cloth interior · Features: red exterior, cloth interior

Payment: finance · Payment: finance · Payment: cash

To compare them, I draw up a decision matrix:

	Price	Payment Method	Mileage	Fuel Efficiency	Aesthetics
New RAV4					
Used CR-V					
Used CX-5					

First, I'll decide how important each of these categories is to me by weighting them. It's kind of like taking a course in college: That one professor who's obsessed with everyone showing up might make class attendance worth 40 percent of your grade, while the ones who DGAF about class attendance will put it at 10 percent and the final exam at, perhaps, 90 percent. You get to decide what contributes most to the final score by giving each category a percentage, which should all add up to 100. In this case, I know I'm going to be driving the car a lot and ideally for a long time, so mileage and fuel efficiency are priorities for me. I'm willing to be flexible on how much and how I pay for it if it gets me the ideal car, so those categories are less heavily weighted. And aesthetics are a solid meh for me; I have my preferences, but they're not deal-breakers.

Next, I'll score the options. I like to score them on a scale of 10, with 10 being the best, just to keep things simple.

	Price (15%)	Payment Method (20%)	Mileage (35%)	Fuel Efficiency (25%)	Aesthetics (5%)
New RAV4	7	4	10	6	8
Used CR-V	8	6	6	9	4
Used CX-5	9	7	4	6	8

How to Judge a Car

Price: The lower, the better, obviously, but you can look up any car's suggested fair market value on the Kelley Blue Book website.

Payment method: Only you know what makes the most sense for you; think about opportunity cost, timeline, and other factors discussed in the previous section.

Mileage: This is a factor only for used cars, obviously, and the lower the better—however, mileage is best considered relative to the age of the car. The average driver puts 12,000 to 15,000 miles on a car every year, so as a rule of thumb, an average yearly mileage below that is good, while an average above that is less so.

Fuel efficiency: You can estimate the yearly fuel costs for individual makes and models at fueleconomy.gov.

From here, I math it out by multiplying each score by the percentage of its weight, then adding the figures for each car to get a final score.

	Price (15%)	Payment Method (20%)	Mileage (35%)	Fuel Efficiency (25%)	Aesthetics (5%)	Score
New RAV4	7	4	10	6	8	7.25
Used CR-V	8	6	6	9	4	6.95
Used CX-5	9	7	4	6	8	6.05

> Want a simple way to crunch the numbers? Download my premade decision matrix spreadsheet at yourrichbff.com/wellclub.

With the numbers crunched, it looks as though I have a winner: the new Toyota. To be sure, I'm not bound to that decision; the numbers are pretty close, and if my gut tells me that I'd rather have the Honda, I can of course go for that one. If I want to get really nerdy about it, I can add more categories (for example, expected resale value, safety, and other factors) and redo my weighting to see if that makes a difference. In the end, though, the *final* final decision is going to have a not-insignificant vibes factor, and that's fine. The decision matrix is here to give you clarity and structure—not to make you ignore your intuition entirely.

Money Management To-Dos for Chapter 3

- If you're in the market for a car, drill down on your situation: Why are you buying a car? What are your driving habits and needs? On the flip side, what does the opportunity cost of paying for a car mean for both your present and your future financial situation?
- Run some numbers to play out your finance options as described on page 63. (Remember, you can download my spreadsheet at yourrichbff.com/wellclub to make it easier!)
- Research car makes and models with your optimization equilibrium in mind: What features actually matter to you?
- Once you've settled on a few make and model options, start scoping out available cars for sale near you and create a decision matrix to stack them up against one another.
- If you're financing, get preapproved for an auto loan through a local bank or credit union; that way you can walk into a dealership locked and loaded.

Chapter Four

Buying a Home

Buying a home used to be the nucleus of the American dream. Emphasis on *used to*. See, for a long, looong time, homeownership was one of the easiest ways not only to create generational wealth but also to move up the social ladder a few rungs. You could afford to buy a home? You suddenly became part of the ownership class *and* owned an asset that was practically guaranteed to appreciate—because in our parents' generation, you could have pretty much thrown a dart at a map to pick a house to buy and it would go up in value.

But life looks really different now. Not everyone wants 2.5 kids and a golden retriever. People want to move around, take job opportunities in various locations, stay closer to cool city locations instead of suburban sprawl or straight-up hit the road and van life it for a few years (or forever). And we're a lot more chill (although we could be chiller, tbf) about prejudging people based on whether or not they own property.

Bottom line: When it comes to the place you call home, security and stability look different for the new generation than it did for our parents—and it doesn't necessarily look the same for any two of us, either. Do security and stability mean the flexibility to break your lease at any time because you've just been offered the most amazing job in London and you need to move *now*? Or is your attitude "Nope, I am building my nest, I don't want to apartment hunt or fight with landlords ever again, I just want to stake my claim on this here corner of Earth and make it home, sweet home"? Is the important thing knowing that if the central AC dies, you won't be the one paying for a new HVAC system, or is it the ability to paint your walls whatever color you want without having to whitewash them before you move out?

I'm not here to preach the gospel of homeownership above all. I've been a renter and an owner at different times in my life and for different reasons. But I'm also not here to act as though the cheapest and most frugal and "most sensible" decision about where to live is always the best one. As I always say, a lot of financial advice is good *in theory*, but we live our lives in practice.

In practice, a home is not just an asset; it's a shelter, a warm place where you can sleep at night. It's a portion of space where you'll spend a ton of your time and create memories. It means more than just the dollars and cents you fork over to live there—and it *should*.

So it's okay if this topic and the decisions about it are partially emotional ones. How could they not be? Like, I don't care how "rational" you are, you cannot make a 100 percent cold, calculated spreadsheet-only decision about where you are going to live, *especially* if you're committing to that place indefinitely. But you do need to understand the fundamentals: how home purchases and loans work, how to budget for homeownership both before and after you buy a place, and how to negotiate like a champ.

I'll cover all those things in this chapter so that you can get yourself on track to whatever home, sweet home looks like for you.

Get Your Mind Right: Home Edition

Homeownership is a lot like being a contestant on *The Bachelorette*: You have to be there for the right reasons, or you're not going to go the distance. And sadly, there's been a lot of brainwashing about homeownership: that it's too late, too impossible, or mandatory in order to be considered a "grown-up." So in the name of pursuing security and stability, let's do a reality check.

Myth Number 1: Everyone owns a home but you, loser.

Homeowner FOMO (say that ten times fast) is real, and social media is making it worse. After skin care, domestic life might be the most distorted topic in #content today. The twentysomething girlies posting "day in my life" reels where they wake up in their perfectly curated bedroom, brush their teeth in their gorgeously appointed bathroom where even the toothpaste is color coordinated, and make their matcha in their spacious gourmet kitchens? Those are basically engineered to make normal people think, "Shit, what am I doing wrong in *my* stupid life that I'm not living like this?"

You're not behind the curve. No matter what the algorithm shoves into your face, everyone and their dog is *not* buying a house in their midtwenties. In reality, the average age when buying a home is forty-five, not twentysomething (and the average twentysomething is *much* more likely to be a renter than a homeowner). On top of that, the typical homebuyer already has a family (because two incomes are better than one when it comes to getting a mortgage and having buying power) and has a place in the suburbs, not the hip city center. And a *lot* of them are *still* making concessions to make room for a home in their budget.

Myth Number 2: You want a home that is already perfect.

This brings me to the second reality check: The social mediafication of homeownership has led people, especially young people, to assume that "home" means "the perfect aesthetic turnkey home with zero compromises." People have become much less willing to buy a house that doesn't 100 percent meet their vision.

On the one hand, I get it. A home is a huge expenditure—why settle? You hustled for that down payment cash, you researched the hell out of mortgage rates, so damn right you're going to buy the best home possible. You don't have to settle for a sad fixer-upper just to have one.

On the other hand, if you tell me you want a turnkey place, you know what that sounds like to me? It sounds as though you're going to have to pay up, or else you're going to have to put in elbow grease. And a lot of people just aren't willing to do that; they want to have it all, but also have everyone else *know* they have it all, to the point that their home needs to be a reflection of their Instagram personality from day one. News flash: That's unlikely to happen unless you have a BIG budget.

Myth Number 3: You'll *never* own a home, you poor slob.

At the same time, there's a large contingency of people with a doomerist view of homeownership: "I will never own a home. The cards are stacked against me. The system is rigged. Woe is me." Do I agree that there are many systemic and historical barriers to homeownership that are real, unfair, and even unjust? One. Hundred. Percent. But also, real talk? I struggle with this kind of throw-up-your-hands attitude. It's a lose-lose mindset, especially when it comes to money. If there truly is nothing to be done to change things—well, then, why worry and suffer twice? And if something, however small, *can* be done, why would you automatically assume that buying a home is out of your control?

If you want to buy a home, you can make it a financial priority. There are more ways than you might think to solve this problem, get a loan, and own your own damn place, especially if you're financially literate (which, based on the fact that you are reading this book, you are or hope to be soon).

Myth Number 4: You *will have to* buy a house one day, because renting past a certain age is weird.

In America, at least, we're socially conditioned not just to value homeownership but to *expect* it. Many people who grow up in middle-class or above families in the United States may not ever have seen their parents rent. They have no mode for what that even looks like. For most of us, adulthood means homeownership and vice versa, period. Renting is something you do temporarily in transient periods of your life.

Personally, I see both sides. The first home I remember being a home wasn't a house at all, but an apartment: I lived in a rental with my mom in Maryland while my dad worked in New Jersey, and he would drive home on the weekends to see us. Money was very tight, and it was what we had to do to make the math work. That first apartment was small, and I remember so vividly when we moved into the next apartment, which was nicer and bigger and in a good school district (the reason for the move). But I remember even more distinctly the move from that second apartment to a townhome—a house my parents *owned*. That townhome, humble though it was, provided a level of pride, joy, security, and stability for my parents that cannot be understated.

Truth of the matter? Renting *or* owning can be the right decision at any given time.

Myth Number 5: Renting is "throwing money away," but owning a home is "an investment."

There's no question that as an investment, real estate does kind of rule. In what other asset class can you fork over only 20 percent (or less!) of the purchase price in cash to start, immediately start using it, and in most cases see its value rise? Like, imagine if you could buy a box of Cheerios on layaway, eat half of it, and then sell it for a 45 percent profit five years later; sounds like a great deal, right?

But let me hit you with this: What if you just don't . . . want to own a home? What if the value of *not* having to save up for a down payment, of *not* having to put in hours of work to find, visit, offer on, haggle on, and actually purchase a place, of *not* having to YouTube "how to fix a broken water main" at 3:00 a.m. can *never* be outweighed by the value of owning a pile of bricks and mortar?

The same way homeownership isn't for everyone (and I mean that in the least snobby way possible), paying rent isn't just paying for shelter; it's paying *not to have to do a lot of chores to maintain that shelter*. And if to you the value of that outweighs the value of your name being on a property deed, then hell no, you're not throwing money away; you're putting it toward something meaningful *to you*.

Real Estate Real Talk: How Buying a Home Works

You're probably familiar with how renting a place works: You fill out an application to live there, the landlord likely runs a credit check and asks your former landlords for references, you get approved, you sign a lease agreeing to the monthly rent and how long you'll live there, you pay a deposit plus your first month of rent (and sometimes the last month as well), and you move in. Basically, as long as your application is approved and you can pay that first/last/security deposit, you're in.

When you *buy* a place, though, the application process is a lot more involved, your monthly payment can vary, and your up-front payment is a lot more. Let's break it down.

Say a great little place goes up for sale in your neighborhood. The location's great, the house is charming, and the asking price is $300,000. You don't have $300,000 in cash lying around, so you're SOL, right? Nope. Typically, homebuyers, even rich ones, don't plunk down the entire purchase price of a house in cash. Instead, you pay a certain amount of money up front (a **down payment**) to secure a **mortgage loan**, which you then pay off over an **amortization period**, a fancy way of saying "term of the loan" (in the United States, a thirty-year mortgage is most common, but you'll also see ten-, fifteen-, and twenty-five-year mortgages). The monthly payments you make over the amortization period pay back the remainder of the loan (the **principal**), plus the interest (more on that in a sec). A typical down payment is around 20 percent of the purchase price (but can be less or more). Saving up for a down payment is a big job, so once you have the cash in hand (or in your bank account), you've cleared the first hurdle toward getting the mortgage and therefore the home.

But the down payment alone isn't enough. Because a mortgage is a loan, the bank puts your mortgage application through a long process of **underwriting** to see, basically, "Is this person real or a catfish?" Unsurprisingly, because mortgages are pretty big as loans go, the bank's deep dive into your finances is going to be *exhaustive*: It's going to ask you for pay stubs, tax returns, bank statements, and more. It's going to pull your credit score *and* your credit report to see what shenanigans you might have been up to with loans in the past. It might even call your employer to ask, basically, "Yo, is this person sketchy?" It's also going to send an appraiser to the property to make sure that the house itself isn't a catfish — that it's genuinely worth the money it's going to lend you to buy it.

This mortgage test is as stressful as it is exhausting, but if you pass it, congratulations! You've won the privilege of owing a bank a lot of money for a big portion of your life, and you're about to make two new financial frenemies: interest rates and closing costs.

Interest is how your bank makes money — it's basically a "Thank you for lending me money 🏦" fee that you pay every month — and is calculated as a percentage of your principal (the amount you borrowed) based on an **interest rate** that is presented to you by your bank at this point.

Then there are **closing costs**, a bunch of administrative fees you pay during the process of going from "I'm interested in this property" to "Whose house? MY HOUSE!" They'll include things such as title insurance fees (a policy that covers your ass in case the seller is a big ol' liar and does not actually own the property—yes, this can happen), document and origination fees (charged by the bank), as well as prorated property and local tax payments for the year. Generally speaking, closing costs can add up to anywhere from 2 to 5 percent of the purchase price.

Finally, the blessed day arrives, and you get to actually take possession of the place at **closing**. You'll sign a ton of paperwork, the seller will sign a ton of paperwork, and you'll have your down payment and closing costs money wired from a checking account to an **escrow account** (think a safety-focused middleman), where it will be verified and then distributed.

From there, grab your keys and pop the champagne, because you're now the proud owner of some multifigure debt, and . . . a house!*

Your Personal Path to Homeownership

Real estate agents like to say that house hunting is all about "location, location, location," but I'd say it's just as much about direction (like, where your life is headed, both literally and metaphorically), timeline, *and* location. Because before you go out to look at individual physical houses, you need to know why you want to buy a house and when you'll be able to afford to buy it; that's the only realistic way to narrow down your options. With that in mind, let's break down how to approach this process for *you*.

---

* Sort of. Technically, the bank owns the home until the mortgage is paid off. But your name is on the title, if that's any consolation!

Direction

Why do you want to buy a home? No, really. Buying a home has been sold to us as both "a good investment" and a flex—but it isn't necessarily either one. Yes, homeownership had a huge impact in building stability for the boomer generation and even Gen X, but it doesn't *have* to be part of how you get rich if it doesn't make sense *to you*. It's worth asking yourself whether you, personally, truly want to buy and own a home or if you're just doing so because you "should." So ask yourself:

- Why do I want to buy a home? As an investment, to create a sense of stability, as a place to shelter my kiddos and dogs from the elements?
- Does homeownership align with my current and future priorities? Namely, how would owning a home (as opposed to renting) make those priorities easier *or* harder to achieve?

Where are you in life right now relative to settling down? People move around a lot in life these days; you might have grown up in one place, gone to college across the country, moved across the country again for your first job, then a few states over for your second, and if you're lucky and you do great work there, then three or four years into your career, you might be asked to go run the London office or the Tokyo office. Buying a home probably doesn't make sense if you plan to continue that nomadic lifestyle.

Yes, people can and do sell houses and move in a hurry when duty calls, but it's a major pain in the ass even when it goes smoothly, and if you think there's a chance that you might need to pull up stakes soon, you should think twice about buying property. A home is what's called an illiquid asset, meaning that you can't just hit them with a magic wand and *poof* them back into cash; you have to find a buyer and jump through a lot of hoops, which can take months or years—all while your money is tied up and you're tied down. Ask yourself:

- Considering factors such as my job, my partnership status, my partner's job, family obligations, and all those kinds of things, am I kind of done moving around from place to place, for the most part?
- Can I see myself living in a home I buy for *at least* five to seven years?

Are you homeownership ready? You don't have to be Chip and Joanna Gaines and repair every leaky faucet and blown circuit breaker yourself, but you do have to be chill with being the one in charge. Unlike being a renter, where there's a landlord or a super who can handle repairs (and your job is to nag them and check in with them until they show up and do the job), being a homeowner means that the buck stops with you and *you're* responsible for fixing things and keeping on top of the financial and legal obligations related to your humble abode. Whether "responsible" means rolling up your sleeves to DIY or googling (and paying for) a handyman to take on repairs is up to you, but either way, you are the captain now. Ask yourself:

- Does the fact that the annual maintenance cost of a home can amount to anywhere from 1 to 4 percent of the purchase price scare me?
- Am I cool with being responsible for stuff such as maintenance and repairs, appliance purchases, insurance, and property taxes?
- If I'm going to outsource the upkeep (think lawn care, pool maintenance, and so on), can I fit it comfortably into my budget?

Timeline

Is your financial house in order? A mortgage ain't nothing but a loan, and to get the best terms on a loan, you've gotta be loanworthy, aka have a good credit score.

> Important to note: While maintaining an excellent credit score is always a good idea, mortgage lenders in particular look at certain aspects of that score and your financial picture with a little more scrutiny: namely, your debt-to-income (DTI) ratio, or how much you owe compared with how much you make. Having a hefty DTI ratio can cause you to be denied a mortgage even if your overall credit score is good, so it's worth taking a look at that component of your credit score to see if it can be improved (i.e., by paying down some of your debt); for a conventional mortgage, a DTI ratio under 43 percent is ideal; an FHA mortgage (see page 97) has a little more wiggle room, but you still want to aim for under 50 percent.

Beyond getting good financial grades, so to speak, you want to make sure that you don't end up *house poor*, meaning that you can technically afford your home, but only if you don't save, don't invest for your future and retirement, and don't do anything fun. As the saying goes, rent is a ceiling (the most you'll pay) but a mortgage is a floor (the minimum you'll pay), and you need to be in a position where you can make a solid monthly mortgage payment *plus* set up a reasonable sinking fund for house-related expenses and still sustain your financial trajectory.

That's not to say that your situation can't change; it's fine to take your foot off the gas pedal in one area in order to gun it toward something else, but you don't want to be cutting into necessities. If buying a house would mean scaling back on your retirement savings, you should give some serious thought to whether your income is at the right level for you to do so. Ask yourself:

- Am I in a solid place, moneywise: not spending more than I earn, investing a portion of my income, with emergency funds and sinking funds set up?
- Are my credit score and DTI solid (and accurate—no mistakes or debts reported that aren't actually mine) or do I need to take time to improve them?
- How much of a monthly payment could I make comfortably, either right now or with some small-to-medium adjustments that won't cut into the meat of my budget?

> ### Credit Score Refresher
> Here's a quick rundown of how lenders see credit scores.
> **800 and up:** Excellent. You're Gucci. No notes.
> **740–799:** Very good. Gold star—not a unicorn, but lenders will still be happy to see you.
> **670–739:** Good. Solid middle of the pack; might have to pay slightly higher interest rates toward the bottom of the range.
> **580–669:** Fair. This is riskier; you might qualify for a loan, but the terms won't be the best.
> **579 and below:** Poor. Sorry to say, this is red flag territory for lenders, and you're unlikely to qualify for a loan without improving your score.

How much and how quickly can you save? Buying a house may not take as much cash as you think (see "Lower-Down-Payment Mortgages" on page 97) but it almost always takes *some* cash to get a mortgage, regardless of the size of the down payment. (As you will recall from earlier, the down payment isn't the only up-front cost; closing costs, plus the seemingly zillion random expenses that will crop up during the process—twenty bucks at Home Depot here, twenty bucks at Target there, they all add up.) Ask yourself:

- How much can I comfortably save per month in a dedicated down payment fund? Is there a chunk of my savings that I can re-earmark from something nonessential (e.g., a vacation) that I could reallocate to a down payment?
- With that savings rate in mind, how long would it take me to save for the down payment, and is that timeline in line with my goals?
- If the timeline feels too long, can I cut back on spending somewhere and/or boost my income?

What is the deal with interest rates now? Anyone who even glances at financial news knows that interest rates have become a national obsession, and for good reason. They're small numbers but with a big impact—maybe bigger than the price of the house itself.

Here's why. Back in 2020–2021, during the covid pandemic, mortgage interest rates were looooow, around 2% to 3%. Fast-forward to 2025, and they were quite a bit higher (despite some medium-aggressive rate cuts by the Federal Reserve in the meantime). Yes, circa 2020–2021, rates were superlow, but homes themselves were pricier. When interest rates climbed higher, to 6% to 7%, buyer demand cooled off and home asking prices pulled back to entice buyers back into the market.

If you were looking just at the price of homes, that seemed like great news: Cheaper prices, right? Sort of. See, a $500,000 home with a 2.5% interest rate and a $310,000 home with a 6.5% interest rate will have roughly the same monthly payment. Basically, when interest rates are high, homes might have lower price tags, but the higher monthly payments will likely mean that you can't afford as much home.

That said, while it's always in your best interest (pun intended) to get the lowest rate possible by shopping around, doing your research, and comparing lenders, ultimately—unless your name is Jerome Powell and you are the chairman of the Federal Reserve—interest rates are out of your control. You aren't obligated to keep waiting and waiting and waiting for the mythical, nonexistent "perfect time to buy," because it's never going to come. Even when interest rates do drop, it rarely happens overnight; based on historical data, you could wait five years and see interest rates drop by only one, maybe two percentage points—and in the meantime, five years of your life will have gone by.

So if you're in the part of your life where you want to own a home (see questions above!), then sure, it might sting a little to know that you're not getting the bestest deal in history, but every day you hold out is another day you could be kicking it in your own home.

Finally, it's worth considering whether an adjustable-rate mortgage (ARM) might make sense for you. While the "typical" American mortgage is a thirty-year term with a fixed interest rate, there are also adjustable-rate mortgages with varying terms available. An ARM works like this: Say you have a 10/1 ARM at 5% interest with a thirty-year term. The first number represents how long you'll pay the stated rate. In this case, it means that for the first ten years of the loan, your interest rate is locked in at 5% (the intro or teaser rate). The second number—the one after the slash—represents how often the rate will readjust after that. In this case, the rate will adjust every year (after the initial ten) until the thirty years is up. The amount your rate will change is based on either a periodic rate cap (a limit on how much it can change every adjustment) or a lifetime rate cap (a limit on how high the rate can go overall). The main benefit of an ARM is that the teaser rate is usually lower than the rates for fixed-rate mortgages, so your initial monthly payments will be lower. The disadvantage is that you don't know how much the rate will change once the adjustments start to kick in, and it could end up being a steep hike.

However, if you know you're going to own your home only for the short term (for example, it's a cozy two-bedroom place that is great for a couple but will be too small when you have kids in three years, or you'll be leaving the area in the near future but still want to own rather than rent), an ARM can make good sense because (in theory) you'll sell the property before the first rate adjustment kicks in.

Ask yourself:

- What are interest rates for mortgages near me? (You can check many banks' and credit unions' websites for a "rates" page.)
- Am I looking for a fixed-rate or an adjustable-rate mortgage?

> **Marry the House but Date the Rate: All About Refinancing**
>
> There's a saying that you should "marry the house but date the rate," and that's thanks to the potential for *refinancing*.
>
> Refinancing is when you redo your financing: You sign for a new loan with new terms; usually because doing so will get you a lower interest rate. You'll pay some up-front closing costs on a refinance just as you would on a new mortgage (for things such as document fees, a home appraisal, and so on), but over the long term, the lower interest rate means less money out of your pocket.
>
> How do you know when it's time to refinance? Keep an eye on market rates; as a rule of thumb, if you can refinance to an interest rate that's 2% below your current rate (and be sure you're checking *refinancing* rates, not new-loan rates—they may differ!), it's almost certainly going to save you money over time. A lower, but not 2% or more lower, rate may still save you money; you'll just want to crunch the numbers before proceeding: Divide the closing costs of the new loan by the amount of interest (in dollars) you will save every month at the new rate; if you plan on staying in the house longer than that number of months, it's a win. The math can get a little complex because of amortization (the fact that the

amount of money you pay in interest decreases over time as you pay down the principal), so check out the refinancing calculator at yourrichbff.com/wellclub to figure out what's best for you.

You can refinance with your existing lender, or you can hop to a new one; it's just a matter of who has the best rates (though sometimes your current lender will offer to match if it's worried that you'll jump ship). You'll also want to have a solid credit score and proof of income to qualify for the best rate, as lenders will be looking at those just as they would for an initial home mortgage loan.

That said, there's never a guarantee that interest rates *will* go down, so refinancing isn't something you should be counting on to make a home purchase viable, but if and when they do, refinancing can mean saving *thousands* of dollars over time.

Location, Location, Location

What do you need in a home? Pretty basic stuff here: Who needs to sleep in, work in, and generally inhabit the home, and what are they going to do there? If you have a pet or a kid (or want to someday), what kind of space are they going to need? Are you down to deal with lawn care, or would you be happy with a town house surrounded by beautiful garden stones? Do you have to have two full bathrooms, or can you get by with one? These questions are important to answer not just so you know what you want but so you can accurately set up your Zillow or Realtor.com filters to start browsing. Ask yourself:

- How many bedrooms and bathrooms do I need? Do I need extras for guests, a home office, or (future or furry) kids?
- How do I feel about outdoor space: necessary or not?
- How much customization and upgrading am I willing (and financially able) to do if a place doesn't quite fit my ideal?

Where do you want to live, and how much do homes cost there? Home value might depend on more than "location, location, location," but location *does* matter, and not just in the sense of "not being next door to a toxic waste factory." The biggie for a lot of people with (or starting) families is going to be the quality of the schools (since public schools are districted based on address), but there are also legitimate aesthetic and logistical factors to consider, such as how close you will be to your job or your hobbies, whether you'll be in a food desert with the nearest grocery store forty minutes away, and whether you will need a car to get around or can be a pedestrian (or cyclist, if that's how you roll) without missing out.

That said, it's also important to keep one of my favorite sayings in mind: You can have anything, but you can't have everything. We've all seen *House Hunters*, and we know that when it comes to location, getting what you want in one domain (good school district, walkability, proximity to family/friends) will likely come with compromises elsewhere (smaller space, road noise, higher property taxes). You'll get the most for your money when you know what matters most to you and what's nice to have but not essential. (You can even use a version of the decision matrix on page 74 if you want to get supertechnical.) Ask yourself:

- What's the vibe I'm looking for in a neighborhood? Quiet suburb? Bustling urban area? Something in between?
- Are the schools in the area good (if kids are part of my equation now or later)? Do I plan to send my kid(s) to public school—because if not, this matters less!
- How far am I willing to live from work, friends, and essentials such as grocery stores and pharmacies? How do I feel about needing a car to do errands and commute?
- Based on my target features from the last question, what are houses going for in the areas I'm considering? How on track am I relative to those purchase prices?

Your Rich BFF Guide to Getting the Best Damn Mortgage Possible

Ready to sign a ton of paperwork? Let's get you the best deal possible. Here's the cheat sheet.

1. **Shop around.** Don't just go with a big bank or the one you already bank with. Don't just go for the first lender you can think of. Don't sleep on smaller places that have only brick-and-mortar locations or (ugh) pen-and-paper applications (yes, they're still out there). Especially try local credit unions; they know the area and tend to play fair. And then *apply at multiple places.* Best case scenario: If you have two good offers in hand, you can play them against each other: "Lender A has offered a better rate, but your terms and service have been much better, dear Lender B, so if you can match that rate, I'll go with you." For some context, Boo and I were speed dating three banks and one credit union before we finally settled on the one that won our business because it offered the best rate and best terms.
2. **Be the best you that you can be.** Do everything you can to max your income and credit score, min your debt, and save for a down payment. If you have a one-off issue or something that may be concerning to lenders (you just started a new job, you took out a loan for a pet surgery), be prepared to spin the story and/or make up for the negative with additional documentation.
3. **Be easy to work with.** Your loan officer is a human being, so make their job easy and they'll be much more likely to go out on a limb for you. Being polite, persistent, and prepared with all the paperwork you need will help, instead of making them chase you for it: Tax returns, pay stubs, IDs, have it all handy and ready to go.

4. **Don't get discouraged.** Setbacks happen (e.g., the seller changes their mind, the house doesn't appraise for the asking price), but that doesn't mean you have to walk away from the house. A lender won't approve a big enough loan because its appraiser did a crappy job and said your house-to-be is in terrible shape? Find a new lender. The seller got a better offer and wants to bail? Offer to match it *and then some* (maybe with money or maybe with a faster closing, whatever you think will sweeten the deal).
5. **Get that shit on lock.** Once you're approved for a mortgage, lock in your rate to ensure you'll get to keep it even if the prevailing rates rise. Even a few weeks can bump rates up enough to cost you over the long term. Most lenders will automatically do this for a set period of time, but it's always good to confirm.
6. **Ask (for discounts) and ye shall receive.** Automatic payments, veterans, teachers, first-time homebuyers . . . there are lots of ways to get discounts, but you do have to look them up and ask for them, because banks aren't just giving them away for free. Use your Google machine or politely ask your loan officer, "Do you have any discounts I might qualify for?" Boo and I were able to get 0.25% off our mortgage rate by making our mortgage lender our primary bank and leveraging a "relationship discount" by moving all of our cash from our other banks to that bank.
7. **Buck tradition.** There are so many more forms of mortgage than the conventional ones that require a standard 20% down payment, so don't forget to research those (read on for more).

Lower-Down-Payment Mortgages

Once you've seen through all the white-picket-fence fantasies that pop culture has mythologized about homeownership, it's worth examining what you "know" about the numbers. For example, most people think that you "have to" or "are supposed to" put 20% down to get a mortgage and buy a home. But in actuality, that's a myth! Some loans require *much* less up front—as little as $0. These are legit options backed by the US government. While they're aboveboard as financial products go, the one drawback is that you'll have to pay private mortgage insurance (PMI), a monthly fee that's required anytime you put down less than 20% as a down payment (with maybe one exception). The good news is that once you have 20% equity in your home, you can have those PMI payments taken off.

FHA loans: These are home mortgages insured by the government and issued by a bank or other lender that is approved by the Federal Housing Authority (FHA). The FHA was established during the Great Depression to make it easier for people to qualify for home loans by creating a government guarantee to ease lenders' concerns about being paid back, and nowadays FHA loans are still considered to have some of the friendliest approval standards out there.

With an FHA loan, you can borrow up to 96.5% of the value of a home if you have a credit score of at least 580. In other words, the down payment is only 3.5%. If your credit score is not the best (like somewhere between 500 and 579), you can still get an FHA loan with a larger down payment of 10%.

Conventional 97 loans: Contrary to an FHA loan, which helps folks with lower credit scores, a conventional 97 is a type of loan that rewards a *high* credit score by requiring only a 3% down payment for first-time homebuyers. You'll want to have a credit score in the 700s or 800s (although a score as low as 620 can qualify), the home price can't exceed a certain amount ($806,500 in the continental United States as of 2025[1]), and the home has to be your primary residence (so you can't use this on an investment property).

USDA loans: If you're more *Little House on the Prairie* than *Sex and the City*, get ready to thank the US Department of Agriculture (USDA) for one of the government's least known mortgage assistance programs. While a mortgage program sponsored by the USDA might seem as though it would be targeted to farmers and ranchers, anybody within the income limits who is interested in buying a home in a rural area is eligible, and the terms are great; low interest rates and no down payments make them a superaccessible mortgage option. The USDA offers three mortgage types:
1. A direct loan from the USDA, which is for low-income and very-low-income families and individuals (as determined by local average incomes).
2. A mortgage guarantee, where the USDA will guarantee a mortgage issued by a participating local lender, similar to an FHA loan. This lets you get a competitive mortgage without having to put any money down (although you will pay PMI).
3. A grant—yes, *free money*, for the purpose of home improvement. You can also combine a loan and a grant for up to $27,500 in assistance.

VA loans: If you can get a VA loan, you should. Seriously. They are truly the best mortgage product available. As the name suggests, these are offered by the Department of Veterans Affairs to current and former members of the US military and their surviving spouses as a way to help give veterans and their families a financial leg up in return for their service. Similar to USDA loans, VA loans allow you to put 0% down on your home. But what makes them the *best* mortgage product is that they are the little exception I mentioned earlier: No PMI is required if you're a qualified borrower. So unlike with all the other less-than-20%-down-payment loans, you don't have to pay mortgage insurance. It's well deserved for all you service members out there, so don't sleep on this!

Money Management To-Dos for Chapter 4

- Review your credit score and debt-to-income ratio, especially if it's been a while since you last checked. You can get a free yearly credit report at annualcreditreport.com. If either your score or your DTI is in the iffy range, take steps to address the issue well in advance of filling out a mortgage application.
- Think through your homeownership journey (with your partner, if they're part of the decision): In what direction is your life headed right now? What's the timeline you're looking at for making a purchase? Where do you want to live—both generally and in terms of specific neighborhoods?
- Evaluate your down payment readiness and timeline: How much do you have saved up, and how does that align with the prices of the houses you're envisioning? What adjustments would you need to make to your savings to hit that number faster (or at all)?
  - *If a 20% down payment seems out of reach, look into*

> *lower-down-payment mortgages (described above) and see if one of those options might work for you.*

- Looking at your budget, how big a monthly PITI (principal, interest, taxes, and insurance—aka your "mortgage payment" once you own a home) could you afford comfortably, either right now or with some minor tweaks to your spending?
- If you're starting to get serious about homebuying, research some local banks and credit unions for today's mortgage rates, and consider applying to be preapproved for a mortgage.
- If you're still weighing whether to rent or buy, download my Rent vs. Buy Calculator at yourrichbff.com/wellclub and run the numbers.

Part Three

Growing Your ~~Family~~ Money Tree

Now that we've covered your most expensive possessions, let's cover your most prized possessions—which are not possessions at all; they're people. (Think about it: If your house was on fire, would you run to grab your laptop and AirPods Max or your kid?) Building and securing a long-term legacy—and possibly even generational wealth—for those you love requires strategic planning that should begin sooner rather than later.

If the most critical usage of your money is putting on your own oxygen mask first (by taking care of yourself both inwardly and outwardly), a very close second is making sure that the people around you can breathe comfortably, too. But that doesn't mean just budgeting to cover their needs; it means navigating some complicated emotional and social situations in which different senses of what's "worth it" can collide (and clash). It might mean being someone's financial, as well as romantic, partner, and it might mean being in charge of the well-being of a small, helpless creature (i.e., a kid or a pet) that cannot itself participate in earning money. It might mean reconfiguring what value is as your life—and your role in other people's lives—shifts and adapts. The bottom line is that building long-term wealth to take care of yourself and those you love starts *now*.

Chapter Five

Marriage and Partnership

If more people treated their relationship like a business, I think we'd all be a lot better off. I know this sounds very transactional and cold-blooded, but hear me out. I treat my relationship like a business because a business succeeds only when you take it seriously, thoughtfully, and responsibly—and the same goes for a relationship.

When I sat down and decided to take Your Rich BFF full-time, it was not on a whim. I made business plans. I did research. I set up the right legal structure for the company. Then, when the business evolved, I dissolved that structure to build a new one that would serve me better. I still work hard at keeping it running every single day: I ensure that the accounting is correct so I don't get audited (and if I did, I'd have the receipts to back up my books); I make sure that the business is flowing cash so I never run out of money to pay the people on my payroll. My business is not just an extension of me; it's its own thing, and it needs to be managed actively in order to thrive.

In my mind, if I didn't treat my relationship with the same responsibility I use in running my business, it would be a disservice to my partner. I treat my relationship like a business because I *value* my relationship.

We don't tend to think of marriage as a financial decision, at least not primarily. I certainly didn't until my mentor told me something mind-blowing: "The most important financial decision you will ever make in life is who you date and who you marry." She was 100 percent correct. Every stage of a romantic relationship involves money, after all, from who pays on the first date to splitting expenses when cohabiting to planning a wedding/creating a prenup and beyond. Money is the number one reason couples fight (sex is at number two, so you know it's serious). The same way you wouldn't start a business with someone by saying "How are we going to turn a profit? Oh, we'll just follow our heart and figure it out!," you shouldn't agree to establish a committed relationship (let alone a marriage, which is a *legal agreement*, remember) while planning to wing it financially.

That said, I do live in reality, and I know that snuggling up together and talking about investment plans isn't most people's idea of a romantic date. I'm fairly confident that most people see their partners completely naked long before they ever broach the subject of money—and do you know how uncomfortable something has to be for getting naked to be the *less* awkward course of action?

So don't mistake this as my scolding everyone for not bringing their most recent tax return along on every first date. For one thing, there is a very real knowledge vacuum that exists around money in our culture; the limited financial education we are given barely touches on the full scope of what people need to do to get their finances into order, let alone how to manage them in tandem with a partner. That's kind of a big issue, since very few of us navigate life alone.

The bigger part is that money just feels . . . *weird* to bring up while dating, especially in the early stages. I would know, because love—let alone marriage, a home, and retirement—certainly wasn't what was on my mind when I met my boo in a dive bar on the Lower East Side of New York City. I was there for a good time, not a long time.

Welp, fast-forward eight years, and it turns out I got both: Greg and I are now newlyweds, fresh off months of wedding planning; we own a home together, have set up 529 accounts for our future kiddos, and have navigated several career shifts as a team.

But we were two of the lucky ones. Greg and I had both mastered our individual finances before we met. We spent responsibly, we had paid down any student loan debt, and we were consistent investors. Much of that was a product of having good mentors and working on Wall Street, but creating our financial infrastructure and building money habits as a duo was truly what allowed us not only to survive as a couple (we spent 24/7 together through two years of a global pandemic, so yes, *survive* is in fact the correct word) but ultimately to thrive together. So even if we weren't comparing retirement projections on our first date, the foundation was there.

That said, building our life together hasn't always been easy. We *still* have to have deep discussions and make judgment calls. We still disagree about things. We still fight! But it would be so much harder without the bedrock of a functional financial system and our shared philosophy that money matters, marriage is a financial arrangement, and we've *got* to have conversations about money to make everything work.

This chapter will help you navigate the biggest financial decision in your life *and* have the conversations that will keep things running smoothly. I can't guarantee that you and your partner will *never* become heated over money, but I can give you the tools you need to make your conversations less name-calling fight and more productive discussion. Because any married person will tell you that being 100 percent blissful 100 percent of the time is not realistic, and it's certainly not what security and stability look like.

Getting Financially Naked: Money Talks

You know the moment in a relationship when you finally stop wearing makeup every time you see the other person, or you finally let them see you in your laundry-day sweats instead of a cute outfit? If they're still psyched to see you, you know you've got a real one. This is like that, but for money. I call it "getting financially naked," and while it might not be as sexy as getting *actually* naked, it's just as important for your long-term chemistry.

Most couples wait until the time they're moving in together to have the discussions that matter about money; you can't lie on a rental application, after all. But that is *way* too late, in my opinion. To quote the cliché, "If you're not dating to get married, you're dating to get your heart broken." In other words, unless you *are* trying to get your heart broken (and presumably you're not), you should be thinking about a future with that person, and that includes how well your financial lives and values match up. You don't want to find out too late, when you're already madly in love with someone, that you two are seriously misaligned on money. Putting off money conversations until you're deep into a relationship can make it that much harder to walk away if the situation turns out not to be right for you.

And no, you can't *not* get financially naked. These conversations aren't optional. You want to be with someone for the long term? Either you can talk about money early and often, or you can talk about it in divorce court. It's your choice.

The final reason to make money talk a consistent feature of your relationship is that conversations about money are really just conversations about sharing and values. And *that's* what solid relationships are built on; that's what true security and stability look like. (And if you can't *ever* have money discussions civilly or without hurt feelings and raised voices, that's a red flag. The occasional heated moment is fine, but consistent yelling? Not so much.)

What do I mean by getting financially naked? I mean disclosing, in no particular order:

- Your debt
- Your savings and investments
- Your salaries
- How you intend to split bills and living expenses

- Your views on gender roles and household labor
- Your five-to-ten-year plan for your career or education
- Whether you want to own or rent a home and where you want to live
- Whether you want to have kids and how many
- Your views on taking care of parents and/or in-laws in old age
- Any potential windfalls or inheritances you expect to receive
- Any past life financial details (child support, alimony, etc.)

Whew. Now, if you're a young twenty- or thirtysomething and dating, I get it. I don't recommend bringing this *all* up on the first date. But I *do* have a stage-by-stage breakdown of what it looks like to get financially naked with your partner in each stage of a relationship and how to make those awkward discussions a little less awkward (hint: wine and pasta help).

Casual Dating

The first money situation you're likely going to have with a potential romantic partner? Who pays for the first date. It's my opinion that whoever makes the invite for the first date pays for the first date. That's it. Obviously, the rules can change as things start to get serious and you get to know each other's finances better, but on those first few dates? You invite, you pay, the end.

Now, have I invited guys on dates and had them insist on paying because chivalry or whatever? Yes. Did I let them? Also yes. It's a thoughtful gesture, it wasn't something I felt like making into a thing, and—in my experience, at least—it didn't come with strings attached (and if I picked up that the dude was looking for some quid pro quo, I'd slap my card back on the table, thanks).

Beyond that, though, the money discussions you'll be having at this stage aren't even really money related. You'll get a sense of where the other person stands just by spending some time with them: learning where they grew up, where they went to school, what they do for work and fun—you know, typical early dating conversations.

Granted, there are some things you won't learn about at this stage, and that's okay. You shouldn't expect in-depth disclosures about their total amount of debt or specific salary numbers (or interrogate them about these, either). But you don't *need* numbers just yet. You know that a date who's an investment banker and a date who's in grad school for museum studies are looking at two very different financial situations and possibly life trajectories—and that's okay. Basically, you want to feel that when it comes to spending—whether time or money—this person values the same things you do.

My favorite way to talk about money but not talk about money? Ask about your date's dream vacation: "If money were no object and you could travel anywhere in the world for a week, where would you go?" It sounds simple (and maybe clichéd), but it reveals a lot. A person who'd go backpacking in Thailand clearly values different things than a person who'd go to Disney World for seven straight days.

Alternatively, you can try a classic such as "If you were handed a million bucks tomorrow, what would you do with it?" If they'd quit their job and live in a van for the rest of their life while you prefer a residence with indoor plumbing, you two might not be on the same page values-wise.

Things to discuss:
- What the other person does for a living
- How they like to spend their time
- Their general career/school plans/goals/dreams

Defining the Relationship (DTR)

Before you get exclusive with someone, before you decide "You and me, we are boyfriends, girlfriends, boyfriend-and-girlfriend, partners, whatever," you need to talk about money in a real way. If you're going to be together indefinitely and if this is going to be one of the top two reasons you guys will fight, you want to get as much ironed out as you can and quickly, right?

For this, I suggest a fun date idea. As you guys are chatting over food and wine, maybe playing Monopoly, you can talk about your views on money. This includes asking questions such as: Do you have debt? Do you consider yourself a spender or a saver? Do you have an emergency fund saved up? Do you have student loans? What would you say is your family's financial situation?

It doesn't have to come off as a probing interrogation, either—because *you* should be sharing, too. These are truly questions that you can position like "You know, transparently, I want to share that I have $50,000 of student debt. I just want to make sure that anyone who's my partner recognizes that I'm going to need to pay that off for the next thirty years of my life, and they know that going into a relationship with me. I'm curious—do you have any debt?"

In fact, for better or for worse, our generation's student debt situation has given us a pretty common talking point to bring up. Not only does it involve hard numbers and interest rates, but it reveals a lot about how a person grew up and what their family situation was like—which is good not because you're out to judge them but because if one day the other person's family becomes part of *your* family, you genuinely want to know what they're like.

For example, I feel fortunate in my relationship in that both my partner and I come from middle-to-upper-middle-class backgrounds and we both graduated without student debt. But we got there in very different ways. He went to Iowa State University, a state school, and his parents did not help him at all. He was a research assistant, so his room and board were covered, and he had a bunch of scholarships to cover tuition so that he graduated with no student debt. Meanwhile, my private college education cost a quarter million dollars. I got a merit scholarship from the school, and I got private scholarships, but my parents had set up a 529 account for me and that money helped fund my education.

Maybe it's just that we're both big finance dorks, but sharing these backstories with each other? It really brought us closer. Highly, highly rec.

The other thing I'd recommend getting out there before you commit to a serious thing? Talking kids or no kids. If you're genuinely on the fence and truly could go either way, maybe you can put it off—but if you definitely do or definitely *don't* want kids and it's a deal-breaker, you need to get that out there. Too many couples skirt the issue and kick the can down the road only to realize two years in that they're really incompatible here—or worse, for the yes-kids partner to wear down the no-kids partner into agreeing to starting a family, which is a recipe for miserable kids *and* parents.

Things to discuss:
- How each of you sees yourself with money (e.g., spender versus saver, frugal versus luxury)
- How you're doing with savings and debt
- Your families' financial backgrounds
- Whether you want kids or not

Moving in Together, AKA Financially Cohabitating

The vast majority of modern couples cohabitate before they get married—76 percent, to be exact.[1] This means that for just about three-quarters of married couples, the first piece of paper legally binding them to each other isn't their marriage certificate; it's their first lease.

Moving in together, whether before or after marriage, is crossing a threshold together, and I don't just mean literally walking in the front door of your new (shared) place. From now on, you're going to have to deal with each other's finances in specifics, on a regular schedule, and with much less room for fudging or hiding; there's no way to get away with ballparking your salary when you're printing out a pay stub to attach to a rental application for an apartment.

That's not to say this full-disclosure moment isn't awkward or uncomfortable or a great way to trigger all your money insecurities, because it totally can be. But it's also a relief. There's no way *not* to talk about money anymore once you're committed to this stage. And if you take the time to establish good dynamics now, you're setting yourself up for success long term.

> ### Don't Become Financially Codependent
>
> PSA: Being part of a couple, even a couple whose finances are commingled, does not mean you shouldn't have your own money. You very much should. Even if you're setting up joint bank accounts, sharing your life with someone, and fully committed to your other half, you still need to have money that is exclusively yours and accessible only to you (as does your partner). Here's why.
>
> Sadly, money can be a powerful tool to trap a romantic partner—especially, but not exclusively, women—in a bad or even abusive situation. Financial abuse has been shown to occur in 99 percent of domestic violence cases, which is terrible but not surprising. Because if your and your partner's finances are 100 percent commingled and you don't have a bank account under your own damn name, how are you going to leave if something goes wrong? Your partner will see where you withdraw money from an ATM. They'll shut off the debit card. You will not be safe. And that sucks.
>
> When you fully sign over access to all of your money to someone else, you limit your ability to control what happens to or with that money. And losing control can be dangerous, for the same reason that rich people have options and poor people don't.

When I say "rich," I really truly mean your individual ability to be financially secure; I don't mean your lifestyle full of fancy shit. Trust me, there are Manhattan wives who are dripping in diamonds, permed and Botoxed and perfectly dressed, and they are so broke that they cannot leave a significant other that they hate. They simply do not have access to the money to do so. They know that if they leave, they will not have a penny to their name.

But it's not just about minimizing the potential for abuse. Even if you're both incredibly happy and never want to leave, leaving all the financial decisions to one person is *not* a wise move. What happens if your partner gets hurt or is incapacitated and all your "shared" money is in their bank account? What happens if they die unexpectedly and you don't know which bank holds your mortgage, which brokerage has your investments, what credit cards are where?

Bottom line: Your relationship cannot be one-sided when it comes to money. It cannot be a scenario in which you do not have access to your key financial information without that person, and ideally, it should not be one in which the entire family unit (yes, two people is a family!) is dependent on one person's income. I say *ideally* only because if anything should happen to the breadwinner, things can get dicey—but I fully recognize that there are situations in which one person earns a paycheck and the other does not, for example, a stay-at-home parent. What's important is that both people are active decision makers when it comes to financial matters.

For couples, the best setup is some variation of yours, mine, and ours. Your paychecks hit *your* individual checking account and are dispersed to joint accounts as needed.

The first question to ask each other is, of course, "Where do we want to live?," immediately followed by "And how much can we afford to pay for it?"

Basically, there are two schools of thought: You can go for an equal split in which everything is strictly 50/50: Each person pays half the rent, half the bills, and so on. Or you can work out another way to divide up the costs: maybe 60/40 or 70/30, or maybe one person covers rent and the other covers utilities and groceries.

Splitting things 50/50 is simple, and it's definitely equal. But when it comes to sharing joint expenses, personally, I think it should be about finding whatever feels *fair*. Because here's the thing about "equal": If Partner A is making $50,000 a year, Partner B is making $250,000 a year, and their annual shared expenses are $30,000, a 50/50 "equal split" would take almost a *third* of Partner A's income but not even a *tenth* of Partner B's, which isn't really fair to Partner A. Even if Partner A is a real trooper and happy to take one for the team, it's hard to imagine that imbalance not causing some kind of friction down the road.

Let's say instead that these crazy kids decide to find a cheaper place to live and get their annual shared expenses down to $15,000. That makes the equal split a lot easier on Partner A's finances. But Partner B might have to make compromises to live in the cheaper place; maybe it's much farther from their job and now their commute is 5ever long; maybe it's too small to accommodate their beloved Peloton; maybe the building won't allow them to adopt a cat. Again, even if Partner B is a good sport, they might really start to feel that they're missing out on what they want out of life and frankly can afford.

What I'm getting at is that an "equal" budget split might be simple mathematically, but it can be a breeding ground for resentment. Too many couples skip the deeper discussion, assume that 50/50 is fair, and only later realize how much whatever compromise they personally made is grinding their gears. So be real with each other and talk this through. Even if you and your partner make close to the same amount of money, you might have different ideas of what's "reasonable" to spend on housing or what you want or need out of the place you live. Here's an example of what this can look like.

> PARTNER A: Hey, I know you're in love with this amazing apartment, and I am, too. But I just do not have space in my budget to cover half of the rent on this place.
> PARTNER B: No worries, I hear you. What are you comfortable spending? I bet we can work something out.
> PARTNER A: Well, right now I'm spending $1,000 a month, and that's about as far as I can stretch. I really don't feel like I can afford more.
> PARTNER B: Okay. Well, I really do want this place. I mean, I'm going to get a lot of use out of that gym in the basement, and I like having a doorman so we don't have to worry about porch pirates. But I don't want you to be stressed about rent just because I want to go work out easily. How about you keep paying your $1,000 and I cover the rest?
> PARTNER A: Hm. Are you sure you're comfortable with that?
> PARTNER B: Yes. I mean, I'm comfortable with it if you're comfortable with it. I don't want you to feel weird either way.
> PARTNER A: No weirdness here. It's a deal.

For the partner who makes less, the takeaway is that you should feel free to approach the conversation with some real talk and frankness about what you can swing. For the partner who makes more, understand that your partner does not want to hold you back, but they also don't want to put themselves into a precarious financial position that could then lead to even more issues in your relationship. For *both* partners, remember, it's ultimately just an apartment, and you love your partner more than you love an apartment. (I hope.)

> Moving in together doesn't have to mean renting, BTW. You can own property together whether or not you're married or plan to ever get married; the key is to make sure you're both legally protected. Case in point: When Boo and I bought a condo, we did it together, and **without** a ring on my finger. Obviously, it was a planned and fully joint decision; we wanted to do it when the timing was good, mortgage rates were rock bottom, and we could snag one of the last covid deals on the market. But we also drafted a co-ownership agreement with our attorney, which outlined that even though we contributed different dollar amounts, we were 50/50 owners of the home, and if either of us were to kick the bucket, 100 percent of the home would go to the other person (instead of to the deceased's estate, meaning realistically the parents of the deceased partner). This in particular is known as Joint Tenants with Rights of Survivorship; another option is Tenants in Common (where if one owner dies, their ownership stake in the property goes to whoever's named in their will—e.g., a parent or a kid).
>
> Regardless of how you define it legally, if you're thinking of co-owning a house or condo with someone who's not your legally wedded spouse, I highly recommend that you work with an attorney to draft and file an ownership agreement. That way, if you two should split up or one of you passes away suddenly, it will make things much smoother at a time when you're likely to be in a bad way emotionally.

As for handling the payments, I highly recommend setting up a joint checking account between the two of you. Anything that's a "both of us expense"—the rent, the groceries every week, the car payments, the

Netflix subscription, anything else you share—you will pay out of this joint account. Just as you divvy up your paychecks to various dedicated accounts for savings or sinking funds, each of you can funnel X percent or $X of your paycheck into that account.

For things that are your own expenses, you can continue to pay with your own money; that way, you can join a pickleball league when your partner has no interest in playing, they can upgrade their wardrobe and shell out for some fresh kicks, and neither of you has to nag the other about money. For shared discretionary spending such as date nights, or weekend trips, or what have you, you can either trade off (one date I'll pay for, one date you'll pay for), add a set amount to the joint account every month, or divide it up by category (I'll cover food and drink dates, you'll pay for concert tickets and movies).

So those are the big convos about present-day expenses. But what about the future? What happens if you can't make the rent one month? Does your partner have the money to cover it? Besides just hashing out the day-to-day bills, you two need to have some real-talk convos about how you'll handle it if things go south. You want to have a contingency plan before—God forbid—the terrible, horrible thing happens.

In practice, this means talking emergency funds. Your emergency fund needs to change as you get older and your expenses grow, and if you're no longer a single twenty-two-year-old surviving on ramen but a coupled-up twenty-nine-year-old with a live-in partner and two kitties, you're going to need a bigger cash reserve to sustain that lifestyle if you lose your income for some reason—and even *more* if your partner doesn't have an equivalent emergency fund.

It's not all doom and gloom, though. You might also want to talk through fun things, maybe making each other authorized users on your credit cards to rack up more rewards points (subject to your trusting them not to rack up your credit card bill too high), setting a budget for a joint vacation, or deciding how much to allocate to gift your respective families each holiday (after all, it's not really fair if one set of parents is getting a brand-new Sony TV and the other is getting a Starbucks gift card).

Things to discuss:
- Where you want to live and how much rent you want to pay
- How you'll split your joint living expenses
- How you'll cover your joint discretionary expenses such as dates or trips
- Whether to set up a joint checking account
- The state of your respective emergency funds

The Happily Ever After

So you've DTR'd, you've moved in together, and you've mutually decided you're in the relationship for the long haul. Whether you're making it legal with the state and getting hitched or just agreeing to be there for each other indefinitely, settling down in a committed relationship can be a huge factor in creating a sense of security and stability in your life.

But settling down doesn't mean settling *in*. The big money topics might be covered, but you're not just going to ride off into the sunset. Forget flowers and back rubs; regular conversations about spending, earning, saving, and investing are truly the key to a happy, healthy, *financially functional* relationship.

I advise you to treat your relationship like a business partnership: not in a cold, transactional way but in terms of transparency and regular check-ins. Just as a company holds quarterly meetings to discuss performance and strategy, you and your partner should have periodic "shareholders' meetings" to review your shared financial goals and progress.

I know how cringey and artificial this sounds. Nobody grows up dreaming of long afternoons of financial review sessions with their handsome prince/beautiful princess. But here's the thing: These conversations are way less painful than the alternative of finding out that your partner has been hiding massive credit card debt or making major financial decisions without consulting you. And by making them a routine, anticipated thing, instead of an emergency "Oh, shit, we have zero dollars in our account, WHAT DID YOU DO?" session, neither one of you will feel attacked, ambushed, or surprised.

Have fun with it. Make goofy PowerPoints. Mix up themed cocktails. Dress up fancy. Just because it's an important conversation doesn't mean it has to be serious. There's no wrong way to have these shareholder meetings; you just have to have them.

Things to discuss:
- Your individual and joint savings goals (vacations, wardrobe upgrades)
- Sinking funds for future expenses (new cars, new appliances, new house)
- Your emergency funds (are they still on track, or do you need to boost them?)
- Your career trajectories
- Lifestyle creep check-in (are you suddenly spending more than you need to somewhere?)
- Insurance and estate planning (*much* more on that in the chapters to come!)

> What if you're committed but not married? Some couples are till-death-do-us-part but don't (or can't) have that piece of paper binding them legally together. That means your financial planning as a couple (or family) will look a little different, but you can still plan ahead thoughtfully and make sure that everyone's protected and taken care of, in sickness and in health, for richer and for poorer . . . and so on.

Your financial obligations:
- Unlike married couples, you're not legally tied to each other's financial obligations (such as debts). If you want to pitch in equally for things such as one partner's student loans or credit card debt, come to a clear agreement on how that will work.
- As a nonmarried twosome, you can open a joint account (for, say, shared household expenses); however, each of you will have fewer legal protections than a married couple would (i.e., if you split up, either partner could *technically* drain the account in full compliance with the law, whereas a married couple's joint accounts are considered marital property and *must* be split 50/50 or however the couple agrees in divorce proceedings).
- Being not married comes with some tax benefits—and some drawbacks. You can't access spousal Social Security or pension benefits if your partner passes away. You also can't file a joint tax return, which can sometimes be a net plus (if you have a kid and one partner files single while the other files as head of household, for example, you might get a larger total standard deduction) and sometimes be a net minus (again, if you have a kid, only *one* of you can claim that kid as a dependent for tax credits . . . and the IRS will not like it if you accidentally *both* claim the kid).

Your legal protections:
- If you buy a place together, consider doing so as Joint Tenants with Right of Survivorship or Tenants in Common (see page 115) and consider how things such as contributions to improvements (i.e., renovations—both dollars and sweat equity!) will be divvied up should you split up and liquidate the place.

- Depending on where you live, you may be able to register as domestic partners, which can grant you *some* legal rights (such as the right to get onto your partner's health insurance) that can be valuable, so it's worth investigating whether that's an option in your state.

Worst-case scenarios:

- Even if you're not married to someone, you can appoint them as your medical and/or financial power of attorney (see page 242), so if your partner is the person you want making those decisions, be sure the paperwork is done up and filed; otherwise, they will have no legal standing to make decisions on your behalf. Because without these documents, it's your biological family—not your partner—who gets to call the shots.
- Unmarried partners don't automatically inherit assets when their partner dies, no matter how long or committed the relationship was (even if the couple had kids together!), so be sure that if you want your partner to get your things and cash should you meet your untimely end, you have an estate plan (see page 235) that makes that clear.

Your Wedding: The Most Expensive Party You Will (Probably) Ever Throw

If you and your SO have decided to make it official and tie the knot, congrats!!! Now you get to engage in planning, funding, and attending the biggest and most elaborate party of your life (probably).

Weddings are very much one of those theory-versus-practice money things. In theory, it is easy to set a budget, choose vendors, and have a wedding—ta-da, the end, pick up your favors on the way out! (Or, cheaper yet, just waltz into city hall and sign the paperwork.) In practice, however, you talk with vendors who all but say, "If you don't get this extra floral design, you are trash and scum of the earth." You get sixteen calls from your mom about why her high school best friend isn't invited even though you've never met this so-called Aunt Cathy. You get a *great* bargain on a dress—that then needs $500 worth of alterations.

Deep breaths. There's a *lot* of weird and emotional shit tied into wedding planning. The reality is, you can have a wedding on any budget. You and your partner just need to take a long, hard look at your lives and think about what matters to you. As is the case with everything else in your life, when it comes to weddings, you can have anything, but you cannot have everything. Here's how to make it work.

Make a budget. I suggest having three budget levels in mind: low, mid, and high. Low is the number that makes you think, "If we got our wedding for this price, we'd be stoked." Mid is more like what you reasonably think is going to happen. High is basically "We cannot spend a dollar more without financially ruining ourselves." Aim for low, expect to land on mid, and know that you may end up on high.

Why three levels? Because everyone I know who's planned a wedding started with a budget in mind—and then went over it. Budgets do change, and you shouldn't feel that you failed just because the cost of chicken cutlets went up from $2 a pound to $3 a pound between when you booked the caterer and when your dinner was served.

You'll also want to account for whether either of your families will be chipping in—and if so, whether that money will come with strings attached.

Know what actually matters—to *you*. To keep the wedding manageable, I suggest that you come up with three categories of event details you want to make sure are top-notch. You can agree on all three as a couple, you can do one each of yours/mine/ours, or you can do whatever combo suits you best and feels fair.

Once you know your priorities, nail them down. Hire the photographer, put a deposit on the venue, book the band—basically, lock in the costs that are your nonnegotiable must-haves. Then, for the things you don't care about as much? Cut corners. Have fake flowers—or no flowers. Have grocery store cupcakes—or no cake. Get your dress secondhand, or wear something from Reformation that costs $300 instead of $3,000. If it isn't mission critical for you, *don't spend money on it as though it is.*

Know that having a big party will be expensive. Even outside of the "wedding tax" (markups on things just because they're "for a wedding"), a big party, such as a wedding party, operates at scale, and scale, well, scales. For example, imagine taking someone to Chipotle for dinner: Chips, guac, a steak burrito, and a margarita will run you $25 or so, right? Now multiply that by a hundred wedding guests, and you're already at $2,500—and that's before you factor in delivery, waitstaff, plates and cutlery, cleanup, and tips. And that's for *Chipotle,* which is a fast casual restaurant!

This is not to say that you should go in expecting to bankrupt yourself (please don't), but if you've never thrown a party this big, you might not realize how quickly the expenses add up. That's not you being bad at planning a wedding, it's just . . . planning a wedding.

Don't forget the hidden costs. There's a whole category of wedding expenses that are easy to overlook but can add up really fast. What these turn out to be will depend on the specifics of your Big Day, but here's a general list to keep in mind.

- Sales tax.
- Insurance or damage costs (for example, if your altar damages

the grass at the venue, you could be on the hook to get it returfed).
- Delivery fees for rentals.
- Tailoring and alterations for your dress or suit.
- Credit card processing fees (some vendors may pass those on to you, to the tune of 3% or so).
- Tips, tips, tips: for your photographer, the DJ, the waitstaff—basically any human being who will be working there on the day of.
- Emergency cash: Do the festivities go slowly and your photographer is out of contractual hours before you've even cut the cake? Having some cash (or a check) to cover that means you won't miss a moment.

Remember that this wedding is for you—plural. Finally, remember: This day is for you. It's not for your mom. It's not to show off to your neighbors. It's for *you*—the two of you. It doesn't matter how much money you spend on the celebration if *you don't like it*, and it doesn't always make sense to scrimp if you'll end up with something you'll hate.

Things to discuss:
- What your overall wedding budget is (low, mid, and high)
- Whether either of your families will want to chip in
- What your three top priorities for the big day will be
- Alternatively, what you couldn't care less about/are happy to skip
- Whether you want to have a registry (for gifts, cash or cash equivalents, or both)

Happily "What If" Ever After: Prenuptial Agreement and Divorce

Money talks in relationships are, generally speaking, a good thing, even if they don't feel that way. But there are two subjects in particular that feel *especially* bad. The good news? They're basically the same chat. The bad news? One of them has to happen when you're still madly in love, and the other . . . does not have great vibes.

I'm talking about a prenup and divorce. It might seem weird to lump these two together, but they're actually two sides of the same financial coin. The core questions are identical: How much do you have? How much do I have? How much do we owe? How much have we saved? What are we splitting?

The difference is that a prenup—or prenuptial agreement if you're being fancy—is having the "what's yours is yours, what's mine is mine" conversation on a sunny day when you actually like your partner versus trying to hash it out after one of you has slowly built up five years of resentment or (even worse) when someone's been unfaithful (i.e., during divorce proceedings).

I know what you're thinking: "But isn't asking for a prenup basically saying you don't trust your partner?" Nope. It's saying that you're mature enough to have tough conversations proactively rather than crossing your fingers and hoping that everything goes well. Think of it as financial insurance for your relationship; nobody would accuse you of *assuming* that you're going to get in a fender bender just because you bought car insurance or *planning* to burn your house down just because you got a homeowner's policy, right?

Plus, research shows that couples who have prenups tend to have easier divorces (if it comes to that) and are *less* likely to fight about money during their marriage. Why? Because everything's on the table from day one. There's a hard stop to how much you can argue about finances when certain things are already codified.

At the end of the day, marriage is a contract, and as with any contract, you want to know what you're getting into and cover every eventuality before you sign on the dotted line. If that ship has sailed and it's time to consciously uncouple your finances, you can follow many of the same principles to do it as smoothly and painlessly as possible.

Prenuptial Agreement

A prenuptial agreement is simply a contract that stipulates how a couple's assets will be allocated in the event of divorce. It is *not* an evil, treacherous thing in which one person is left a king and the other person is left destitute. It is also *not* a sign that you don't love your partner or that you don't trust them. No, if anything, a prenup is a sign that you don't trust your government. Because here's the thing: Even if you don't sign a prenuptial agreement, you have one. It's just dictated by the government instead of by you and your spouse.

Now, I don't know about you, but I don't think the government fully understands my wants or needs. I don't think the people in power are smarter than I am. In fact, I am absolutely certain that they are less smart and less attuned to my needs and often deliberately vote against my best interests. I don't care if you are left, right, or dead center; I am sure that you do not agree with everything our government does. So regardless of how you feel about your partner and regardless of how you feel about the government's rules, why not make the rules yourself?

That's all a prenup is. You are making your own rules instead of saying, "Sure, I'm happy with whatever the government thinks is fair, even though I have no idea what that is." (For example, the government might feel that my business—that I founded, grew, and run myself—should half belong to any ex-spouse I have, but I don't. Neither does my husband. So we wrote our own rules.)

So if your spouse-to-be suggests getting a prenup, it doesn't make them the Devil. If they get the ball rolling, you roll along with it. Make sure to consult your own personal attorney—not the one who is working for your fiancé(e)—to ensure that the prenup is legally binding and that your interests are truly represented.

What if the topic hasn't come up? You can broach the subject yourself—and I promise that you won't burst into flames if you do. Try this script: "Hey, babe. I was reading up on how marital property laws work and I want to make sure we're both protected in case something unexpected happens. I know prenups can be a sensitive topic, and I obviously don't plan for us to ever get divorced, but if that did happen, I would much rather that you and I make the rules for what happens instead of letting the government make that call for us. Would you be open to discussing the possibility of getting a prenup?"

From there, you'll want to enlist some legal help—again, each of you should have your *own* lawyer—and have an agreement drafted.

Things to discuss:
- What's yours, what's mine, and what's ours? Clearly define what's "separate property" and will stay that way (i.e., go back to its original owner in the event of a divorce) versus "marital property" (to be split between you). This can also be future facing for property you don't yet own but anticipate getting one day (e.g., an inheritance, a pension).
- How will our future assets be divided? If you buy a house, a car, a yacht, who's going to get what?
- How should debt be assigned? Typically you'll want each party to remain responsible for any debt they bring into the marriage (e.g., student loans), but you may choose to split mutual debts assumed during the marriage (e.g., a mortgage).
- If you have any business interests—whether you're a full-time entrepreneur with an LLC or a creative type with an Etsy side hustle—you'll want to stipulate what right, if any, your ex-spouse would have to those entities and their proceeds.

> Similarly to planning your will (see page 244), you can save a lot of time (and money) by having these documents done online, then hiring a human lawyer to review them and ensure that they're in good shape, as opposed to retaining a lawyer from the get-go. Of course, what's most important is that the documents are done right, so don't cut corners if it leaves you feeling unsure that you're truly protected legally!

Till Debt Do Us Part: Divorce

Here's the thing about divorce that nobody tells you: The only guaranteed winner is the lawyers. When you go to war with your family, you're both going to have to pay up—literally. Even if you "win," you've lost one of the people closest to you and probably dropped a small fortune in legal fees. Hardly a triumph.

Divorce is essentially a really intense financial audit that happens while you're in a pretty gnarly emotional state. Again, the questions are the same—How much do you have? How much does the other person have? What did you build together? What will stay separate?—but you're more than likely feeling emotionally exhausted and frustrated while trying to answer them. So the smart move is to treat divorce like the business transaction it ultimately is. Here are a few tips for doing so.

Be organized. Just as with any audit, the better organized and more transparent you are from the start, the smoother the process will go. The smartest thing you can do, even if you're blissfully happy right now, is keep clear financial records throughout your marriage. It's like having a clean house; it's much easier to maintain it as you go than to declutter frantically when your housekeeper is ten minutes away from arriving. (Except in this case, the housekeeper is your divorce attorney, and the hourly rate is *much* steeper.) Especially if your future ex-spouse tries to pull anything sneaky (such as hiding assets so they don't have to share), having receipts to prove both your individual and your joint financial status at any point in time will keep things from veering into hearsay.

Make sure you have your own individual copies of the following in a place where you and only you can access and modify them (e.g., a password-protected cloud folder or storage drive, or a safe deposit box for physical copies).

- Identifying documents: photo IDs, Social Security card, marriage certificate
- Contracts: mortgages, deeds, leases, vehicle titles, insurance policies
- Financial records: bank statements, investment account statements
- Income documentation: pay stubs, tax forms, tax returns, employment contracts, business paperwork
- Bills and debt records: credit card statements, loan statements, medical bills

Be collaborative. I know, this is *so* much easier said than done, and you might be feeling more "scorched earth" than "conscious uncoupling." But fighting over every single ATM withdrawal so that your future ex will get screwed isn't just petty, it's expensive as hell. The extra hours your lawyers spend arguing over who gets the air fryer? That's money that could be going toward your fresh start—so don't screw *yourself* over in the process.

As hard as it is to swallow, the goal isn't to "win" the divorce; it's to get through it with your finances (and hopefully your dignity) relatively intact. Investing in therapy to get through those feelings rather than duking them out in the courts isn't just likely to be cheaper in the long run; it's healthier for you and less likely to hang over your head for the long term. Because at the end of the day, your ex might be out of your life, but the legal bills can really linger, and carrying that expense will keep your new happily ever after that much farther away.

Be pragmatic. A divorce isn't the end of the world, even if it feels like it. But it *is* a major financial event, and your lifestyle may need to change once you're single (and single income) again (especially, sorry to say, if you're a woman; after a divorce is finalized, women's average household income falls by 41 percent, compared to men's 23 percent). You no longer benefit from economies of scale on expenses such as rent and utilities, you may no longer have shared benefits from your ex-spouse's job, and you might have a sizable legal fee to pay off. This might mean a downgrade all around, from where you live to how much you spend on fun stuff (or even necessities), but ultimately, your long-term emotional health and happiness are more important.

Finally, it's good to remember that not everyone walks out of the divorce attorney's office like Nicole Kidman. Even the smoothest and most amicable of divorces is not a fun thing to go through. There doesn't have to be animosity or bad blood to make it hard to deal with. Think of Ted and Michelle on *Ted Lasso*: Ted was sad. Michelle was sad. Both of them were sad, even though it was a no-fault divorce! Change is hard, and even a "nice" divorce involves an adjustment period that people don't factor in. Do your best to treat it like any other big life change: your first day in a new city, your first day at a new job. It's strange and awkward and hard, but it does get easier with time—it just *takes* time, and that's okay.

Money Management To-Dos for Chapter 5

- If you're in a relationship and you haven't yet gotten financially naked with your partner, now's the time to do so. If you're

playing catch-up, you don't have to jump in at the stage you're in; you can work your way up from previous stages.
- If there are wedding bells in your future, congratulations! It's time to budget. Sit down with your partner and work out your low-, mid-, and high-level budget amounts, and nail down your three nonnegotiables (whether three things that you *both* really want, one each that you both want and one mutual—or however you want to divide them).
  - *If either partner's parents are likely to want to help pay, discuss the ground rules and boundaries with your partner ahead of time so that you can present a united (and grateful!) front.*
  - *Once you've decided on your nonnegotiables, start researching price quotes for those ASAP, and book your vendors; that way, the service is locked in, and the earmarked money is spoken for.*
  - *For everything else, research quotes and dial your expectations up or down depending on how things fit into your budget.*
- Speaking of marriage, wedding planning and prenup planning can happen simultaneously. Here's how.
  - *Start by getting acquainted with your state's "default" prenup (i.e., how the law divides martial property after a divorce) for background knowledge, then bring up the topic with your partner.*
  - *Review the questions on page 126 and get your (individual) answers squared away.*
  - *With those questions answered, research local family law attorneys and schedule consultations to get a vibe check. (Remember, each spouse-to-be should have their own legal rep.)*

Chapter Six

Kids

The decision to have kids might just be the most popular bad financial decision out there. I'm not saying *not* to have kids; I'm just saying that having kids will make you poorer. The thing is, both of these truths can be, well, true. To borrow a line from my mom, if I've said it once, I've said it a thousand times: Financial advice operates in theory, but people live their lives in practice. And for many people, my future self included, the deep joy and meaning that come from raising a couple of tater tots is priceless (or at least worth what they'll pay in keeping said tots fed, clothed, and housed). Having security and stability isn't *just* about having lots of zeroes in your bank account, after all; it's about feeling that you're living the life that means the most to you.

That said, if you're going to take the plunge into parenthood, you need to come to terms with this reality: Kids are expensive. They represent a massive, ongoing, nonnegotiable expense for *at least* the next eighteen years of your life. Maybe you already have that general idea that "kids cost money" in your head, given that almost one in four millennials and Gen Zers cite their relative financial freedom as the top reason they *don't* have kids;[1] what you now need to understand is the *scope* of that cost.

The biggest mistake prospective parents make is underestimating the impact that growing, birthing, and raising children will have on their finances. According to NerdWallet, 44 percent of prospective parents in the United States think that their baby's first year of life will cost them less than $5,000. The real average amount? *Four times that much.*[2] Not only that, but most people have no idea what makes babies so expensive: the same survey found that half of parents-to-be expected diapers to be their number one cost, when in reality diapers were less than *one-tenth* the *actual* biggest cost (spoiler alert: childcare).

The point is, it's easy to assume that you'll be throwing in just a few more line items: diapers, clothes, a new stroller and car seat, and so on. But the real financial considerations in baby having and child-rearing aren't expenditures on things you can pick up at Target. You're looking at major ongoing expenses such as childcare, which in some areas can cost as much as a mortgage payment. You'll likely face career trade-offs, especially if you're the one getting pregnant, as parental leave and career pauses have downstream effects on your earning potential. And medical costs can quickly spiral, whether from routine care or unexpected health challenges.

Again, I don't say any of this to discourage you from having children, although if you're childfree by choice, more power to you. Live that beautiful stain-free, disposable-income life. Rather, it's about helping you make an informed decision and preparing thoughtfully if you *do* choose to become a parent.

On that note, there's another financial reality of parenthood that a lot of people tend to overlook, one that's more deeply entwined with the idea of building security and stability. That is the reality that if you do things right, your kids are going to be better off than you are. Possibly *much* better off.

When my parents were teens, they were suffering under the Cultural Revolution in China. When *I* was a teen, I was given a beat-up Honda Accord with the paint chipping off. It might have been a little hard for them to hear me complain about not having money for Abercrombie everything, you know? By the same token, if you work hard, invest wisely, and build a good life for yourself and your family, you'll likely see your kid being able to afford things you never could yourself. That's also the financial reality of being a parent. It doesn't just mean footing the bill; it means being the source of security and stability for someone else, even when they're frustrating you or driving you nuts or just *don't know how good they have it*. It means modeling what good (not perfect) financial habits look like and finding the sweet spot between "spoiling" and "neglecting." (I for one know that when my future kid's a teen, I'm not buying the kid a Ferrari, but I'm not sticking them in a twenty-year-old clunker, either.)

In this chapter, I'll lay out how to use your resources and money to bring your kid into the world as comfortably as possible, do nice things for them, and be their financial role model. We'll explore the true costs of raising children, from conception through college, and look at strategies for managing these expenses while still building wealth for your family's future. I'll also discuss options such as fertility treatments, adoption, and surrogacy and their associated costs. And I'll help you figure out how to raise kids who are themselves financially literate (and not spoiled little Richie Riches).

In *This* Economy?: How to Afford Having a Baby, Short and Long Term

There are two categories of things that make welcoming a new baby into your family expensive. The first is all the stuff you need to buy: clothes, diapers, gear, basically anything you'd see on the gift table at a baby shower. The total cost for this category can vary a lot depending on how bougie you want to be (trust me when I say that some strollers cost more than a used car), but you're looking at somewhere between $2,000 and $10,000 for those major onetime and miscellaneous ongoing expenses (e.g., diapers, wipes, food). Preparing for those is similar to saving up for any other big onetime purchase: You have to look at your budget and adjust your spending accordingly.

The second category of things that make babies expensive is one that's easier to overlook but arguably has a bigger impact: Having a baby doesn't just add to the ways money flows *out of* your bank account; it also almost always stops money flowing *into* your account, at least temporarily, when one or both parents take leave from work, either to recover from birth and bond with the baby immediately postpartum or over the longer term to care for the kiddo in their youngest years. With that in mind, let's break down how to tackle each of these money stoppages and minimize the impact to your take-home.

The Short Term: Parental Leave

Ask any new parent if it's possible to work full-time while taking care of a newborn, and they will probably laugh-cry right in your face. Taking some amount of time off work is going to be necessary just to keep that little peanut alive and in clean diapers. Plus, if you're the one who grew and birthed the little cantaloupe, you'll need time to rest and recover because childbirth is no joke.

So in that short-term newborn period, you've gotta figure out a way to cover your expenses while *not* actively working. Unfortunately, the odds that you'll get enough paid time off to do these essential things—or any paid time off at all—are not in your favor. The frustrating truth is that in America, we've created a dystopian *Hunger Games* kind of system in which your parental leave options often depend on what district you live in—I mean, sorry, where you work, what state you live in, and whether you've hit the employer benefits lottery. Some companies offer weeks or months of paid leave, while others basically expect you to pop the baby out and be back at your desk before the epidural wears off. Some states have programs that will pay you part of your salary while you're home taking care of your newborn, while others shrug and tell you to pull yourself up by your bootstraps. And depending on the size of your company, the length of time you've worked there, and how many hours you normally put in per year, it may even be legal to fire you for taking time off, leaving you without an income indefinitely.

There is far from enough space here to lay out all the flaws (and benefits) of this convoluted system, and it's going to be highly dependent on where you live and who you work for, among many other factors. Basically, though, the name of the game is to find out exactly what you're entitled to, max that shit out, and not take no for an answer.

Ways to Get Paid While on Parental Leave

- **Short-term disability insurance:** It's weird but true: Recovering from childbirth counts as a "disability" for insurance purposes. A policy that covers that postpartum recovery period when you're unable to work, offered through your employer, can cover as much as 60 to 70 percent of your salary for six to eight weeks. Pro tip: Sign up for this *well before* you're pregnant if your job offers it; otherwise you'll almost certainly be denied.
- **Your company's paid family leave:** This is a perk and totally optional for companies to offer, but if yours does, for the love of God, *use it*. Even if you're not the one physically delivering the baby, many companies have general parental leave available to anyone welcoming a new bundle of joy, so don't be shy about using this benefit. It's part of your comp package!
- **State benefits:** Some states have their own paid leave programs. You'll need to have worked in the state long enough to qualify. Moving there when you are eight months pregnant won't cut it.
- **Accrued personal time off/vacation/sick time:** If you're thinking of procreating in the near future, you might want to start banking your vacation time. How you use it (and

> stack it with any paid leave from your company or your state) will depend on your company policies, so read the employee handbook carefully.

Once you've determined how much money you could potentially receive for a period of parental leave, you need to figure out how much time that money would cover you for—and if it's less than you want (or need) to recover from childbirth and/or spend with your new arrival, you need to start crunching numbers and possibly making some tough calls.

The simplest option is to take additional unpaid time off. If you can save up money beforehand, cut back on some expenses, and/or have another nonjob source of income to cover any gaps, this is a reasonable way to go.

The one thing to make sure of is how much of that additional unpaid leave would be job protected, meaning that your employer can't fire you for taking it. The federal **Family Medical Leave Act (FMLA)**, for example, covers you for twelve weeks, but only if both you and your employer qualify. Some states have additional protections, especially if you end up with a documented condition such as postpartum depression that qualifies as a disability.

If you can't get additional unpaid time off, you can ask if your employer could work out a part-time return schedule, during which you would work a few days a week for less pay, thus having days at home with your baby. You could do some freelancing or consulting or pick up a side hustle that's flexible on time and will bring in a little cash (or see if your partner can).

The Long Term: Career Hiatus

There are tons of valid reasons to take time out of the workforce when you have kids. Even after you or your partner is healed and your baby is sleeping more than two hours at a stretch, you might just want to be home with them while they're little. I'm not going to join in on either side of the mommy wars. No one can unilaterally say what is and isn't right for another family, especially without knowing all the details. Again, this is an emotional decision as much as a financial one, and that's fine. If security and stability mean knowing that you'll get to see your kid all day every day, that is valid. What I *can* say is that there is a cost to stepping out of the workforce, even temporarily, and it's not as simple to tally up as most people make it seem.

THE CAREER COST

Let's look at dollars first. Often, what tends to happen after a kid enters the picture is that Mom and Dad look at the cost of childcare, look at their salaries, and ask themselves, not unreasonably, "Why is one of us going to work if our whole paycheck *or more* is essentially going to day care?" The math maths; one parent (usually Mom) decides to stay home, sometimes with the idea of returning to the workforce in a few years once kindergarten rolls around and the family budget adjusts itself accordingly.

The problem is that the wealth you build from your job isn't linear; it compounds over time—not just literally, in the case of contributions to retirement accounts, but in terms of your lifetime earning potential.

Say you're a twenty-eight-year-old woman making $50,000 annually who decides to stay home until your kid goes to kindergarten—say, five years. Obviously, you'll be giving up $250,000 in wages. But you'll also be forfeiting about $252,383 in wage *growth* due to raises over the course of your career. And if you contribute to a 401(k) (say 5% on your end with a 2% employer match), that five-year break would cost you $167,731 in retirement assets and benefits.[3]

In other words, the equation is not as simple as whether or not you can afford to reduce your household income by $50,000 a year for five years. It may also be a question of whether you want to earn well over half a million dollars less—$670,114 to be exact—over the course of your career.

Maybe it's your only option. Or maybe you have a choice and decide it is worth it to you. You just need to make an informed decision. The Center for American Progress has a calculator at interactives.americanprogress.org/childcarecosts/ that can estimate what a work break of various lengths would look like for you depending on your age, salary, and projected length of time out of the workforce and will give you a better picture of the real effects of staying home.

That said, it's not all or nothing, and there are ways to earn money while still being able to spend time with your kid: part-time work, consulting, freelancing, side hustling. The options are often there; you may just need to get creative about how you manage your time and balance your work and life.

THE RELATIONSHIP COST

If you're coupled up, one partner's deliberate step away from their career can also lead to a shift in how you as a partnership approach money and teamwork—and it's important to be aware of that. As I always like to say, marriage is a group project. It's not 100 percent equal 100 percent of the time, and you can't expect it to be. But when kids enter the picture, the group project dynamic shifts. Often one person becomes the "breadwinner," and the other becomes the "homemaker," and the mentality about who gets to call which shots can subtly change.

But here's the thing: Even if only one person's pulling in a paycheck, both parents are making that paycheck possible. The job-having parent is putting in the hours and getting the W-2, and the home-staying parent is doing all the things that make the job-having parent's work possible by being the caretaker, the chauffeur, the cook, the housekeeper, the nanny, the keeper of the schedule.

And yes, that household shit is truly valuable. Unfortunately, whether because housework is typically done by women and the world is sexist AF or because no one's being cut a check for doing this kind of work, it's easy to overlook the fact that it creates value—but it does. Studies have found that the economic value of the unpaid housework done by women globally amounts to some $10.9 trillion.[4] In other words, the stay-at-home parent deserves to enjoy the financial benefits that a traditional breadwinner does, because they are making the joint life possible. The argument that "I made the money, so I can choose how to spend it" is total bullshit; you wouldn't have been able to make that much money had your significant other not stayed at home and taken care of all of the other stuff! You think you can come home every single night to a hot meal on the dinner table, just because, like . . . magic?

Long story short: If you're the stay-at-home parent, you should have an equal say in where the money goes, and you shouldn't be denied your own spending just because you're not pulling in a paycheck. Because, again, you guys are partners. You are doing this because you can lean on each other. It is a group project. This is why it's so crucial that as you build your family, you and your partner discuss not just how you'll keep the family income sustainable but how you plan to run the household. How will *both* of you contribute, and how will you recognize the value the other is creating, even if they're not earning a salary?

The New Normal: IVF, Surrogacy, and Adoption

Like many young couples, after my husband and I got married, we started thinking about our family planning journey. Unlike a lot of couples', though, our position was somewhat unique.

I don't have a traditional W-2 job. I work for myself, which means I do not have paid time off, I don't have maternity leave coverage, and other people work for me and rely on me for their livelihoods. Moreover, I am only as good as my last post, my last podcast episode, my last book. I have to get while the getting is good and hustle. Slowing down to have a kid could suddenly put me and others I care about at a financial disadvantage. Combine that with the news that some of our friends were having some fertility struggles at the ripe old age of thirty, and we decided that it would make the most sense for me to freeze my eggs now so we could start our family later. Even though our decision-making process was unique, Greg and I aren't actually special in that regard. Across the board, people don't make families the way they used to.

This is a good thing, a great thing, in a lot of ways: The number of babies born thanks to reproductive assistance is on the rise, making more people happy parents. In vitro fertilization (IVF), intrauterine insemination (IUI), and surrogacy enable parents with infertility issues to become pregnant, same-sex couples to have biological children, and individuals to become single parents by choice. And IVF makes it more likely for women to have successful pregnancies later in life than they otherwise would.[5]

But the changes in how and when people are having kids—and what it takes to do so when the time comes—are ultimately tied to money. Our peak earning years tend to overlap pretty squarely with our peak fertile years: Starting younger gives you better odds of conceiving but might mean you have less money to support your new family, and waiting for great financial stability means that the odds of conceiving get worse and worse. (Fun fact: Did you know that an over-thirty-five mom-to-be is referred to as a geriatric pregnancy? Love that for us.) For us women, the older and more educated we become, the more likely we are to seek fertility services.[6]

In short, focusing on earning money, which you need to raise a kid, can ironically make it harder to conceive that kid in the first place. It's the ultimate high-stakes time-versus-money trade-off.

The good news: There are solutions to make conception easier, whether that's on a later timeline or because of fertility issues. The bad news: They cost money.

In my case, we were out roughly $20,000 for the egg-freezing process, $6,000 for the medications to make it happen, and then, when the time comes to actually put the embryo into my body, it'll run another $10,000 or so. If you want or need a surrogate, that can cost anywhere from $100,000 to $250,000.

These numbers look staggering. They *are* staggering, but take it from me: The sooner you come to terms with the costs of these procedures and the reality that you may need to avail yourself of them, the sooner you can lay out a road map for your future. Here's how to do so.

1. **Plan ahead financially.** IVF is extremely expensive, with costs potentially reaching $20,000 to $30,000 per cycle. Adoption costs can vary from a few thousand dollars when the adoption is done through a foster care system to $60,000 or more when done through a private agency.[7] Start saving early if possible, and redirect some savings toward this goal; it's short term and time sensitive, so it isn't the end of the world.
2. **Look into your company's benefits.** Some employers offer coverage for IVF treatments or adoption costs that can defray some of the expenses. Even if yours doesn't, try asking. I had a girlfriend who took a competing company's fertility benefits policy to her HR department and straight-up said, "This is what they get at ABC Corp. What can we do here?" Her employer ended up going for it.
3. **Consider using personal loans instead of credit cards to finance IVF.** Personal loans almost always have lower interest rates than credit cards do, meaning that you'll spend less on interest fees and will likely be able to pay off the debt sooner. Even better, some medical practices (including the fertility clinic I went to) offer 0% interest financing, so you can plan your family in your younger years and pay for the process over a longer period of time at no penalty to you.
4. **Explore free egg-freezing options offered by donation programs,** but carefully consider the ethical implications. Cofertility, for example, offers a free egg-freezing treatment, but you'd get to keep only half of your eggs, while the family sponsoring you would get the other half. Your genetic material would be out there for other couples to use to create *their*

babies. Maybe you're okay with that (or even stoked about it!), and maybe you're not. Just be fully clear about it before you decide.

5. **Be prepared for both the financial and emotional toll of the process.** Fertility treatments can tap out both your wallet *and* your mental health.
6. **Research and understand the tax implications.** Some fertility expenses may be tax deductible, and most out-of-pocket costs should qualify to be covered by a flexible spending account (FSA) or health savings account (HSA) if your medical insurance plan offers one. Adoption expenses may qualify for the Federal Adoption Tax Credit, and some states offer adoption assistance programs.
7. **Be open to discussing your plans with close family members.** Yes, it's awkward to talk about sperm and eggs in front of your parents or beloved auntie, but they might want to help out financially.
8. **Stay informed about the latest advancements in fertility treatments,** as new options may become available. Depending on your medical profile and demographics, you might even qualify for clinical trials for new procedures or methods at lower or no cost to you.

Childcare

If you think having a baby is expensive, just wait until you need someone to watch it while you work. First, much like parental leave, the childcare system in the United States is kind of a hot mess—and by "hot," I mean "expensive." The cost of childcare has tripled since 1991,[8] and according to the Department of Labor, American families spend anywhere from 8.9 to 16 percent of their annual income on full-time childcare.[9] In dollar figures, this amounts to $6,552 to $15,600 per family per year (although probably more, as the most recent published data are from 2022). Where you fall on that spectrum will depend on your area as well as the age of your kiddo: Tiny babies cost more to watch than four-year-olds do (because smaller kids require more attention, and more supervision means more staff to pay), and urban day cares tend to be pricier than rural ones.

Unfortunately, way too many new parents and parents-to-be seem to have a major blind spot about childcare, either not thinking about it at all or having a "It's one banana, what could it cost?" attitude about it. This makes sense: Childcare is a prime example of what I call a **net new expense**—a completely new category of spending rather than a build-out of one you're already paying for. Unlike buying baby clothes or food, the prices of which you can somewhat estimate by extrapolating from your own expenses for adult clothes and solid food, childcare will be an entirely new budget line item.

The challenge is compounded by the fact that for most working parents, childcare is nonnegotiable; babies aren't cats you can leave at home with some kibble and water, and most employers frown on your bringing your newborn to the office (even if that office is at home—lots of employment contracts stipulate that you *must* have childcare even if WFH). On top of that, childcare costs hit at the same time that many families are dealing with reduced income due to parental leave or career adjustments. You're simultaneously earning less while facing one of the biggest new expenses of your life.

In short, there's no real way around this ugly surprise expense, but you can make it less ugly (and less of a surprise) if you start planning for these costs well before you have children. Here's how to do so.

Start planning for childcare early. Socking away cash for childcare is a smart move, and so is finding a carer. Wait-lists at day cares can fill up before most of the babies are even born, so you're going to want to research, tour, and size up the options in your area well before you're actually a parent (possibly before you're even expecting, depending on your area). Don't hesitate to put your name onto as many wait-lists as possible; it's much easier to get *off* of one than it is to squeeze your way in later.

Explore all your options. Day care centers are one option, but so are nannies (or nanny shares, where you split the costs with another family) as well as in-home day cares (which can still be state licensed and inspected). Part-time day care and swapping off with a spouse or partner can be a decent option for some people. Hiring a reliable local student (or retiree!) a few afternoons a week can be, too. It takes legwork up front, but a patchwork solution can be feasible and less expensive.

Use your employer benefits. Look into whether your company offers a **Dependent Care FSA**, which allows you to contribute pretax dollars for childcare expenses, but be realistic about its limitations; the maximum annual contribution is usually far from enough to get you through a year of childcare. Bigger employers might also have negotiated rates with childcare centers in your area, which is definitely worth looking into.

Call in your family. If you have parents or in-laws who are local, willing, trustworthy, and available, don't disregard them as potential babysitters. A grandparent who can afford to spend some of their time watching their grandkid is the greatest gift and genuinely a form of generational wealth. It doesn't have to be for free, either; you can pay your parents for their time (yes, even through your Dependent Care FSA!). That said, accepting family help can also mean accepting family *input*, so you might need to grit your teeth through some boomer parenting insights. Only you can know if the trade-off is worth it!

Don't count childcare against just Mom's salary. This is more of a mindset tip than a practical one, but it's important to state. Childcare is a family expense, not just a "working mother's" expense. If both parents are working, childcare allows *both* of them to work. It's unfair and not realistic to mentally deduct it from *either* parent's income alone.

Know that childcare won't be needed forever, it's not all or nothing, and it's an investment. For average, healthy kids, full-time day care is a temporary state. Not to get all "Slipping Through My Fingers" by ABBA, but your kids won't be tiny forever, and they will eventually go to school and take some of the pressure off you.

Day care also doesn't have to be a full-time commitment. Again, if you're able to string together a variety of caregivers during your workweek or return to work part-time when the kids are smallest and day care is priciest, you can find a solid middle ground that will work for you.

Finally, you can think of day care expenses as an investment. You're paying now to ensure that you will be able to keep your job during what are likely your peak earning years and keep moving up in your career. Even though it feels like a lot (and probably *is* a lot) now, you're making that expenditure with the aim of eventually coming out net positive. (Not only that, but you're showing your kid what it means for you to be a loving parent while juggling an awesome career: role model material.)

Investing for Your Kids

Did you ever hear the phrase "Santa loves rich kids more"? Well, the same is basically true for investment accounts: Rich kids have them and get the most out of them. Luckily, you don't have to raise a trust fund baby to set up an investment strategy that will give your kiddo the building blocks of their future. The goal isn't just to hand them a pile of money; it's to set them up with both resources and financial literacy that will serve them throughout their lives. So in this section I'll cover funding their education, teaching them to invest, and helping them to be responsible with their money.

529 Plans

A 529 plan is an investment account designed to encourage saving for future education expenses by providing a small tax advantage. If you withdraw the money to cover qualified costs for a specific person you name ahead of time (a *beneficiary*), you will be exempt from certain types of taxes. Typically, the beneficiary will be your kiddo, and those expenses will be college tuition and related costs—hence why a 529 plan is often called a "college savings account."

But a 529 plan is so much more than just a piggy bank for college. You can open one before your kid is born, attach *your* SSN, and start contributing, potentially enjoying state income tax deductions each year (about two-thirds of states offer that benefit). Your investments will grow tax free, waiting for your future bundle of joy—and once they arrive, you make *them* the beneficiary. If your kid goes to private school for K–12, you can withdraw up to $10,000 annually to cover the costs, and you can withdraw an unlimited amount to help fund their higher education in college, trade school, culinary school, or other types of educational institutions.

If one kid manages to get all the way through their schooling and still has some money left over in the account, you can switch up the 529 beneficiary *again* to help out their sibling—or even yourself. (Cooking classes at the Culinary Institute? Spanish at the local community college? So long as the course is run by a qualifying educational provider, you're good.)

Finally, if you don't want or need to spend the money on educational expenses (your kid received a scholarship, they chose not to go on to higher ed because they became a famous YouTuber, whatever), you can roll some of it into a Roth IRA for the beneficiary, tax and penalty free, up to $7,000 per year (the same as the maximum annual IRA contribution) as of 2025 for a lifetime total of $35,000.

The one quirky thing about 529 plans is that their tax benefits come at the state, not the federal, level. The contributions you make won't reduce your federal tax bill (what you pay to the IRS) but can save you on state income taxes through either a tax credit or a tax deduction. (Granted, since some states don't have personal income tax to begin with, that might not end up saving you anything.) 529 plans don't have yearly contribution limits, but there *are* state-prescribed aggregate contribution limits for how much you can put into one in total that range from $235,000 to $550,000 as of this writing, depending on the state.

All that said, don't get paralysis by analysis. If you think a 529 plan makes sense for you and potential future babies, open one, start with yourself as the beneficiary, and start contributing.

UGMAs and UTMAs

These two alphabet soup accounts are two options for setting up a custodial investment account: The account benefits a minor (your kid) but is controlled by an adult (the custodian). They're sort of the training wheels of the investment world.

Why does a kid need a custodian? Well, legally, children under eighteen can't hold assets directly or do their own investing—but that can get sticky, especially if there's something like a life insurance payout. If you die and your minor child is the named beneficiary on your life insurance policy, their access to the money will be held up in legal proceedings until the court appoints a custodian.

UGMAs and UTMAs give you a simplified option to transfer assets to your children without having to set up a formal trust fund (more on that later). UGMAs and UTMAs are pretty straightforward to set up: A financial institution can help you do it, no lawyer needed.

UGMAs came first, with the passage of the Uniform Gifts to Minors Act in 1956, and UTMAs followed, with the Uniform Transfers to Minors Act in 1986. The difference is that the *gift* account can hold only cash and securities (i.e., stocks, bonds, and mutual funds), while the *transfer* account can include all that plus assets such as property (cars, homes, and so on). Also, UTMAs aren't available in South Carolina or Vermont. Random but true.

Creating one of these is simple: You establish a UTMA or UGMA account with your brokerage of choice, naming your kid as the beneficiary and a trusted adult as the custodian. You can then fill up the account in one of several ways. One, you can fund it as you would a regular brokerage account and buy securities. The investments will grow over time and will be transferred to your kid once they're of age (between eighteen and twenty-one years old, depending on the state). Or two, you can name the UTMA or UGMA as the beneficiary of your assets, for example, your life insurance policy. Should you meet your untimely end, the death benefit will hang out in that account, managed by your custodian, until your kid is of age. This will not only ensure that your kid will receive the money but also keep the government's nose out of your business! (And if your chosen custodian gets shady with the money, your child will be able to sue them, so there's that, too.)

To be clear, these accounts aren't *just* for life insurance; you can name them as a beneficiary of pretty much any asset: cash, real estate, even patents and royalties. This is just one example of how they can work to the benefit of your kiddos before they come of age.

Custodial Roth IRAs

You might remember our old pal the Individual Retirement Account. It comes in both a traditional and a Roth variety (remember that traditional = no taxes now; Roth = no taxes later). Well, adults aren't the only ones having investing fun; a custodial Roth IRA is basically Roth IRA, Jr. If your kid is earning income, whether from baby modeling or mowing lawns, they can be saving for retirement—with your help.

These accounts, like UTMAs and UGMAs, are custodial, meaning that an adult (you) will act as the custodian in charge of managing the funds and assets within, but your kid will be the one to reap the eventual benefits (when they're eighteen, or twenty-one in some states). Your kid gets all the tax benefits of a Roth IRA, *plus* they get a huge jump start on compound growth by starting to invest so much earlier.

A custodial Roth IRA can be a great teaching tool, too: The maximum contribution is your child's total compensation for the year (or for 2025, $7,000, whichever is less), but the contributions can come from anywhere, so long as you have a clear ledger of the hours worked and where the earned income came from.

And while the money in an IRA is usually locked up until age 59.5, in this case, there's a loophole. *Roth* IRAs allow qualified withdrawals of contributions (money you put in) at any time for any purpose and withdrawals of earnings (money your money makes you) on your investments without a penalty (but not without tax) for certain expenses such as education, birth, or adoption, purchasing your first home, or even to help in the aftermath of domestic abuse. So there's some added flexibility there, too.

> Which account is best? Again, don't let analysis paralysis hold you back; *any* investment in your kid's future is a good one. Personally, I like UTMAs for several reasons: They don't need to be used only for education expenses (what if your kid becomes a TikTok influencer?); they can hold both traditional and alternative investments; unlike a custodial Roth IRA, they can be funded with money made by the parents as opposed to the kid; and they're tax advantaged because they're usually taxed at the child's lower tax rate (unlike most cases with a standard custodial brokerage account).

When and Why to Get Your Kid a Credit Card

No, I don't mean giving your child a credit card and letting them charge as many Robux as your credit limit allows. But putting your kid onto a credit card can give them a serious financial leg up for basically free.

As you may recall from my first book, your credit score (the financial report card that tells lenders how worthy of loans or lines of credit you are) is calculated partially based on *age of accounts*: the older, the better. For most of us, our oldest account is either a student loan or the first rinky-dink credit card we got around the time we started our first job. But rich kids have credit histories stretching back to their kindergarten years if not earlier, and it's this little hack that does it.

All you need to do is add your child as an authorized user to a credit card you have in good standing (that last part is crucial—a delinquent or maxed-out account will *not* help their credit reputation). Many card issuers have no minimum age requirement, so you could theoretically pop Junior on there as soon as you get his SSN in the mail. A better option, though, is to do it *and* explain to your kids why you're doing it as a little intro to the idea of credit history. You could even agree that they're allowed to use the card for certain expenses up to a set limit (like an allowance) or can use it freely as long as they pay you in full for whatever they buy by the statement closing date, essentially making the Bank of Mom and Dad the middleman between your kid and the credit card company. Or you could simply sign up for the card, stick it into your sock drawer, and never let them touch it; it will still build their credit history based on your own spending, as long as you pay the bill in full on time every month.

Teach Your Children Well:
How to Raise Money-Smart Kids

For the longest time, the default way of teaching kids about money was "Don't—until you suddenly have to." Every time little Johnny asks how much money Mom and Dad make at the dinner table, he's told, "That's tacky, don't ask." When he's curious about how much the family house costs, same thing—no one will answer. Over and over, these natural moments of financial curiosity are shut down, only to suddenly dump a massive money decision on him when he goes to college.

The important thing is not to make your children obsess over hoarding wealth or give them a weird money complex but rather give them the tools to understand, manage, and not avoid money and thinking about money—while also making sure that their needs are met. Because the way you give your kids money and material support is a lesson in itself, and especially as they start to get older, it's worth being thoughtful about how much support is helpful and when it starts to turn into enabling. Basically, there are three schools of thought about how much financial help—both education-wise and dollars-wise—to give your kids.

Help them as much as possible. Let me tell you the story of a kid I'll call CJ the DJ. CJ had basically unlimited money. He was attending the University of Chicago, one of the best (and most expensive) schools in the country, but he clearly did not take his education very seriously, because as far as I know he never darkened the door of the library during his whole time there. Instead, he ended up becoming the de facto DJ for his frat, complete with a full turntable setup and tons of expensive audio equipment. After graduation, instead of getting a job like all the other overgrown frat boys (many of whom ended up very successful and responsible, I might add; it was the University of Chicago, after all), CJ took his DJing professional. Was he talented? Well, talent is subjective. Was he hardworking? Mm, I'd say *not likely*.

Did he have so much money that it didn't really matter because his parents never cut him off? Yes, yes, he did.

I will give you one guess where that man's DJ career went: nowhere. Even though at some point in time, there had been someone in his family tree who was good at making, saving, and investing money, CJ did not ultimately benefit from that financial savvy. He ended up flaming out in the entertainment business and is now thirty-five or so years old with no work history or transferable skills to speak of.

This is, I would argue, the *wrong* way to help your kids. When money is the only thing passed down, as opposed to an education about how to *use* and *grow* that wealth, the kids often don't live up to their potential. No, they won't suffer materially, but they won't thrive, either.

CJ may be an extreme example, but it's kind of a "same problem, fewer zeroes" situation for more average-income parents who happily open their wallets for any and all asks from their kids without question. The *real* generational wealth is knowledge—and your kids aren't going to get that by taking handouts their whole lives.

Let them struggle. Then there's the opposite side of the coin, where parents don't want to give their kids *anything*. Social media is full of parents like this for some reason: posting all about how they don't do allowances, don't give their kids "fancy lessons" or even birthday presents. And that's honestly grim as hell!

I find it fascinating that these people are *so* interested in building generational wealth but hate to see it used. Ultimately, I'd argue that the reason you work so hard is to provide yourself and your loved ones the best possible life, right? And the best possible life includes making sure that your kid is healthy, fed, dressed appropriately for the weather, sent to school, *and* offered opportunities outside of their baseline needs. If they want piano lessons, ballet classes, soccer camp, whatever interest they want to pursue, being able to provide those things is important. That's . . . kind of the whole point of earning money.

More than that, when parents say, "I'm not helping out my kid; I had it hard, so they deserve to have it just as hard," it can become a self-perpetuating cycle. It's the same thing you see in high-pressure industries obsessed with "paying your dues": You were reamed out by your boss when you were a lowly assistant, so now that you're the boss, you're going to make some *new* assistant's life hell. But to what end? It's not going to incentivize them to work harder. It's definitely not going to make them like or respect you. In fact, it's just going to lead to their making the same mistakes you made—which, given that you've already made the mistakes and can essentially give them a speed run and cheat code through that, *makes no sense*.

If you want to transform generational curses into generational wealth, the one way *not* to do it is to make your kid's life equally as hard as yours was. Pushing your kiddos out of the nest with no knowledge or resources isn't going to build their character, it's just going to build their resentment.

Provide them with skills, experience, and a privileged upbringing but limited money. The best (or maybe just the most famous) example of this? The Gates family. Bill Gates, one of the richest humans ever to live, a man with hundreds of *billions* of dollars, has repeatedly made it known that his kids will be getting $10 million each as an inheritance after he dies—that's it.

To be sure, he gave them allllllll the advantages and resources growing up; most of the kids went to ultraelite colleges, they can get their foot into the door for any interview they desire—so they'll be able to pursue whatever career path in life they want to. But $10 million, which sounds like a lot to any normal person, is a fraction of a fraction of his net worth; given his net worth of $117 billion, a $10 million per kid inheritance is the same as a parent with a net worth of $500,000 leaving their kid about $42.50.

So in the grand scheme of things, they won't be walking away with anything close to their parents' fortune. They've been given a lot of advantages, yes—they grew up being Bill Gates's daughter or son in social circles most people can barely dream of—but with ten mil, they're not going to be able to continue the same lifestyle indefinitely. They'll never starve, but they probably won't live in the kind of home their parents raised them in, either. In other words, they'll have security and stability—because that's what security and stability are. They're not the *absence* of any problem. They're not the ability to snap your fingers and have an In-N-Out burger flown into New York just because you feel like it. They're the bedrock knowledge that you will be okay, on the whole, in the long run.

This is where I personally land—kind of the "teach a man to fish" philosophy. This approach creates kids who have a little grit but are still armed with the tools to succeed in any environment, as well as a sufficient support system so that they'll never be in real danger or make risky decisions because they're worried about money. From what I can tell, the Gates kids are independent, motivated, and successful, and I think part of the reason is knowing that if they wanted a life similar to the one their parents provided, they could not rely on their inheritance alone.

Bottom line: Have open conversations about finances, give your children agency over financial decisions in age-appropriate ways, and pave the way for them to have security and stability without living life on Easy Street.

Critically, *you* don't have to be perfect with money yourself to start teaching your kids to be. In fact, sharing your own financial learning experiences (including your mistakes) can be incredibly valuable. Modeling healthy money behaviors is, in and of itself, a way of teaching. And being that teacher for them? That's generational wealth in play.

Money Management To-Dos for Chapter 6

- If you're planning to have kids in the very near future, figure out what the impact on your earnings might be. For example:

- *What paid leave options are available to you, if any? Can you save up for your time off work to cover any gaps?*
- *If you're considering taking a longer career gap, look at how that will affect your long-term earning trajectory. You can use the Center for American Progress's calculator to start ballparking at interactives.americanprogress.org/childcarecosts/.*
- If you choose to postpone having kids or know that you are likely to encounter fertility issues, will need reproductive assistance, or plan to adopt, research the costs and providers of the services you need, and figure out which payment avenues (financing, saving, work benefits) might work for you.
- If you're about to add a kid to your family (or have some in the mix already), look into 529 accounts, UTMA and UGMA accounts, and custodial Roth IRA accounts and set up whichever one(s) make sense for your financial situation and your kiddos.
- If you have a credit card in good standing, add your kid as an authorized user to start building a credit history for them. (Whether you give them the card to spend with is up to you—but you certainly don't *have* to.)
- If your kid is old enough to chat with, don't shy away from money conversations. When they ask kid-level questions about how much things cost, how much you earn, or similar, answer them honestly—but with appropriate context and scale. Here are a few ways to start off your responses.
    - "That's a great question. What don't you understand?"
    - "I'm glad you asked. Why do you want to know?"
    - "That's interesting. Where did you hear that?"

Chapter Seven

Family and Friends

When I was on Wall Street, I had a colleague, a fellow newbie analyst, named Andre. Andre was a gentle giant, a first-generation college student who'd gotten an Ivy League athletic scholarship and used his education as a springboard to a job at JPMorgan. His path to working in finance had been very different from that of the people around him. Most of the *other* up-and-coming analysts came from families with money because, one, it takes a lot of money to go to the feeder schools for trading or investment banking, and two, how do you even know that this kind of thing is a career option unless your Uncle Rob works on Wall Street? A few handshakes later, and *boom*: you've gotten your first internship. Your family pulls you all the way up.

For Andre, it was the opposite. His family hadn't given him a leg up into the finance world; *he* was helping support *them*. He sent money home to help his mom pay her rent or make her car payment. And on our analyst paychecks (which weren't a lot after you factor paying rent on a postgraduation apartment plus the insane cost of living in New York) most of us, including Andre, were just making ends meet, with *maybe* a little bit of savings. So when I heard that his family was counting on him like that, it was a moment of perspective change for me.

True, I didn't come from family money. I wasn't one of the silverspoon, manor-born trust fund kiddos who woke up one day with an entry-level job at Goldman Sachs thanks to her parents' connections. I already felt like an outsider because my parents didn't have a place in the Hamptons, and frankly, I could barely find the Hamptons on a map—I didn't come from that background.

But that guy was dealing with all those same realities *and then some*. For me, family had always been a source of support; my parents weren't bankrolling any kind of lavish lifestyle for me, but they had paid for my education, which was huge, and had always made sure I had what I needed. More to the point, they weren't asking me for money. I wasn't expected to be their source of security and stability, only the other way around. In my mind, it had always seemed that the natural order of things was that parents paid for their kids, who then paid for kids of their own, and so on and so forth. While *my* first analyst bonus was the reason I was able to escape my cockroach-ridden apartment and get a little breathing room, Andre's helped his mom fix her water heater. That man was probably running on empty and still sending gas home.

For a lot of us, our relationships with our family and friends are one of the biggest areas where money goes from being a simple numbers game of saving versus spending to being a complex web of emotional and financial obligations. Yet it's something we don't talk about; nobody throws up a "My mom needed help with her mortgage payment" story on Instagram alongside their "I just bought my first house!" post, after all.

That's why it's important not to sweep these things to the side. Finding the delicate balance of setting up your own safety net while still being there for the people you care about will look different for everyone, but no matter your situation, *not* putting some conscious effort into planning and setting boundaries is almost guaranteed to get you into a sticky situation or two. Because as great as it would be to give your nearest and dearest help infinitely, you also can't set yourself on fire to keep others warm.

Having "The Talk" with Your Parents

There are two pivotal moments that shape your relationship with your parents. The first usually comes in your tween or teen years, when you realize that they aren't infallible, all-powerful beings; they're just people, doing their best. The second, more sobering realization comes later, often in your thirties or forties, when you're forced to confront their mortality. This might be triggered by a health scare, one of your parents' friends getting sick or passing away, or conversations about wills and trusts. It's at that second point that some of us discover that our parents don't really have a retirement plan.

Statistically speaking, for people in our parents' generation, there's about a one-in-five chance that they have no retirement savings[1]—zero—and it's a coin toss whether or not they have a will.[2] This means that many people reading this book will eventually face difficult conversations about supporting their parents financially or what's going to happen once their parents pass away. And if your parents are struggling, they aren't likely to mention that struggle directly or just hit you up for cash; instead, they might mention that their lease is up and they need a place to live or end up in the hospital with no way to pay the bill. You won't find out that your parents are in a tight spot until they're desperate and you have no choice but to bail them out.

Having financial conversations early, while everyone is healthy and clearheaded and there's still time to take some kind of action, can prevent the need for crisis management later. But even if everyone involved is hale and hearty, these discussions are still inherently challenging; at the very least, they're a little awkward, and at the most, they're a full-on role reversal in which you, the kid, have to help your parents do, well, grown-up stuff.

But—assuming that there's no estrangement or other factors changing the dynamic—that role reversal is ultimately the fate of every parent-child relationship. Your parents raised you from a wee tiny helpless thing to an independent adult; now, as they gradually become more dependent and helpless, you step up to the plate.

Here's how to have that conversation—or, rather, series of conversations—and avoid being on the hook for everything while still making sure your parents get what they need. While there's no perfect (or even typical) way to navigate this new frontier in your relationship, being prepared and proactive is far better than waiting for an emergency to force your hand.

Broach the Topic

Best-case scenario: This is a short conversation. Your parents have retirement savings, a will, and maybe some bonuses such as long-term-care insurance. They give you their attorney's business card with a sticky note that says "CALL THIS NUMBER WHEN WE'RE DEAD," and that's that.

Realistic scenario: They're only partially where they need to be—or nowhere close to it.

It's an awkward conversation to be like "Hey, Mom, hey, Dad, have you been giving any thought to how old and close to death you're getting?" but it's really better to be proactive. You can ease your way into the conversation with any number of segues ("I just read that about half of people your age don't have a will. Do you guys have one?") Then listen. Be empathetic, active, and curious without being overly pushy.

Talk Productively

Not to play into age stereotypes, but chances are good that your parents are of the "talking about money is rude" generation, which means that you might get a lot of "Money's tight, but we'll manage" or "We're taking it one day at a time" kind of nonanswers.

When it comes to estate planning, the best way to get the ball rolling might just be . . . going first. For example, my dad was not very keen on doing any kind of estate planning, but when Greg and I set up our wills and trusts with an attorney, I went ahead and passed his info along to my dad. When the two of them got on the phone, my dad really put the guy through his paces, as though Papa Tu was convinced that his Google knowledge was better than that man's law degree and forty years in the business. After a long talk, finally it led somewhere, and my parents agreed to get their financial house into order. They actually logged in to every single account they had and showed me exactly how much money was in each one, along with the deed to their house and their car paperwork. They set up the right infrastructure so that when the time does come, we'll have an exact plan in place and I won't have to prove anything to a judge to get their affairs in order.

Help Where You Can, but Keep Boundaries Intact

Much as with kids, there's a lot of "teach a man to fish" tactics you can use with your parents to help them without literally giving them money.

- **Help them budget.** You don't have to sit down and go through their bank statements line by line, but there are lots of young-person money-saving hacks (e.g., negotiating bills) that could help reduce their annual cash outflow.
- **Help them set up catch-up contributions.** If your parents will be fifty or older by the end of the calendar year, they're eligible to make what's known as "catch-up" contributions to certain retirement accounts. (Yes, the money will have less time to compound before they retire, but every little bit counts!) Here's what that looks like for 2025.

Parents aged 50–59*	Parents aged 60–63	Parents aged 64 or older
For an **IRA/Roth IRA**: $1,000 catch-up contribution in addition to the $7,000 base limit (for a total of $8,000)	For an **IRA/Roth IRA**: $1,000 catch-up contribution in addition to the $7,000 base limit (for a total of $8,000)	For an **IRA/Roth IRA**: $1,000 catch-up contribution in addition to the $7,000 base limit (for a total of $8,000)
For an **employer-sponsored plan** (e.g., 401(k)): $7,500 catch-up contribution in addition to the $23,500 base limit (for a total of $31,000)	For an **employer-sponsored plan** (e.g., 401(k)): $11,250** catch-up contribution in addition to the $23,500 base limit (for a total of $34,750)	For an **employer-sponsored plan** (e.g., 401(k)): $7,500 catch-up contribution in addition to the $23,500 base limit (for a total of $31,000)

* Meaning the age of your parent on the last day of the year.

** The higher "super catch-up" amount for ages 60–63 is a new provision from the SECURE 2.0 Act, but is optional for plans to offer, so check with the plan administrator to see if this higher contribution is available.

- **Help them research assistance programs.** Besides Social Security and Medicare, there are lots of public and private programs, grants, and groups that help older people cover costs, lower utility bills, even get boxes of farm-fresh produce. Research your parents' state and county department of aging to see what's available and help them out with the paperwork (or online applications, as the case may be).
- **Help them avoid getting scammed.** Sadly, the older you get, the more you become a target for all kinds of financial scams, from "I'm Brad Pitt, and I need your money to get out of this hospital" to "This is the FBI, send us $3,000 in Target gift cards immediately." Sharing examples of these stories with your folks (without judgment) can help them keep their eyes open.

- **Help them downsize.** Volunteer to help go through their stuff and clear out what they don't need so it's less of a mental burden. If they've been meaning to sell one of their cars and just haven't gotten around to it, help stick that thing up on Craigslist. If they're thinking of selling their house to live somewhere smaller (and cheaper), offer to be on hand as an additional helper. And speaking of houses . . .
- **Help them keep rent money in the family.** A Family Opportunity Mortgage (FOM) is a type of loan designed to help you buy a home for your elderly parents or disabled adult children. This can be a solid option if your folks are in need of housing and you have the cash for a down payment, because rather than their paying rent to a landlord (or a retirement home), they will pay you, the owner of the property. What's more, FOMs tend to have lower interest rates and lower down payment requirements (as low as 5% of the purchase price), so if it suits your situation, this could be a win-win. Your parents will get to live somewhere more homey, while helping you gain equity in a property!
- **Help them earn some extra cash.** Fun fact: There's nothing in the rule book that says you can't hire your parents. If you have kids (or plan to), you could pay one of your parents to be a nanny while you work. If you're going out of town and need someone to watch Rover, offer to pay your parents for boarding your dog at their place. If one of your parents has a unique skill set (former plumber, retired English teacher), pay for their expertise fixing leaky pipes or proofreading your résumé. For many older folks, not only does this help them avoid the feeling of receiving a "handout" but gives them a fun task to keep their minds and bodies active.

"But We're Family": Navigating Boundaries Around Monetary Help

My friend Mei was basically raised by her aunt and uncle, two Chinese immigrants steeped in cultural tradition. Mei's uncle liked three things a little too much: making money, smoking cigarettes, and gambling.

Because Mei was raised by those two, when she got her first big-girl job in the city and had a nice paycheck to match, she would send them some of her money to help out with bills. And even though it was very much the twenty-first century, Mei's aunt deferred to her uncle to manage it—because in the patriarchal Chinese society, the husband was the head of the household.

Mei's family hailed from South Jersey—very close to the Sin City of the East, Atlantic City. So when Mei sent them money, Mei's uncle would take the money and gamble with it. The bills wouldn't be paid, Mei's aunt and uncle had literally nothing to show for it, and Mei would be out however much money she'd sent them.

For the longest time, Mei had no idea that that was happening. Eventually, Auntie revealed where the money was *actually* going, so Mei started passing the money directly to her. But then Uncle found out, would somehow get the money from Auntie, and would gamble it away anyway.

When you start to get a reputation as the "financially savvy" one in the family or just start earning a big paycheck, you might find yourself beset by family members asking (or expecting) you to give them money. It might be your "seniors," such as parents, aunts, or uncles, or it might be your "peers," such as cousins or even siblings. And while most of us are (blessedly) not the Roy family from *Succession* with all the siblings backstabbing one another over inheritance and family assets (or even the Featherington sisters from *Bridgerton* sniping at one another over their choice of husband), lending family members money can end up in a very give-a-mouse-a-cookie situation. Suddenly, borrowing your car once in a while turns into borrowing your car once a week and then into borrowing your car whenever they want to and asking you for gas money. Or, in Mei's case, it ended up being scooped away on a craps table.

But Mei pulled a pretty genius move in the end. She concluded that she could not give *money* to her aunt and uncle anymore. She was still going to be generous with them, but on her terms and in a way that couldn't be misused. Now she takes Auntie on a luxurious vacation once a year, paid directly to the cruise line. When her uncle needed surgery, she arranged to have the hospital send the bill to her. But direct gifts of cash? A thing of the past.

The moral of the story is, obviously, know your boundaries and hold firm, ideally before too much money ends up being frittered away. But the *other* moral is that when it comes to helping your family financially, there can often be a middle ground.

Start by following the rule of the three C's: If they're asking for the money to obtain convenience, comfort, or consumerism, you should think twice about lending (aka giving) it to them. Beyond that, here's how to handle some specific situations that crop up.

If They Keep Trying to Mooch Off of You

"But we're faaaaamily" is not a sound reason to give someone an interest-free loan—let alone a straight-up gift.

- **Do set your terms up front.** "I'm happy to let you borrow my car if you put gas in the tank when you're done." "I'd love to meet up for lunch. I paid last time, so are you good to cover this round?"
- **Don't ghost them or make them guess.** If you're not going to give them what they want, say so. Until you put a firm

stop to their asks, they're just going to keep trying, and that's uncomfortable for both of you.
- **Do offer an alternative.** Your sister claims to need $500 for an emergency shopping trip? Bet. "I don't have any money left for gifting in my budget right now, but if you need something to wear for your date, I can lend you a dress."
- **Don't fall for guilt trips or low blows.** No one knows how to push your buttons like close family, but that doesn't mean you have to stoop to their level or give in. "Typical. You always were selfish as a kid." Okay, sorry you feel that way. "If you loved me, you would." Nope, boundaries are loving, too.

If They Genuinely Need Your Support

That said, there are some situations in which your fam needs money and you want to give it. Maybe they're disabled or need long-term care, maybe they need money to help get a divorce or otherwise get out of a bad relationship, or maybe they're struggling with addiction and need financial help to get back on their feet.

- **Do think of any money you put toward helping them as a gift, not a loan.** If they do pay you back one day, great (though you can still politely refuse), but treat that money as out of sight, out of mind from the get-go, and you'll have your expectations locked in.
- **Don't just cut a check or hand out cash.** Instead, pay service providers (doctors, attorneys, caretakers, residential facilities) directly to ensure that the money goes where it needs to.
- **Do set up accounts.** This can be as simple as helping them get the ball rolling on a high-yield savings or brokerage account or helping them establish a 529 plan for their kids (which Auntie or Uncle You can contribute to, too). For family members

with disabilities, Achieving a Better Life Experience (ABLE) accounts are tax-free savings accounts that can be used to cover disability-related expenses without being counted toward their assets for determining SSI eligibility (for the first $100,000).
- **Don't add them to your accounts.** Don't cosign loans for them, don't make them an authorized user on your credit card (without cutting up the card with their name on it), don't do anything that will commingle your monetary picture with theirs and potentially jeopardize *your* financial health.

If They're Just Making Dumb Money Decisions

It's downright annoying to see people you love make stupid decisions. Whether it's buying shitcoins, getting sucked into MLMs, or just generally spending like there's no tomorrow (when, in fact, there is a tomorrow; it's the first of the month, and rent is due), ill-advised money decisions by the people you love hit differently when *you* know better.

- **Do point them in the right direction—gently.** By appealing to your shared values, sensibilities, and even inside jokes, you're much more likely to make headway with some tidbits of financial advice. Throwing in some humility helps, too: A "Lol I just realized I never signed up for my company's 401(k) plan" text might prompt a "Lol me neither, what even is that?" reply, and *boom*, you've got an easy entry into a bigger conversation.
- Conversely, **don't be a know-it-all.** You know the saying "There's no zeal like that of the converted?" Sometimes finally getting up to speed financially can make people a little, um, insufferable about their newfound knowledge. Throw that on top of existing family dynamics, and you're more likely to piss off your bro or sis than get them to see the value of what you're saying.

- **Don't take the bait.** Your sister's flaunting her Birkin bag while all you've got to show for *your* last few paychecks is a stable place to live and a maxed-out 401(k)? Yes, you'll have more to show for your decision *eventually*, but in the moment, it's sort of hard to beat something with nothing. Solution: Don't play the game. Be the bigger person: Compliment her bag if you must, but resist the urge to add commentary, no matter how "helpful" it might arguably be.
- **Do live and let live.** Look, at the end of the day, it's their money, and if they're going to F around, they kinda have to find out for themselves, you know? As long as they're not in any immediate danger, there's only so much you can (or should) do. Keep your eyes on your own balance sheet, and Thanksgiving will be way less stressful.

Do Me a Solid: How to Navigate Friends, Money, and Favors

At our place in New York City, Greg and I have an extra bedroom, so occasionally friends come and stay with us. No problem—we're happy to host, we have the space, and New York hotels are expensive as hell. Plus, it's an easy way to see our friends when they are in town, so win-win.

For a while, we had one friend in particular who stayed with us regularly. He traveled pretty frequently for work and came to the city a lot. Which, again, was fine—like, the room is there whether he sleeps in it or not, we're happy to share. But after a while, instead of making a nice, small gesture to say thanks, such as taking out the trash or bringing a bottle of wine to share, he started to Venmo us $50 per night.

Now, I am not keeping a mental balance sheet of who owes whom in a friendship, and we don't need to count pennies between friends.

But those $50 Venmos felt . . . not good. I felt taken advantage of in a way I wouldn't have, had that same friend brought us a $50 bottle of wine or even picked up some take-out tacos for everyone.

So what gives?

When it comes to friends, generosity, and giving gifts—whether of money or of objects—I'm a firm believer in the "favors economy" model. The favors economy existed much more in our parents' day: Your parents' neighbors would drive them to the airport because Uber did not exist. Then your parents would feed your neighbor's cat when they went out of town because Rover did not exist. It wasn't about matching the other person dollar for dollar; it just meant showing some social grace, doing a favor, and not taking other people for granted. Everyone mutually agreed that they'd help one another out from time to time and all get square in the end.

Which is why I think those Venmos rubbed me the wrong way. It felt as though they had cheapened the friendship to a tit-for-tat transaction instead of recognizing the aspect of community at play. And whether we're the giver or the taker in any given friendship situation, that is so important to remember. (Also, what hotel in NYC charges $50 a night? Give me a break, ya cheapskate!)

The reason this matters financially is that as we get older, there often comes a time when our income levels start to diverge from those of our longtime friends. Different careers, different life circumstances, different lots of things can mean that one person from your friend group might be earning three times what another person is.

If you're the richer friend, maybe you scored courtside seats to a Knicks game or have a spare ticket to the symphony and want to take your pal along. No strings attached, no expectation of being paid back, just a gift. Or maybe you know your friend straight-up needs money, and you want to be the one to give it to them. But if you're the not-as-rich friend, accepting that money, gift, or favor can feel weird, especially if it's considerably generous and even if you really need it.

This can get awkward, but it doesn't have to. Take it from me, someone who's made a career out of being a Very Online millionaire literally called "Your Rich BFF" but still has friends in a wide variety of careers and on a wide variety of income levels: It is possible to share good times (and good things) with your friends without it putting a strain on your relationships.

Thinking in terms of a favors economy can help us be generous givers (or gracious receivers) and leave both parties feeling happier than they did before the exchange of goods or services—which, ultimately, is what money should be doing in our lives. We can leverage what's basically the Uno reverse of the reciprocity principle I talked about back in chapter 1 and allow everyone in the friendship to feel that their dignity stays intact.

If You're the Giving Friend

I once heard this anecdote about a mom who asked her daughter to run over to the neighbors' and ask for a cup of flour. The kid knows they have three bags of flour in the pantry, so she's like, "But, Mom, why do I have to go to the neighbors for something we already have?" So the mom explains that their neighbors had fallen on hard times and their family had been helping them out to pay the bills. "If the neighbors give us something we need, they won't feel so indebted to us. Flour is cheap, and they probably can spare some. Now go ask."

I think that's a beautiful depiction of how to think of giving people you care about a gift, be it of money or of stuff. People don't want to be pitied; they want agency. They want to feel as though they're contributing in the same way. It's about finding ways they can give you something in return that doesn't put them out.

For example, when my friends and I go out to dinner, I'll usually pick up the tab. I feel totally fine doing this, because I look around at my friends and think, "Okay, you are a surgery resident making $60,000 a year, working 120 hours a week. Both of you went to business school, so I know you're each six figures in the hole. And you just got your first job as an attorney after five years of Teach for America, and let's be real, we don't pay our teachers enough, especially at TFA. I got this one."

Then, later, when we're going out, I'll ask, "Can I borrow that top?" It costs them nothing to lend me that top, and you can bet that you've never seen someone throw a top at me so quickly. Or if I'm passing through their city, I'll ask, "Can I stay with you at your apartment?" even though I could easily book a hotel room. It makes them feel that they're doing something for me, and it allows me to continue treating them to some of those bigger dinners without their feeling that the dynamic has completely changed; it also gives us yet another shared experience—which is the whole point of friendship, right?

If You're the Receiving Friend

From a social graces standpoint, if you're the one receiving a gift, the onus is on you to be gracious—and that means accepting gifts as they are given, without too much insistence that "it's too much" or resistance overall. Making a small gesture of reciprocation is a good idea, too: even if your friend doesn't give you a specific opening to do them a favor, just keep them in the front of your mind and look for something nice to offer them in return. Again, it's not about dollar value here, it's about "I was thinking of you" or "I saw a way to make your life nicer."

More than that, though, receiving gifts when there's a big (or even medium to small) wealth disparity in the friendship can feel as though it's shining a light on said disparity and specifically that *you* are on the light end of the financial teeter-totter. But real talk? Your friend does not like you purely because you give them some calculable material benefit. You have value to them beyond nickels and dimes.

Maybe you're kind, compassionate, or generous. Maybe you're giving with your time. Maybe you're the best hype man or woman and make your friends feel awesome. Maybe you're really supportive when shit gets rough or you're the first person your friends trust for advice. All of that has value, even if you can't attach a price tag to it.

Pets Are People, Too

We millennials and Gen Zers love our pets. And I mean love. Our relationship with our pets has evolved dramatically from our grandparents' generation, when pets were either working animals or a luxury reserved for the rich, and even our parents' generation, when animals were seen more as additions to the family rather than full-fledged members of it. Now people feed their pets human-grade food, dress them up like children, and push them around in strollers. People are out there putting coats on huskies—sled dogs literally bred to run in the snow.

As someone who has recently been googling "dog adoption near me" a lot more than I'm willing to admit, I have to acknowledge that much like having a child, having a pet is going to make you poorer—and that's especially the case in this age of pet obsession. (If you're one of the nearly two-thirds of young adults who has a pet,[3] I suspect this is not news to you.)

Frankly, the decision to bring a pet into your home is a bigger moral responsibility than most of us realize. Unlike human children, who will eventually grow up and (fingers crossed) become independent, your pet will rely on you financially for its entire life. Also, unlike human children, who are eventually able to care for themselves and take on tasks that you previously spent money to have done on their behalf, a pet's quality of life is directly correlated with how much money you're willing and able to spend on it, especially as it ages and needs more medical care. (Santa loves rich pets more, too.)

That said, it's not wrong to want a pet, morally or financially. But as the postpandemic glut of abandoned pets in shelters showed us, wanting a pet and actually being able to care for it are two different things.

Here's how you can ensure that your furry li'l friend has the best life possible without sending you into serious debt.

Get a pet that fits your lifestyle. If you have a teeny-tiny city apartment, getting a teeny-tiny dog makes perfect sense. Getting a Border Collie that needs two ten-mile walks a day does not—and if you get one but have a busy nine-to-nine work schedule, you're going to be paying handsomely for someone to give that dog its exercise. Beyond that, if you're not sure you'll settle in the area permanently—or if you anticipate moving for work or school soon—having a pet in tow will make moving a lot more expensive. Waiting until after the big move will save you both money and stress.

Be aware that healthier pets are cheaper. Unfortunately, the way many animals are bred now means that they often come with health complications. Brachycephalic (smooshy-faced) dogs such as pugs and French bulldogs are apt to have breathing problems. Scottish fold cats (with the cute little ears) are prone to degenerative joint disease. Dalmatians can go deaf or blind due to a genetic mutation. You might have your heart set on a certain breed, but a mutt might be hardier in the long run.

Set up a sinking fund before you adopt. When your dog decides to be an idiot and eats the chocolate under the Christmas tree, then runs to eat its own throw-up after being given medicine (real story btw), the last thing you want to be thinking is "Can I afford to save this dog's life?" Socking away some cash before you're head over heels in love with your new pet—and regularly contributing to the fund—will help you forestall those kinds of heart-wrenching judgment calls.

Choose a real local vet. Over the past few years, there's been a nationwide trend of private equity firms buying out a bunch of small veterinary practices, sweeping them all into an umbrella group, and fixing the prices in a geographical area at a higher rate.[4] It's shitty, but it's happening. Before establishing care with a veterinary office, do some research to see who actually owns it and whether they might be more profit motivated than care motivated.

If you do have an emergency, finance it wisely. When your sweet little kitty's life is hanging in the balance, it's very easy to get swept up in the moment and sign on whatever dotted line the vet puts in front of you, but don't let your hot emotional state see you neglecting to read the terms. Some vets may subtly push you toward signing up for a third-party health care credit card—not because it makes it easier for you to pay but because that third-party health care card pays the vet faster.[5] If you can work out a payment plan directly with the vet's office, that can be the best option. Health care–specific loans and credit cards aren't terrible, but read the terms closely; remember that the interest rate, not the monthly payment, is what affects how much you pay in the long run, and a 0% introductory interest rate often expires pretty quickly (in six months or less) and then the interest rate skyrockets.

That said, pet insurance is also a thing and can be a very smart thing to have; check out page 229 for how it works.

Don't forget net new expenses. Again, dogs and cats aren't children, but they do have this in common: They add a whole new category of cost to your budget. Food and a doggie bed are one thing; dog walkers, boarding them while you're on vacation, and routine grooming appointments are another. Figure out expenses based not just on how you'll live with a pet on the boring, stay-at-home days but on the unusual days as well.

Try before you buy. Fostering pets—giving them a place to live until an animal rescue can match them with a forever home—is a great service and a defined time commitment. By definition, those dogs and cats aren't yours to keep (or yours to pay vet visits for), but you still get all the fun parts of having a pet, and it is a solid way to test-drive whether having a pet is feasible for you right now.

Have animals make you money. Alternatively, dog walking and cat sitting make excellent side hustles: You can hang out with cute animals and get paid for the privilege. If you own your place or have a chill landlord, you can even board animals overnight at your house. Apps such as Rover and Wag make the process easy, but you can also hang out a shingle the old-fashioned way by letting friends and family know you're in the pet-sitting biz. If you want, you can even put the money you earn into a dedicated pet-of-your-own fund.

Money Management To-Dos for Chapter 7

- Have "the talk" with your parents. Get a read on their overall situation, the state of their estate planning (if any), and their readiness for retirement.
- If you have a family member who's asking for money or otherwise needs your support, run the three C's test: If it's for *convenience, comfort,* or *consumerism,* lay down your boundary. If not, proceed with caution, and follow the steps on page 164 to ensure that your money is actually being spent where it's needed.
- If a pet is in your future (or your present), set up a sinking fund to cover emergency pet expenses (if you don't already have one).
    - *If you're still weighing whether or not to get a fuzzy friend, commit to fostering or pet sitting for a set period of time before you make the decision.*
    - *For existing pets, you can also look into taking out pet insurance (see page 229).*

Part Four

Securing Your Legacy

Making the most of your time on Earth means planning for when that time is up, too—or even just starting to reach the final years. Almost all personal finance gurus, myself included, like to bang on about retirement, retirement, retirement as some kind of ultimate goal, but almost no one seems to talk about what that means. What is happily ever after? Riding off into the sunset means what, exactly? And when you do eventually shuffle off this mortal coil, it's true that you can't take your money with you, but that doesn't mean you should just dump it all onto your loved ones with no preparation or plan.

With thoughtful futurecasting, some deep digging into what you really want out of life, and some knowledge of the ins and outs of things such as estate planning, life insurance, and handling big chunks of money (such as inheritances), you can make sure your money is optimized to get you the life you want the whole way through—and even beyond. Securing your legacy starts now.

Chapter Eight

Retirement

Sometimes it feels as though the world is dying and nothing really matters. Okay, a lot of the time it feels that way. And when the future looks so bleak, it's not unreasonable to wonder why you should even bother thinking about retirement.

At least, that's how a lot of the media says we young people are thinking these days. If you've ever been to a comments section or just existed in the world in general, you'll probably agree with me that millennials and definitely Gen Zers have a reputation for being nihilists and doomers—and therefore "irresponsible" with their money.

Except that we actually aren't. We are, in fact, *better* at investing for our future than our boomer and Gen X friends are. A recent report by the brokerage firm Vanguard found that workers aged eighteen to twenty-four were 32 percent more likely to invest in their workplace retirement plan than their older colleagues were at their age. Other studies have shown that one in four Gen Zers started investing before they turned eighteen, just over half of them consider funding their retirement to be a high priority,[1] and only 13 percent of millennials with investment accounts think they won't have enough money to retire.[2]

Although younger generations have been criticized for being lazy, stupid, and pessimistic and not caring about the future, we are very much not that way. We've had it harder than previous generations, yet we've emerged more, not less, financially literate. (Also, thanks to the beauty of compound growth, starting earlier means that Gen Zers will also likely be that much more financially ready for retirement when the time comes; those precious early years are a gold mine!)

At the same time, just because we're doing it doesn't make it fun. Delaying gratification is *hard*, and human brains are wired to respond to immediate rewards, not long-term returns. Plus, chronic stress can make us more likely to stick in our habit ruts rather than take action to achieve our long-term goals,[3] and with the state of the world being what it is, who *isn't* chronically stressed? For a lot of reasons, when the world around us is going up in flames, it can be that much easier to second-guess why we're socking away so much in an account we won't be able to touch for three or four decades.

The biggest hurdle to saving for retirement is undoubtedly getting started, which is why, in my first book, I broke down exactly what it means to save for retirement (aka invest). But knowing how to do something and actually doing it are two different things, and there are lots of less-than-rational forces (from geezers moaning about "kids today" to the collective postpandemic and climate-related trauma we're all undergoing) that can make it so easy *not* to do what you need to. So as you work to build up security and stability in your life, it's worth making sure that you're doing right by future you and setting yourself up for a bangin' retirement.

Because that's the other crucial misconception to dismantle about retirement: It's not a sad stretch of years where you gradually wither away (or some creepy *Midsommar* thing where the people in your town throw you off a cliff). Retirement isn't reaching some magical age where you suddenly stop working, stop being relevant to the wider world, and start playing bingo. It's simply a stage in life in which working for money is optional. By the same token, retirement *planning* isn't about shoveling away cash so you can afford to stay alive in your later years (well, it's partially that) but about creating options for your future self.

With that in mind, let's rethink what your retirement *could* be, break down what dollar figure it'll take to get you there, and how to course correct if you're not quite there yet.

And They All Lived Happily Ever After: Rethinking Retirement

When you have a home in Florida, you spend a lot of time around old people, and in my building in Miami, I am *by far* the youngest person living there. Most of my neighbors are at least in their sixties, if not well into retirement.

Perhaps you'd think they'd be a calm, quiet, slow-moving crowd. Perhaps you'd be *wrong*. These ladies all wake up around 5:00 a.m. They get dressed in cute little workout clothes. They go for a walk. They have a coffee chat. When I'm ripping my eyes open at 8:57 to run to our building's 9:00 a.m. Pilates class, they are strolling in well ahead of time.

After that, they have a leisurely brunch. Then they go to bridge club or bingo. Then they take *another* workout class and go sit by the beach with a book. At night, they cook a whole meal for themselves and their husbands (or boyfriends), and *then* they go out to the community events we have: movies on the lawn, disco dance parties, casino night. (Meanwhile, I—young, active, allegedly full of life—do not participate in *any* of these community activities, despite paying for them through my amenities fee.) The point is, these senior gals are living it up. If all you saw was a blow-by-blow of their day in the life, you'd think *they* were the professional TikTokers.

That's not to say that these older folks are all living bustling lives of *leisure*, however. I used to walk on the treadmill every single night alongside the same guy. He was eighty-five, he had come to this country from Colombia, and he had ended up becoming a very successful real estate investor: commercial properties, medical facilities, office buildings. One day while on the treadmill, he told me that he drives from the beach to the city every day and checks on his units. He has a property manager—someone whose full-time job is *checking on the units*—but still, every day, without fail, he puts on his black tracksuit and drives through rush-hour traffic *both ways*. That's how much he values being able to do something with his time in retirement— essentially, to *keep working*.

What I've come to realize from seeing how the other half of the human age spectrum lives is that the word *retirement* is a misnomer. There's nothing *tired* about it. Seeing these people two or three times my age being just as busy as I was (and consistently happy about it) has opened my eyes to the fact that retirement is not, no pun intended, a dead stop.

But unless, like me, you see this last-quartile lifestyle up close, it's hard to conceive of retirement looking that way when you're still decades away from it yourself. When you're in your twenties and thirties and forties and even fifties, grinding it out at work all day, maybe taking care of a family at night and on the weekends, you get a little bit of spare time and all you can think about is sitting around like a bump on a log. Yet when you finally get to the point of having all the spare time you want—of retiring—the *last* thing you want to do is be a bump on a log. You want to have stuff to do during the day. You want to wake up and have purpose.

What does any of this have to do with dollars and cents? Well, to figure out how much money you'll need in retirement, you'll need to know what that retirement is going to look like. And to do that, you've got to know that retirement can be whatever you want to make of it. It can mean having days jam-packed with yoga classes and book clubs and power walking. It can mean putting on your best tracksuit and going about your business as usual. It can mean living like my mom does—doing contract consulting jobs a few months out of the year, then chilling or traveling with my dad for the rest. All it has to mean is that you have freedom of how to spend your time.

So rather than thinking about retirement as the end of your productive years, think of it as the beginning of a new phase in which you will have complete control over your schedule. Maybe you'll teach part-time, serve on nonprofit boards, volunteer at causes you care about, or, hell, spend three hours a day in rush hour just to feel *alive*. The key is getting specific about what you want (or think you'll want) to do with your time so you can take steps now to build the financial freedom to make those choices on your own terms when the time comes.

Here are some guiding questions that can help you visualize what your retirement life will be all about. While I've put these in a rough order, there's no wrong place to start, and you should expect the process to be iterative, with your initial responses being revised as you narrow down your priorities in other areas. This plan should be a living document, one that you can aim for without being locked into it, especially as your life (and you) change. Remember, people still grow *as people* pretty much until the day they die. You've got a lot of living left!

1. **What will your major expenses be in retirement?** While your needs might stay roughly the same, your expenses to cover them might not. That, and you will certainly have some net new expenses come up as you age in earnest: Independent or assisted living (i.e., a retirement home), in-home caregivers, and other assistive services should be factored in. Obviously, you're not going to be able to arrive at an exact figure—and that's okay. You're going to be benchmarking off of averages, so the best practice is to take a realistic look at your life on two fronts: one, your standard of living as it relates to the average for your area (you know, because the guy living in the largest house on the hill will not have the same retirement as the person in the average condo), and two, your familial medical history. If all four of your grandparents lived until age ninety, then there's a nonzero chance that you'll live longer than the average person and stay healthier longer, but if there are (kinda morbid here, sorry) several people in your family who have chronic illnesses

or otherwise lived less long than average, it may be good to take that into account and make some worst-case scenario assumptions.

2. **Is anybody going to be retiring with you?** Obviously, if you're partnered up and intend to stay that way till death do you part, retirement is a two-body problem, and you'll want to factor in your SO's needs and desires as well as your own.

3. **Where do you want to retire?** It's the real estate market all over again: location, location, location. Obviously, you know that basics such as rent or a mortgage and groceries will be pricier in NYC than in Oklahoma (for example), but you also need to consider the price of net new costs in retirement (such as independent living facilities), and don't discount the effect that state-level taxes can have on your overall financial picture (seniors don't love Florida *just* for the sunshine, after all; there's also no state income tax and thus no tax on retirement income). Research the basic cost of living, but also the cost of senior care, because that can vary wildly across the country and not the way you might expect (for example, average assisted living expenses in Vermont are almost twice those in Utah—who knew?).

4. **Will you work? If you will, how much income can you expect to make?** Maybe you like the idea of quitting your day job at sixty-five but doing part-time work as a consultant in your field until you *truly* want to stop working. Maybe you're done with the career treadmill forever but would love a gig serving on a board for an organization, walking dogs, or selling crocheted tops on Etsy.

5. **What are some things you want to prioritize in your retirement?** These can be as big and broad (family! travel!) or as specific (owning a condo with an east-facing balcony to see the sun rise every day) as you wish. Either way, identifying your priorities can help give you clarity between two options

that otherwise seem equally good or eliminate ones that are incompatible altogether.

Give Me a Number

You can't put a price on happiness (allegedly), but you damn sure can put a price on a retirement home. So how do you know that you've saved enough for the last chunk of your life? This is the million-dollar question—or more accurately, the several-million-dollar question. No, we can't see the future, but we can get pretty close by using some strategic calculations and educated guesswork.

I've talked before about the FU number, the amount you'd need to have in your investment account, assuming normal/average market returns for the future (which I'll clock at 4 percent annually), that would be sufficient to support you if you stopped working. The FU number is the simplest answer to the "How much?" question. As a refresher, here's the formula:

Your total annual spending ÷ .04 = FU number

If you know how much you spend every year, you probably just ran these numbers and audibly gasped—because that number might seem huge. Don't panic. This is very much back-of-the-envelope math, and we're going to get a little more specific—especially now that you have a clearer picture of what you want out of retirement.

To be sure, this is a number that can and will change over the course of your life—as your priorities, expenses, and assets change—so it's not something you need to nail out of the gate. You'll want to redo your numbers periodically (and certainly after a big life event such as getting married, having kids, etc.) to take the temperature on your progress, and you'll also want to stay calm about the whole thing, even when the numbers start looking big.

That said, let's break down how to arrive at your refined, more accurate retirement number by diving into the details that will help you refine your target: numbers about you, numbers about your current money, and numbers about your future money.

> I've made it easy to do the math by making a spreadsheet version of this calculator; you can download it at yourrichbff.com/wellclub.

Numbers About You

Investments are all about your time horizon—the amount of time you have to let them grow—and a time horizon is always personal. At the absolute maximum, your time horizon will be equal to your mortal lifespan, but since you will probably want to retire sometime *before* you die, you'll need to do some figuring. Ask yourself:

- How old am I?
- At what age do I plan to retire?
- How long do I think I'll live?

I know, it's kind of grim to contemplate, but again, an educated (or optimistic) guess is fine. It's actually probably better to *overestimate* how long you'll still be kicking around, because, worst-case scenario, you die earlier than expected and there's a little cash left in the bank. *Underestimate* and you could be left with a lot of living to do and no money to do it with: not great.

As for your desired retirement age, the "default" in America is 67, because that's when you become eligible for Social Security benefits (although if you can hold out until, say, age 70, the amount of benefits you get increases). However, you become eligible to start withdrawing funds from designated retirement accounts—401(k)s, 403(b)s,

IRAs—penalty free at age 59½. (In fact, you can withdraw funds penalty free—but not tax free—at age 55 if you lose or leave your job that calendar year, but only from the 401(k) plan of the employer you left.) And if an HSA is part of your retirement strategy, you can withdraw those funds at any time as long as you use them to reimburse documented and qualified medical expenses. (Or, if you're super-duper-healthy and don't have any medical expenses to speak of, you can use the account like a standard IRA and take funds out starting at age 65, paying income tax on them.)

That said, I suggest holding out as long as you can before counting on *any* of those sources of income, for a few reasons.

For starters, I am not optimistic about Social Security. As of this writing, projections are that the Social Security program will have exhausted its reserves by 2035 (and while there would still be money to pay out benefits, they'd be cut by at least 20 percent). Even if the program does still exist by the time the rest of my Zillennial friends and I retire, the full benefit we'd receive will be equal to about 40 percent of our current income.[4] Even removed from all of that context, Social Security is inherently a *promise*, not actual money in the bank, and I don't think that relying on any government program that could be wiped away with the stroke of a legislative pen is the best strategy. (As a supplement? Fine, great. As the core of your retirement plan? Ehhhh.)

Second, and more generally, time is money, and the longer you let your investments hang out to compound, the more money your money will make you. That said, by the time you're in your late fifties to early sixties, you'll ideally have your investments overwhelmingly in lower-risk, lower-return assets such as bonds rather than stocks, so it's not as though you'd be missing out on huge #gainz. Still, every penny counts.

With these numbers in hand, you can estimate how long you have to keep saving and investing (retirement age minus current age) and how long you'll need the money to last you (age when you kick the bucket minus retirement age).

Numbers About Your Current Money

What are you working with? Ask yourself:

- How much do I earn every year?
- How much do I spend every year—and what kinds of things am I spending it on?
- How much do I currently have saved (invested) for retirement?
- How much am I adding to that retirement savings (investment) every month?

The last two numbers will help you calculate how big a number you'll hit by your retirement date. Your earnings and spending, on the other hand, are going to help you assess that progress—and recalibrate it if necessary.

Knowing how much you earn versus spend gives you a rough surplus (hopefully) or a deficit (not hopefully). If you're spending at a deficit, that is a problem to be corrected immediately, and it's high time to revisit your budgeting method to see where things are going screwy. (If you need help budgeting, check out chapter 3 of *Rich AF* for tips.) If you're not, phew—those extra dollars (the ones that aren't going into your retirement accounts but aren't covering annual expenses) are potentially something to shore up and throw toward retirement if you're not on track to hit the number you need to.

The reason it's important to know not just your total annual spending, but your spending *categories* is that the way you spend your money now isn't the way you'll spend it when you're older, and not just because you'll qualify for senior discounts. Some expenses naturally fall away over time (such as childcare as your kids grow up) or disappear once you stop working (such as commuting costs). Having a rough sense of what kinds of spending *won't* persist into your golden years can help you estimate more accurately what your annual cash needs will be when the time comes. That said, you're probably going to want to be generous here and round up. It's better to prep for a worst-case scenario (or, okay, the least ideal, if not superdire, situation) than one that's totally lean. As a quick gut check, you can run the numbers to see how close your current retirement savings and savings rate are to getting you to your FU number.

But if there's still a big gap, don't panic. There's one more step to go.

Numbers About Your Future Money

By nature, these numbers are going to be the most guesstimatey of them all — but you can still be pretty accurate even for ballpark figures. Ask yourself:

- How much will I need per year in retirement?
- How much money will my money make me?

You're already halfway there on the first question, since you know how much you're spending now. As a very broad rule of thumb, most people need about 75 to 80 percent of their working income in retirement to maintain their standard of living. But this is just a starting point. You can go ahead and eliminate those not-for-old-people expenses you identified in the last step. But you should also consider which expenses might *start* during retirement (good ol' net new expenses rise again) and which might stay present but change.

This is where your vision for your retirement comes in. Use that beautiful dream to scale your spending accordingly. For example, you'll still be paying for housing, but maybe you plan to sell your family home and downsize to a smaller condo. Maybe you plan to buy a huge property in Florida. Maybe you'll stay where you are, but your mortgage will be paid off. You might still want to travel, but way *more*, once you have time on your hands.

It's also important to think about medical costs, which tend to escalate the older you get. As with all things health care, your mileage will vary *wildly* depending on what kind of human body you inhabit, but generally speaking, getting old comfortably—the operative word being *comfortably*—isn't cheap: According to recent estimates by Fidelity Investments, a sixty-five-year-old retiree nowadays can expect to pay around $165,000 on out-of-pocket health care costs over the course of their retirement,[5] and with health care costs currently rising at about 3.8 percent every year, that would mean a millennial retiring in 2046 would need just shy of $375,000 to cover out-of-pocket health care costs.[6]

Finally, you need to factor in how much you can expect your money to grow over time. I say *expect* because—as your brokerage's disclaimer has surely told you—investments can and do lose money, and there is no guarantee of performance results. *However*, there is a lot of historical data, and that allows us to make estimates. Not only that, but because you're just making projections here, you can look at a few growth rates to see a bigger range of potential outcomes.

There are two main ways to calculate potential future growth: You can take a single average rate of return and run the numbers once, or you can take a range of rates of return and run the numbers for each rate in that range separately, then look at the spread (the difference between the lowest and highest outcomes) and see what you've got. The latter option is what's known as a Monte Carlo simulation (named after the fancy casino in Monaco where high rollers lose thousands of euros on craps tables and hide their assets from their home countries' governments).

If you want to keep it simple with option 1, you can assume a 4% rate of return over time. That's a *conservative* average—a portfolio that's 60 percent stocks, 40 percent bonds has earned about 6.8% per year on average since 1997[7]—but, again, it's better to have money left over when you die than come up short while you're still kicking.

If you want to get fancy and roll a few dice, you can try three different rates of return: the best case, the likely case, and the worst case—say 6%, 4%, and 3%, respectively. If you're still hitting your target at the worst-case rate, you are golden. If not but you're looking okay at the middle number and just fine at that higher number, I wouldn't be too worried. And if you're going to make it only if the best-case scenario happens, it's time to rethink a few things.

The Grand Total

Got all your numbers? Here are your equations.

For projected retirement savings:

$$FV = P(1+r)^t + \frac{M \cdot ((1+r)^t - 1)}{r}$$

Where:

- FV = future value of retirement savings (total at retirement)
- P = current savings (invested) for retirement*
- r = annual return on investments (as a decimal)
- t = years until retirement, calculated as retirement age − current age
- M = monthly contributions to retirement savings

For required retirement savings:

$$FV_{required} = \frac{A \cdot ((1+i)^n - 1)}{i(1+i)^n}$$

---

* This should include only cash or near-cash equivalents, such as investment accounts; it should *not* include things such as equity in a house. Otherwise, you could run this calculation with zero dollars in the bank and a decent house and think you'd have enough money to retire—but that would really be possible only if you throw your house up on fire sale, find a tiny, cheap new place to live, and still make all your benchmarks. Not ideal—or advisable as a plan.

Where:

- $FV_{required}$ = total retirement savings required to sustain desired annual expenses in retirement
- A = desired annual expenses in retirement
- i = annual inflation-adjusted withdrawal rate
- n = length of retirement (years in retirement), calculated as life expectancy − retirement age

> If the equations above gave you a traumatic flashback to algebra class and you no longer have your graphing calculator from high school math, remember, I got you: Grab my retirement calculator spreadsheet at yourrichbff.com/wellclub.

Finally, if this all feels overwhelming, breathe deeply. This retirement number—hell, your whole retirement plan—should be more of a living document than a onetime answer, something that will evolve as your life does. Getting married? Time to recalculate. Started a new job with better benefits? Crunch those numbers again. Received an inheritance from Great-aunt Mabel? You know the drill. The goal isn't to achieve perfect precision; it's to give yourself the best odds.

Help Me, I'm Poor: How to Adjust When You're Not Going to Hit That Number

So you've visualized, figured out your numbers, done the math, and—you're short. Possibly *way* short.

Take a deep breath. You have not made any dramatic, life-altering mistakes. If anything, you're very much on the right track, because by thinking about this now and taking necessary action ASAP, you're leveraging the most powerful tool you have on your side: *time*.

You have also not succumbed to some kind of moral failing. Maybe you stopped saving for retirement because you were having cash flow issues and needed to buy cute little things such as food and shelter, maybe you didn't get started as soon as you could have because you didn't know what a 401(k) was or your job had shit-tier benefits and no retirement plan, or maybe you had to draw down your accounts to cover a major unexpected bill and you're trying to build them back up.

No matter what, don't beat yourself up, and don't freak out! It's going to be okay. The only *bad* thing you can do from here on out is nothing. Here's what you should do instead.

Stay calm and assess the damage. First off, while no reduction in retirement savings is "good" per se, some are less bad than others. If you're closer to retirement, for example, a break will impact you less than if you were younger, because your assets are probably earning less to begin with (if you're rebalancing them to lower-risk, lower-return as you get older, which should happen if you are invested in a target-date fund). Conversely, if you're younger and weren't saving all that much to begin with, you still have time to make up ground, and you have a longer time horizon for that savings to grow.

Look hard at your two numbers (what you'd need for retirement and what you're likely to end up with when the time comes). If you jump back in at a "conventional wisdom" savings rate (10 to 15 percent of your annual pay), will that close the gap? If so, excellent. If not, there's still plenty of options.

Scale back now. I know this one's hard, and I'm not trying to get all "give up your daily latte and end up a millionaire" on you, but facts are facts: Spending less on goods and services now will free up cash you can invest for later.

Look at your budget, and scrutinize every line item: Can you reduce your spending in some areas or eliminate those areas entirely? (This is a great place to use the red/yellow/green categories I talked about in *Rich AF*.) Even smallish stuff can add up over time; if you're willing to forgo one $35 happy hour tab per week (have seltzer and be the DD!), that's already about $1,800 more you can save for retirement every year—which, after thirty years at 4 percent average annual growth, would amount to closer to $5,800. (Invest five years' worth of happy hour cash, and you'd have over $27,000.) Once you've identified a potential cutback, go ahead and rerun the numbers to see what the long-term effects of that short-term sacrifice could be, and it'll feel a lot more motivating.

Scale back later. Of course, you can also adjust the number on the other side of the equation: the amount you'll need in retirement. If you know that your retirement vision was pretty ambitious (bicoastal mansions and a private jet), you can certainly scale back to something that still scratches the itch but costs less (just *one* li'l beach house and business class). That said, I don't recommend digging *too* deeply into your future self's pockets; it's hard to anticipate what kind of curveballs life will throw at you between now and then, and it's much better to have more money than less, especially when your ability to earn money will likely decline somewhat, at least toward the very end of your life.

Commit to catching up. If incremental changes aren't feasible to get you there at this moment, the most realistic plan may be to catch up on retirement savings later—by *not* increasing your spending even when your income goes up. You can, for example, pledge to put at least 50 percent of your future raises into your retirement fund. If you get bonuses (or any kind of windfall, really), you can promise yourself that you will put some (or all) of that future money directly into your retirement investments: Do not pass "go," do not spend $200. Yes, it takes discipline to see these commitments through, but at the same time, if you can pull the trigger quickly enough and get that money invested, you won't really miss it, because it'll be as though you never had it in the first place.

Get a better gig. Remember that you can save only, at most, 100 percent of what you earn, but you can always earn more. Well, it's time to do that. You don't have to reinvent your whole career or start a business, either. Just asking for a raise (which you should have done way back in book 1, chapter 2, but there's no time like the present) or switching to work for a competitor can boost your pay meaningfully: studies have shown that Americans who switch jobs more frequently see almost double the salary increases as those who stay in their positions longer.

But it's also worth job shopping with retirement benefits in mind. If your current job has a crappy (or no) retirement plan, another job with the same pay—but those added benefits—could make a big difference. Don't ignore government jobs, either; benefits for federal government employees (health insurance, paid leave, and retirement) are an average of 43 percent higher than benefits for the same roles in the private sector,[8] and governments—whether federal, state, or local—are the rare employers in this day and age that might actually still offer a *pension plan*; almost 90 percent of state and local government workers have access to one.[9] Not to mention that a government job can provide other under-the-radar benefits, such as *total* forgiveness of your student loans after ten years under the Public Service Loan Forgiveness program or drastically lowered tuition for kids of public university employees. The trade-off, whether you work in the public or the private sector, may be fewer *other* benefits (such as PTO, flexible schedules, or fun perks), but if you're okay to make those sacrifices, the benefits down the road could be huge.

How Balanced Is Your Portfolio?

When you're staring down the road to retirement, it's not just the value of your portfolio that you want to look at but also its asset mix. If your portfolio is too conservative (containing lots of assets that are unlikely to lose value but that are not going up a whole lot, either), it might not grow fast enough to support you when you're ready to retire. But go too aggressive (lots of high-risk, high-reward assets), and you risk seeing everything wiped out if the market takes a big turn when you're least prepared to absorb it. Basically, the older you get and therefore the less time you have, the more you should lean in to fixed-income investments (such as bonds) rather than equities (such as stocks).

As you probably know, this is why I am a big fan of robo-advisors and target-date funds for most regular schmegular investors; they do the rebalancing for you. Over time, they'll swap out riskier (but higher-income-potential) investments with more stable (but lower-return) ones. If your retirement funds are invested in one of these funds, you're golden. If not, I have a rule of thumb you can use to figure out if you're on track with your asset mix. Here's how it works.

1. Take your age and round it to the nearest 5.
2. Subtract 10 from that number.
3. That's the percentage of your portfolio that should be in bonds and other fixed-income investments. The rest goes to equities, i.e., stocks—ideally in an index fund that tracks the broader market.

For example, say you're 34 years old: Round up to 35, subtract 10, and you get 25 percent. This means that your portfolio should be about 25 percent bonds and 75 percent stocks. Or maybe you just hit 51: Round down to 50, subtract 10, and you're looking at a 40/60 split between bonds and stocks.

> Caveat: If you're super-super-behind, you might want to increase your percentage of equities. Yes, this means accepting more risk, but if you're playing catch-up, you likely have a longer runway until retirement since you'll need to be working (and investing) for more years anyway.

Money Management To-Dos for Chapter 8

- Write out some of your dreams, goals, and possibilities for what your retirement looks like, answering the questions on page 181.
- Pull together the following:
  - *Numbers about you: your present age, your projected retirement age, a rough guess of how long you'll live*
  - *Numbers about your current money: how much you earn and spend per year, how much you have saved for retirement, how much you're adding to that savings every month*
  - *Numbers about your future money: how much you think you'll need per year in retirement*
- Using the equations on page 189, calculate your projected amount saved at retirement and your projected required amount for retirement. (Or use my spreadsheet at yourrichbff.com/wellclub).
  - *For the projected amount saved, you can use the 4 percent rule or a Monte Carlo simulation (see page 183).*
- If your current retirement savings plan is coming in under where it needs to be, consider which of the catch-up strategies might work for you and put them into action.

Chapter Nine

Inheritances and Windfalls

I vividly remember the first five-figure bonus I got after I started working in ad sales. It was back in my BuzzFeed era, and in the BuzzFeed ad sales department, bonuses were a *huge* deal, because the more we sold, the greater the bonus we earned—and if we seriously hustled (which I very much did), we could be seriously paid. (For context, by my last year there, my base salary was less than 20 percent of my overall compensation; everything else—almost 80 percent!—was bonus or commission. That's how much they moved the needle.) In some respects, the lower base salary was great because we learned to live on less, which made the bonus a huge windfall. On the other hand, the bonus was never guaranteed so in a potential down year, there could be very little windfall (a problem if you are spending anticipating the bonus coming).

At the time, though, I was still kind of a baby salesperson, so it was going to be my first-ever big-time bonus, and I was stoked. That day, I happened to mention my excitement to a very senior manager whom I was chatting with.

"Oh, what are you going to spend it on?" she asked.

Me being me, I was like, "Well, I'm going to save part of it, max out my 401(k), probably sock some away for a future down payment, blah blah blah," but before I could finish, the manager stopped me. "You have no idea what I would give to have had this attitude at your age," she said.

I asked her what she meant, and she explained. "When I started out getting these bonuses, I was making more money than ever. I might have doubled my income year over year. But you know what I did? Every time I would get that check for forty grand, I would immediately go buy a car or buy clothes or buy bags. And do you want to guess whether I have any of that stuff now?"

She did not. Also, what she didn't have was what that money could have gotten her if she'd diverted it differently way back when: compounding; dividends; security and stability through nothing more than the power of time and putting her money to work.

That conversation made me realize just how much these windfall moments are what separate the men from the boys—or the upwardly mobile adults from the stuck-where-they-are children. When we're faced with a sudden influx of cash, the stakes get very high very fast, and all our financial prowess (and impulse control) is put to the test.

While we may think of random windfalls as the kind of thing that happens only to lottery winners or Adam Sandler in *Mr. Deeds*, the fact is that a good number of us young adult–aged people will receive some kind of windfall during our lifetime.

We are on the cusp of the greatest generational wealth transfer in history. Baby boomers are set to pass more than $68 trillion on to their children. In fact, 52 percent of millennials who are expecting to receive an inheritance from their parents or another family member said they expect to receive at least $350,000.

This money has the potential to be life changing—or create big regrets. When you're only ever used to seeing numbers that big on your student loan statements, it can be genuinely hard to conceive of how much an inheritance, big bonus check, or (hey, why not) lottery win actually is—or isn't. See, human brains are kind of bad at understanding numbers on a large scale, because of our tendency to estimate, which is more about *comparing* than it is *counting*. When numbers get big and aren't tied to something concrete or immediate, our eyes can start to glaze over (think of how mind-numbing it is to decide whether you need 128 GB or 256 GB of memory in your new phone; like, IDK, man, how many Spotifys is that?).

But if you can get yourself locked and loaded ahead of time—as I did back in my first-ever-bonus-check days—you can not only lay the foundation for security and stability over the long term but in a sense use that money to its fullest. When I earned that bonus money, I *earned* it, with all the blood, sweat, and tears that extra client calls and late-night emails can take out of a person. As such, leveraging it to get to where I am today in my career feels so much more validating and self-actualizing than it would have if I'd just gone out and bought a car. Same with inheritances, maybe even more so: When someone has bequeathed you a chunk of their worldly goods, they probably did it because they cared about you and wanted you to have the best life for the longest time possible. Using that windfall wisely will be making their wishes come true—even if they don't live to see it happen.

Windfall Pitfalls: What Not to Do

If you've never seen that many zeroes in your bank account before, it's surprisingly easy to blow through a big sum when it hits all at once. While it's often reported that 70 percent of lottery winners go bankrupt (or just run out of cash) in five years, the actual figure is unknown—but there are plenty of anecdotes that show how suddenly gained wealth can suddenly disappear, and not just for sad reasons such as having a gambling addiction or buying way more luxury cars than one person can ever drive. Some people bankrupt themselves while trying to help other people—a perfect example of what happens if you don't "put your own mask on before helping others."

The point is, with high dollar amounts come high stakes and sometimes high anxiety. Let's nip that in the bud by laying out the major mistakes and how to avoid them.

Pitfall 1: Failing to Plan

Again, I hate to sound like your middle school gym teacher, but this point is real. The ultimate reason most people end up as living examples of "Mo' money, mo' problems" boils down to not having a plan. Not planning makes it easy to see your windfall as a big chunk of money that will never go away rather than a finite sum that can (and will) be exhausted if you spend it willy-nilly. (That's why, in the event that you *do* win the lottery, I suggest you strongly consider speaking to an estate planning attorney, accountant, and certified financial planner *first thing*.)

Pitfall 2: Coming in Hot

Remember hot and cold cognition? They're very much in play here, too, because acting emotionally is *so* easy in these situations. Getting an inheritance, for one, always means that someone you know is dead, and that's rough (even if you had a complicated relationship) and can leave you in emotional turmoil. But even a positive windfall can have you feeling some kind of way; winning the lottery or getting a surprise bonus will activate many of the same physical systems in your body that strip away processing resources from your rational decision-making brain. You lose literally nothing by letting the money sit in a high-yield savings account (HYSA) for a few days or weeks and giving yourself some time to cool off before making any major moves.

Pitfall 3: Quitting Your Job

Sorry to say, but unless you truly snagged multimillions, you probably did not just get "quit your job" money. Yes, even if you invest it.

For starters, your windfall won't likely go as far as you think. Even a chunky sum of a half-million dollars would amount to only $20,000 per year in income (assuming you invested it and stuck to the "4 percent rule" for annual withdrawals). What's more, leaving your job doesn't *just* remove your income stream from the equation, but could take away things such as insurance coverage and retirement fund matching—which you'd then be on the hook to pay for out of pocket.

Pitfall 4: Upgrading Everything

Lifestyle inflation is the easiest way to go broke, and it's extra tempting when you have more money than you've ever seen burning a hole in your pocket. The thing about lifestyle expenses is that they, too, compound over time, even if they *look* small and one time only at the outset. Say you get a chunk of change and decide to trade in your car for something newer. Not only will your monthly payment go up from, say, $300 to $500 (not *so* bad), but your insurance premium might jump, too. The new car might need higher-octane gas or more expensive maintenance, or you might need to start paying for an indoor parking space—and suddenly you're looking at hundreds of dollars more in expenses per month, let alone per year.

Pitfall 5: Rawdogging It

Some of this stuff just might take a professional, especially if you end up in probate (the legal process for inheritances to be distributed amongst legal heirs) because your Great-aunt Betsy never wrote her ex-husband out of her will. If there's any murkiness around the inheritance or any family conflicts that might flare up as assets are divided, an attorney can be a knowledgeable, neutral third party.

So You Won the Actual Lottery

On the very slim chance that you're the next Mega Millions jackpot winner, congrats! You *definitely* do not want to do this alone. Here's your step-by-step.

1. DO NOT SIGN YOUR LOTTERY TICKET. You want to stay anonymous.
2. Take digital photos of your ticket. Scan the ticket front and back as well.
3. Put the actual ticket somewhere *very* safe, such as a safe deposit box in a bank safe.
4. Reach out to an attorney specializing in lottery winnings, who can help you see how long you have to claim and ideally help you claim your winnings anonymously.
5. Reach out to an accountant. You'll have to pay a hefty tax bill, and that is not something you want to screw up on this scale.
6. If your state doesn't let you claim anonymously, it's time to ghost! Make all of your social media fully private and change your phone number. I'd also look into changing any property records from your legal name to a trust, so people can't easily just look up where you live if you own a home.
7. Get that bag, and claim your winnings (ideally anonymously)! Then go to the decision tree in the next section (see page 205).

Pitfall 6: Telling Everyone You're Rich Now

This is not just because bragging is tacky. Seriously, I don't care how long you've known a person or how far back you go, people *change* when big money enters the picture. The exception (obviously) is your spouse, because their finances are legally entwined with yours (although, hopefully, y'all anticipated this situation and have a prenup to account for it), but beyond them, telling people is *strictly* on a need-to-know basis—and besides a lawyer and/or accountant, there isn't anyone else who *needs* to know (even, tbh, your kids). That's not to say you can't decide to give things or money to people you care about thanks to your newfound wealth (I'll get there in a sec!), but you don't want to make it weird (or make it sound as though you're available for no-interest loans . . . that will more than likely turn into gifts).

Pitfall 7: Not Doing Anything Nice with the Money

Yes, you can spend a little (as a treat). In fact, I think you should do so, for two reasons. One, money should make our lives more secure, stable, and enjoyable, and just because those first two things are top priority doesn't mean that the third doesn't exist. Two, a relatively smaller splurge can be a good way to scratch the itch to spend, thereby staving off bigger (dumber) purchases you'll come to regret. I suggest allocating max 5 percent of your windfall to whatever makes you happy, no matter how "impractical" it is, whether it's a red-light skin care mask or a trip to Bali. (Just be sure that that 5 percent covers all the expenses, including whatever upkeep it'll take to use.)

Bonus Buck$: When You're Not Paycheck to Paycheck Anymore

I mentioned up top that when I worked at BuzzFeed, most of my income came from bonuses, but frankly, this has *always* been the case for me given the career paths I've chosen. On Wall Street, in sales, in real estate, in many, many industries where you eat what you kill, people see the vast majority of their annual income arrive in the form of a bonus. Even outside commission work, the more performance based or executive level you become, the more dependent your income will become on the back end (i.e., in bonuses) as opposed to a baseline salary; that's just how those employment agreements tend to be structured.

What this means is that the further along you get in your career, the more likely you are to start seeing a serious percentage of your income come to you in the form of, essentially, windfalls: large sums at somewhat irregular intervals that may or may not be the same size every time.

This can be very good or very bad, depending on your self-control—which, to be fair, you need in both situations. For example, say you work at a tech company as a software engineer, you're good at what you do, and you earn a base pay of $250,000 plus some stock options that may or may not be worth something if your company goes public. Your comp isn't performance based beyond your being smart and good at what you do, so you are paid portions of that $250k regularly throughout the year. In that case, you have to be really diligent about saving from every single paycheck, but you also don't have to sweat too much if you overspend from any one of those pay periods, because the next one's just two weeks away.

On the other hand, if you're in a performance-based job such as sales, you have might to be extraconscious of your budgeting day-to-day because your base pay is just enough to cover the essentials, but you also have to resist the twin temptations of borrowing from Future You ("It's okay to put this on my credit card now even though I don't have the cash; I'll be getting a bonus in a month") and going out-of-control nuts on spending when your check does hit. In fact, sometimes having that leaner base salary with the promise of a fat bonus to come can make it harder to resist temptation when the check does arrive; research has pointed to the idea that self-control is like a muscle that gets worn out the more you use it (through a process called ego depletion) and decision fatigue is real (that's why Steve Jobs wore the same outfit every day—so he could save his brainpower for other tasks).

So when it comes to planning around bonuses—which, as you ascend your professional ladder, are more and more likely to be part of how you earn your money—my best advice is to make things as automatic as possible so that you don't have to muscle through them.

Start by thinking of these periodic windfalls as something to help you get ahead, not catch up. When I was earning those chunky bonuses, I didn't always get one every quarter. I couldn't live big and assume that I'd pay my bills later, because the dollars might not be there when I needed them. Instead, the bonuses were what allowed me to make a deep dent in my plans for the future—to map out a path to security and stability.

Next, precommit to how much you'll allocate and where, even if you don't yet know the exact dollar amount of what you'll be getting. Saying that you'll put X percent toward debt or Y percent toward a sinking fund for a new car maps out a plan without locking you into specific numbers. (This is a great place to make sure you build in some kind of "fun" spending—with a limit. You'll be less tempted to bump your treat-yo-self purchase up by 5 percent if it means decreasing another, more meaningful category by that much.)

Finally, understand how taxes on bonuses work—because they're not intuitive, and they're not fun. It's true that your bonus is initially taxed at a higher rate than your base compensation, so less of it ends up in your bank account the day the check is cut. However, this does not make the guy from your high school who took remedial math correct in his soapboxing about how "you should never take bonuses or overtime pay because it's taxed more and you'll make less."

That's not true. What does happen is that bonuses, and the big ol' additional dollar value they add to your income, can and sometimes do push you into the next tax bracket, and in that next bracket, all the dollars you earn over the threshold are taxed at a higher rate than the base pay you traditionally make. This makes the government nervous, because it knows that people don't understand our tax system, so when bonuses are issued, your employer issues them separately from your traditional regular payroll, marks them as bonuses, and withholds taxes on them at the highest applicable rate, as if you earned that much money all year round. But—and this is key—when tax time comes around and you file your return—the government will see that you weren't actually earning that bonus-level money fifty-two weeks out of the year, and it will send you a nice refund for what you overpaid.

Does this mean that the government's getting an interest-free loan from you? Yes. But it's really silly to claim that you're getting less overall, because you're not; you just have to wait a little longer to get it. That definitely doesn't mean you shouldn't actively be working to get the biggest bonus possible, but it does mean that you should think ahead in terms of cash flow and be conservative when estimating how much liquid money you'll have in your hands after those bonus taxes are taken out and before they're refunded.

The Windfall Decision Tree

Now that you know what not to do, what comes next? Don't worry; I brought a system. And it's a two-parter.

First, you're going to CASH that windfall: **Calculate**, **Account for taxes**, **Secure it**, and **Hold it** (for part two of the process).

Calculate

How much money are we talking? Is it cash, or is it some other kind of asset, e.g., an inherited retirement account or a physical asset such as real estate?

For a noncash asset: Decide if you want to liquidate it or hold it.

> There's a reason that books on tax and inheritance law are so thick and dense: Almost every case described in them is an edge case. Among factors such as multiple heirs, multiple state laws, and even the time of year, inheriting assets (especially noncash assets, such as a house) can become complex *fast*, and there's no way I can cover every possible scenario here. While the process I describe is a solid order of operations, you can get more personalized guidance on specific options via my Ask Dolly app—where you can get information on the basics and talk to a live, human certified financial planner (CFP) to build a great foundation to bring in when you meet with a tax or estate planning attorney. Check it out at AskDolly.com.

Account for Taxes

When it comes to the IRS, out of sight is out of mind, and getting this taken care of first means you won't end up spending money that's actually Uncle Sam's. Depending on the nature of your windfall, you might owe:

- **Inheritance tax:** This is paid by you in some states; check your state's laws for how and how much to pay.
- **Estate tax:** This is taken out by the estate *before* the inheritance is distributed, so should not be your problem.
- **Capital gains tax:** This applies if you sell inherited assets (such as stocks and real estate) for a profit, but only *after* you hold them long enough to appreciate.
- **Income tax:** If you're receiving a bonus from your employer, double-check that your payroll processor has withheld the proper amount of tax (which will be higher than usual!) from your bonus. If you're receiving a payment from a nonemployer

source (such as a book advance, hey!), it *may* be treated as self-employment income and be subject to income tax *plus* Social Security and Medicare taxes (as well as any state taxes). You'll want to set that aside to avoid a surprise come tax time.

Secure It

With taxes taken care of, you'll want to stick the money somewhere secure and liquid (e.g., a high-yield savings account) so that it's safe and sound—and earns a little interest.

Hold It

Congrats—the money left over is yours free and clear! You can sit tight with it as you plan the next step.

With everything CASHed out, it's time to STRIP. (No, I don't mean on a pole, although if that's how you get your bag, go for it.) You're going to address your priorities in the following order: **Savings**, **Total debt**, **Retirement**, **Investments**, and **Planning**.

Savings

You'll want to set aside three to six months' worth of living expenses, put it into an FDIC-insured high-yield savings account so you're getting the most out of your money, and then proceed to the next step with any money left over.

Total Debt

Pay it down! Rank your debt from the highest to the lowest interest rate, *not* the total amount owed (you can refer to chapter 6 of *Rich AF* for a breakdown), make the minimum payment across everything, and then any additional dollars you want to use for paying down debt, you can put toward your various debts in their order of interest rate from high to low.

> What if your debt is at a *super* low interest rate? If you were one of those lucky ducks to score, say, a pandemic-era mortgage of 2.5%, you might not want to pay it off in a hurry; what you *do* want to pay off is high-interest-rate debt (such as credit cards). Follow the **7% rule**: If the debt has a 7% interest rate or higher, pay it off before investing. Then start investing *while* paying off the debts with lower than 7% interest rates at the same time. This works over the long term because there's a *positive delta* (you're bringing in money faster than it's flowing out). The 7% comes from the fact that investing in an index fund that tracks the market will return you an average of 8% to 10% annually, so by following this rule, you'll be positioned to *make* more investing in the market than you'd *save* by paying off your low-interest-rate debt.

Retirement

Have you maxed out your tax-advantaged investment accounts—Roth IRA, 401(k)—for the year? If not, then contribute what you need to in order to hit the annual maximum or adjust your per-paycheck contributions if it's an employer-sponsored plan.

Investments

Once the money's in those accounts, you want to make sure you *invest* it, not just let it sit around in cash. You can self-direct and pick out broader market index funds that track the overall performance of the market or target-date funds that automatically rebalance according to when you plan to retire, or you can use a roboadvisor to get a more personalized portfolio tailored to your situation and goals.

But don't forget to invest in *yourself*! Maybe now's the time to get that certification or next degree—or even just upgrade how you take care of yourself in the day-to-day.

Planning

If you're still sitting on some money, the world is your oyster. What are your money goals? Getting hitched, buying a house, starting a family? Don't limit yourself to the immediate future: Definitely plan that culinary tour of Europe you've always dreamed of, but also look five to ten years out and think of what Future You might want or need at that point. Will your car be on its last legs? Will you maybe want a puppy to run around the backyard of the house you buy?

Money Management To-Dos for Chapter 9

- If your job compensation includes bonuses or your life otherwise involves semiregular miniwindfalls:
  - *Precommit to what percentage of that chunk of change will go where.*
  - *Calculate the potential tax burden* ahead *of time so that you don't budget to spend money you won't have.*
- If you've received a windfall:
  - *CASH it: Calculate, Account for taxes, Secure it, and Hold it.*
  - *Then STRIP it: Tackle Savings, Total debt, Retirement, Investments, and Planning.*

Chapter Ten

Insurance

In the online financial space, insurance has gotten a sexy reputation as of late. People DM me about it all the time: Vivian, what about insurance??? bc I saw this guy in a skintight polo shirt who looks like he tans under a hot dog heat lamp tell me that I could have infinite banking and lend to myself and be rich beyond my wildest dreams just by . . . buying insurance??? he said only idiots, the uncultured swine, the RUBES of the world buy stocks or index funds, but the REALLY smart people are buying insurance.

I'm sure you've seen something along those lines, too. And I bet you're now very curious: Does doing this actually work? Are the claims true? In a word: no.

I don't know how else to say this: If it sounds too good to be true, it is too good to be true. If it walks like a duck, if it quacks like a duck, it's probably a fucking duck, right? So no, sorry, insurance is not a one weird trick money cheat code that can get you infinity number of dollars. But insurance *is* very valuable, and it's something that if you're trying to build that security and stability in your life, you really can't afford to skip.

Why? Because insurance has always been about *protection*. The OG "insurance policies" were (arguably) those of organized crime groups, including the Mafia, which established themselves as private protection firms—and no, I don't mean extortion money in the "Nice little shop you've got here . . . be a shame if something happened to it" sense, but as literally money to ensure protection. In the late nineteenth and early twentieth centuries, when businesses owned by immigrants opened in big US cities, they were usually in the dicier neighborhoods, and they'd often be vandalized and/or robbed, which was obviously not great for business. So in the case of the Mafia, the Italian butcher, the Italian baker, the Italian candlestick maker would pay the Mafia to act as a backstop, not to stand guard outside the store like a bouncer but more to act as the "find out" in Fuck Around and Find Out, if you know what I mean. When gangs would come and steal meats or breads or candles, the Italian Mob would . . . pay the perpetrators a visit, let's say. In its own *Godfather 2* way, the system gave the business owners peace of mind. I know it was also often via extortion, but you get the gist, so roll with me.

Today, and in a much more regulated industry, insurance is still a product created to give you peace of mind. Fundamentally, insurance is simple: You pay a company a little money each month to protect something—your house, your car, your health—and in exchange for that money, the insurance company agrees to pay you an agreed-upon amount if something bad happens to the thing you want to protect.

Sounds like a sweet deal, right? In theory it is, because insurance is also *supposed* to be win-win. For you, the consumer, it's a load off your mind and a financially wise move: It will *almost always* cost less to pay into homeowner's insurance, for example, than go uninsured and have to pay for a whole new house yourself if yours catches fire or blows away or floods. For the insurer, it's profit: Its team of statistics nerds, called actuaries, runs a bunch of numbers and calculates how much to charge you (and everyone else) so that even if the company *does* have to pay out for damages in individual cases, it will still be in the black.

But here's the reality: Insurance as we know it is fundamentally broken, especially when it comes to homeowner's insurance, where the math isn't mathing anymore. Those teams of actuaries, whose entire job is to calculate risk and determine appropriate premiums to charge customers? They're quickly discovering that their traditional calculations don't reflect the reality of our world. People are living longer but also getting sicker—which costs insurers more. Natural disasters are becoming more frequent and catastrophic than any of the models had predicted—which costs insurers more.

As a result, when it comes to homeowner's insurance, companies are pulling out of high-risk areas, rolling back or flat-out denying coverage, and making it harder to get claims approved. They're looking for more and more ways to shrink coverage, complicate policies, and jack up premiums. We're seeing this play out dramatically with homeowner's insurance in places such as Florida and California, where it's become insanely expensive to get coverage, if coverage is even offered (and good luck getting a payout if your house is leveled). The insurance industry as a whole is stuck in a vicious cycle. Because, at the end of the day, insurance companies are like any other business. They're for-profit companies. They can't *not* try to make money or even "just" break even. They need to grow, quarter after quarter, year after year. And if their costs are rising, that means they'll have to make up the difference on the back end: that is, in what they give to you.

This is why insurance isn't and can never be the financial hot girl that online get-rich-quick gurus swear it is. It is not, I repeat, *not* a way to *make* money. But it is a way to *avoid losing more money than necessary*, and that is both realistic and a good idea.

None of this is to say that you should avoid insurance altogether. Quite the opposite: In the name of security and stability, there is arguably nothing as critical as solid insurance coverage. There's no point in building a life you care about and enjoy if you're not going to protect it. (And even after your life is over, insurance makes it possible to take care of the people you love.) It just means that getting the right insurance requires you to understand the basics, learn how to evaluate what's on offer carefully, and buy exactly the coverage you need—no more, no less. In this chapter, I'll break down the different types of insurance and what they cover, how to get the best coverage for your situation, and, most important, how to protect yourself in a system that increasingly seems stacked against the consumer.

Homeowner's Insurance

If you have a mortgage on your home, you're going to have to get homeowner's insurance. Why? Well, since technically the home is the *bank's* home until you've paid off the loan, the bank very much wants to make sure that if something bad happens to its property, its investment is protected. Without your taking out homeowner's insurance, it may have a hard time recovering the money it lent you, and if there's one thing banks don't play around about, it's collecting their due. You'll get home insurance when you buy your house (to prove to the bank that you have it before they cut the seller a big ol' check), and you'll typically pay the premiums out of escrow, or lumped in with your monthly payment to the bank. In other words, you pay the bank, then the bank pays the insurer.

Homeowner's insurance typically covers three (sometimes four) main things:

1. Dwelling Coverage (AKA the House Itself)

Your home insurance covers your home—groundbreaking. That said, there's an asterisk here: Your home is covered under "normal circumstances," but what's "normal" is relative, and the more likely something is to happen in your area, the less likely it is to be covered under your homeowner's insurance policy. For example: If you live in Ohio and a random hailstorm breaks your window or damages some roof shingles? Covered. If you live in Florida and get hurricane damage or you're in Tornado Alley and suffer tornado damage? Probably not going to be covered.

The actual dollar amount of this coverage is going to be pegged at replacement cost, or what it would cost to rebuild the house from scratch if you had nothing but a bare patch of land. This will probably *not* be the same amount as you paid for it or even the market value of the house. You'll want to have your home insured for at least 80 percent of replacement cost, and your insurer will calculate that cost by asking a bunch of questions about your home's features and materials.

2. Your Stuff Inside

This is also fairly intuitive: Your homeowner's policy covers the contents of your home from theft or damage—again, *under normal circumstances*. Usually, this amount will be anywhere from 50 to 70 percent of your dwelling coverage, but if you own really fancy stuff and have a not-so-expensive house, it might be worth adjusting the coverage to ensure that you can afford to replace things, especially stuff that's mission critical, such as computers you need to work.

3. Liability

This is one of the biggest protections your homeowner's insurance can offer, but not one that most people think (or even know) about. Having liability coverage means that if someone comes to your house, trips on a floorboard, breaks their nose, and sues you, your homeowner's insurance will cover the cost of that lawsuit.

Nice, right? Insurance companies can afford to cover liabilities because they're usually not catastrophic and don't happen en masse (like, the odds that every single home on your street has someone slip, break their elbow, and sue at the exact same time are the same as the odds of your hitting it big in Vegas and never having to work again—not very high). However, because the liability coverage is tied to legal action, you usually have to *actually be sued* to get a payout, which can be a hassle. (Remember the "Worst Aunt Ever" who went viral for suing her nephew after he hugged her too hard and she fell? She *had to* sue in order to get her injury claim covered by insurance.)

4. (Sometimes) Accessory Dwelling Units

Accessory dwelling units (ADUs) are more or less what the name suggests: a place on your property where, though it's not the main residence, someone could conceivably dwell. These are your garage apartments, your basement rentals, your "in-law suites," and so on.

Typically, homeowner's insurance covers structures on your property under what's called "other structures coverage," which usually amounts to about 10 percent of your main dwelling coverage. So if your house is insured for $500,000, it includes about $50,000 of insurance coverage for your shed, garage, and *potentially* that ADU.

But that is a big "potentially," because insurance companies can be *really* picky about ADUs. If you're renting out that space, for example, you're now running a business from your property, which could void your homeowner's policy or at least leave you in the lurch for coverage of anything that happens to or in that space. The same might be true if you're using that cute little shed as a home office (again, it technically becomes business use). There's also the risk that the previous owners had that sucker installed, um, under the table, and didn't conform to local building codes and regulations, which is a must if you want insurance to cover it. If you have an ADU and your homeowner's policy does not cover it, your insurance company might require you to:

- Buy additional liability coverage (bumping up the dollar amount on your existing policy with an addendum)
- Buy a landlord policy (a separate policy entirely that covers the ADU)
- Make fixes to the structure to bring it up to compliance with the building code

- Or . . . buy a completely different type of insurance altogether (your mileage will truly vary)

Obviously, this applies only if you have an ADU on your property, but if you do, you'll want to make sure it's not falling through the cracks.

That said, here are the things that are *not* covered by a standard homeowner's policy—and that can come back to bite you if you're not careful.

Flood Damage

If you live in a flood zone, that is. People who live in low-lying areas and floodplains as designated by the Federal Emergency Management Agency (FEMA) and have a mortgage backed by the government, which is most mortgages, are not only legally required to have separate flood insurance but to buy it from the government under the National Flood Insurance Program (NFIP), which is part of FEMA; the policies are issued by private companies, but they're regulated so that the companies can't price gouge.

Other Natural Disasters

You know why I know that climate change is real? Because the math nerds at insurance companies think it's real—and they aren't paying for it.

That sounds harsh, but it makes sense when you consider their business model. The fundamental problem with catastrophic events such as hurricanes, wildfires, and mudslides is that they wipe out entire neighborhoods at once. When every house in a zip code is destroyed simultaneously, the insurance payouts are enormous, so insurance companies have either stopped covering these risks entirely or require separate, specific policies for them. Unfortunately, this has led to a lot of scary scenarios where people's homes are getting destroyed, they don't qualify for an insurance payout, but they're still on the hook for their mortgage payment. The bank doesn't care that your house is gone and your insurance won't pay; it just wants its money.

If you live in a high-risk area for any of these natural disasters, you can look into what's called Difference in Conditions (DIC) insurance to cover catastrophic events. This coverage essentially bridges the gap between what homeowner's insurance covers and what might actually happen and could make the difference between financial ruin and a clean slate after a scary loss. (Though I do want to be honest: It can be very pricey, so be sure to run the numbers before you sign up.)

Edge Cases

There's a figurative gray area around your house where your property stops being your property but things breaking there can still affect the condition of your property: specifically, water and sewer lines, which are owned by your local municipality and water/waste authority but aren't covered by your homeowner's policy. Here's where that gets tricky: If there is a big tree on your lot, say, and its roots have been growing into the surrounding ground for years and years, they could infiltrate those utility lines and break them open, causing a nasty backup into *your* innocent house or property. Or the lines could become corroded by the dirt in your yard or just break down from wear and tear. None of these is covered by standard homeowner's policies, but all of them involve, um, "backup" onto your property—so not only will you have to pay to repair the damaged water or sewer line (which can cost a few thousand dollars), you'll also have to deal with damage to your stuff. Fortunately, you can pretty easily add what's called a "rider" (bonus coverage) to your homeowner's policy to cover water backup and/or service line replacement, usually for just a couple of extra bucks per month.

No matter what your situation (the size of your house, your location, the state of the global climate) the most important thing is to understand thoroughly what your policy does and doesn't cover—*before* you need to make a claim. Review its details carefully and ask questions about specific scenarios that worry you. It's much better to be aware of your coverage gaps ahead of time than to discover them after a disaster.

> ## What About Renter's Insurance?
>
> It may seem kind of unfair that you have to buy insurance when you don't own the property you live in, but buying renter's insurance is a good idea regardless. Yes, your landlord has insurance on the property, but it's a different kind of insurance that doesn't cover the same things that an owner-occupier homeowner's plan would.
>
> **Landlord's insurance covers:**
>
> - Damage to the building itself from fire, water, etc.
> - Liability for harm caused by *their* negligence (e.g., not fixing a broken walkway that causes someone to trip and break their leg)
> - Lost rent in the event the unit becomes uninhabitable (sometimes)
>
> **Renter's insurance covers:**
>
> - Damage to *your stuff* inside the building (or sometimes out of it, too: example, your laptop gets stolen out of your car)
> - Liability for harm caused by you and your actions *on* the property (e.g., you don't clean up a spilled drink in the kitchen, someone slips and bashes their head on the counter and decides to sue)
> - A place to stay (such as a hotel) if the unit becomes uninhabitable
> - Damage you cause to the property (oops) and legal costs if your landlord takes you to court over them

> Fortunately, renter's insurance is typically a fraction of the cost of homeowner's insurance ($25 a month or less on average), so even if your lease doesn't require it, given all the protection it gives you, there's no reason *not* to have it. As for coverage levels, that $25 a month cost will get you about $30,000 in personal property coverage (based on national averages) with a $500 deductible, but your mileage may vary (depending on where you live and other demographic factors).[1] You'll typically be able to choose coverage levels (higher or lower) depending on your needs; just be sure it actually covers all the stuff you can't afford to replace out of pocket and you're golden.

Car Insurance

While a home is almost always the most expensive thing we ever buy, motor vehicles often come in second. Car insurance doesn't just protect the physical object of your car; it also covers your ass in the event that you hurt someone or something *with* that car, and for that reason, it's a must-have (and usually legally required) if you're driving.

That said, car insurance does come fairly à la carte, and there are various layers of coverage that you can opt into or out of, depending on your state. However, just because you *can* strip your car insurance coverage down to the bare bones doesn't mean you should, especially if you rely on your car (to get to work to make money, for example). That's why it's important to know the different aspects of car insurance so you can put together a policy that makes sense for you.

1. Liability Coverage

If you have a car, you're probably going to have to have this; it's mandatory in every state except, weirdly, New Hampshire, which doesn't require *any* auto insurance, and Florida, which requires only *property* liability. Regardless of law, it's an absolute must in my book. Liability coverage breaks down into bodily injury liability (if you hurt a person) and property liability (if you drive into a mailbox, for example). If either of those things happens, this coverage will pay out for expenses such as medical fees (theirs, not yours), legal fees, and repairs to property.

Is it required? Yes, in most states.

How much coverage should you get? At least your state's minimum, but beyond that, experts recommend $100,000 per person and $300,000 per accident for bodily injury liability, and $100,000 for property liability.

2. Collision Coverage

This is (in part) what covers your actual car: After a crash, this coverage will pay for damage to your vehicle. If you're leasing or financing your vehicle, you probably won't be able to opt out of this; since you don't own the car, the dealership or financial institution is going to want to protect what's theirs—but that really just covers your own butt in the long run, so it's for the best.

Is it required? Usually, if you're financing or leasing; otherwise optional.

How much coverage do you need? The amount of coverage will depend on the value of your car, but you can choose your deductible (how much you'll pay out of pocket before insurance kicks in). And since lower deductible = higher premiums, I suggest getting the highest deductible you could comfortably afford in the event of an accident.

3. Comprehensive Coverage

There are some things collision coverage can't buy—and for everything else, there's comprehensive. This will cover you if your car is damaged or stolen by anything that's *not* a traffic accident (such as flood, fire, vandalism—although you should always check the specifics of your coverage). Again, if you're leasing or financing, this may be required in your contract, but it could still be a good idea even if your car is paid off; if your car is especially fancy and high value, for example, or if you live or work in a kind of sketchy area and would rather have the peace of mind.

Is it required? Usually, if you're financing or leasing; otherwise optional.

How much coverage do you need? As with collision, the amount depends on the value of your car, but you can choose your deductible; go with the highest one you can afford.

4. Personal Injury/Medical Payments Coverage

Liability insurance has your back for any injuries you cause to someone in another car, but your passengers (and yourself) would be covered only by this. It can do more than just pay for a neck brace, too: things like lost wages or even the cost of temporarily replacing you at work might be covered.

Is it required? If you live in one of twelve "no-fault" states or Puerto Rico, personal injury coverage is mandatory. If you live anywhere else, you can opt into medical payments coverage.

How much coverage do you need? At least your legal minimum, obviously. Beyond that, consider how much medical insurance you have; if you have a plan that'll cover most injuries, you might not need a high-dollar coverage limit or any at all.

5. Uninsured/Underinsured Motorist Coverage

You know how when you were learning to drive, your parents would say, "Honey, it's not *you* we're worried about, it's all the other drivers out there?" This is that, but in insurance form: It protects you from *other people* not having coverage.

Yes, not having car insurance is against the law. So are jaywalking, littering, and underage drinking, and people do those things all the time. About 14 percent of drivers on the roads *don't* have insurance—which maybe doesn't sound like a lot, but pull up to a Starbucks with twenty cars in the lot, and three of the drivers are likely to have no coverage. If you're in an accident and the other driver has no coverage, you're basically SOL unless you have this coverage.

Is it required? Yes, in twenty-two states plus DC.

How much coverage do you need? Match whatever your own liability coverage is to keep it simple.

Valuable Articles Insurance

When my husband proposed to me, it was everything I ever dreamed of. Not just because we were on the shore of Lake Como on a gorgeous Italian day. Not just because the ring was stunning and exactly my taste. Not just because he is my ride-or-die and I was stoked as hell to spend the rest of my life with him. Because when he gave me the ring, and I said yes, the first thing I said *after* that was "Do we have insurance on this?"

Reader, he said yes. He got insurance way before he even proposed, because he knows me that well; he knows that I want to protect my valuables, and he knows that I am historically known for having . . . really, really *not* dexterous hands. I'm clumsy, you might say. So taking that gorgeous rock and handing it to me on the bank of a body of water was a *bold move* (or would have been without the insurance).

Besides your home and your car, you probably own one or two things that are worth a lot of money *and* irreplaceable. Jewelry, an antique heirloom, even your gaming PC or top-of-the-line electric guitar—all of these might be worth insuring under a separate policy, which can go by various names: valuables insurance, jewelry insurance, personal articles insurance, and so on.

It's true that your homeowner's policy will cover loss, theft, or damage when your stuff is *inside* your home. But once you're out and about in the world with your things—wearing your engagement ring, taking your guitar to gigs, whatever—they're no longer in the zone of protection your homeowner's policy gives them. So if I fly to LA, walk the red carpet for an event, and look down at my hand only to see—oh, shit—that the rock has fallen out of my ring setting (remember when that happened to Keltie Knight?), I'm SOL. With insurance, I'll be able to file a claim (along with whatever documentation my insurer requests, such as a police report in case of theft, for example) and get reimbursed for the replacement cost of my ring.

Does every valuable thing you own need to be insured? No. I *could* buy insurance on some of my designer bags, for example, but for those, I'm fine shouldering the (relatively low) risk that something will happen to them and paying out of pocket to replace them should the worst happen (since by the time I pay the insurance premiums, I might be halfway to that dollar amount anyway). But for things that are worth beaucoup bucks and/or are hugely meaningful to you, it's worth paying a few bucks a year to insure them.

Many insurers that write homeowner's and auto policies also offer valuable articles insurance with a bundle-and-save type of discount or can hook you up with a broker who does, so it's worth starting with your existing insurers to see what they can do for you. There are also newer, stand-alone companies that write only this kind of insurance that you can investigate. You'll also need to have some kind of documentation of the cash value of the item in question: If you bought the item yourself, a receipt and certificate of authenticity may do the trick, but for anything you inherited or otherwise didn't pay cash for, you'll need to have it appraised. Many jewelers, for example, will do this for a small fee; just go in and ask.

Life Insurance

Life insurance is different from homeowner's and auto insurance; it's not about risk management per se (since, you know, 100 percent of people will die) but rather about taking care of the people who *don't* die: your family, your loved ones, and anyone else who either depends on you or will be taking care of the aftermath after you pass away. It's a way to make sure they don't have to deal with emotional distress *and* financial distress.

This is also the type of insurance that the borderline-scammy online gurus are peddling as The Best Investment Ever! Let me say it once more: Life insurance is *not* an investment. Life insurance is life insurance, and you should consider it—and buy it—accordingly. Folks online may try to sell you on (emphasis on *sell*) life insurance as an investment, but as you'll see shortly, that doesn't make a ton of sense.

There are two main kinds of life insurance: whole life and term life. Term life is relatively straightforward: You take out a policy for a defined term, say twenty years. Every year, you pay premiums to your insurance company, and if you die during that twenty-year term, your beneficiary receives a lump-sum payment as defined in your policy. If you die *after* your term expires, however, there's no payment.

Whole life is a bit more complicated: There is still a death benefit, one that doesn't expire after a certain time period as it does in term life, but there's also a cash value, which increases as you continue to pay premiums. This is why you hear about insurance being an investment vehicle or even as part of a retirement plan—about which you should be very wary.

While it's true that there are tax benefits to paying for whole life insurance as opposed to investing in stocks, the returns from contributing to a whole life insurance policy are far lower than what you're likely to get in the stock market—and the money in the policy is illiquid, meaning that you can't easily cash it out. If you withdraw your money from a whole life policy within the first fifteen or so years, you'll pay a steep penalty. Whole life insurance *can* make sense for very-high-net-worth individuals; while it's a pretty low-return "investment" product, if you're part of the 1 percent, odds are that you're making significantly riskier investments than the average person is (private equity, angel investing, being on *Shark Tank*, etc.), so it's often nice to diversify into a product that is lower return but also lower risk. However, if you're not, spending your investment cash on a whole life policy instead of putting it into the market means that you likely won't make the return you'd need to hit most of your financial goals (such as . . . retirement). So if you don't *already* have a lot of money, it's likely not a good use of your dollars, and if you need life insurance, term life is likely the better bet.

Your employer may offer you life insurance as a benefit; that's great if it does and worth signing up for if it offers it; make sure that the beneficiary is up to date considering your current life situation. However, the max payout on an employer policy tends to be relatively modest— usually a year's salary—and if you're the breadwinner of your family or otherwise want to ensure that there will be more than that on hand after you die, you might want to purchase an additional outside policy.

Climbing the Ladder:
How Much Life Insurance to Get and When

How much life insurance do you need? An easy rule of thumb for term life coverage is to multiply your annual income by ten. But the truly pro move is what's called *laddering*: Instead of buying one big term life policy, you'll buy several different term life policies with staggered expiration dates so that your coverage automatically adjusts as your life and income needs change. (It's sort of like a DIY target-date fund, but for life insurance.)

To create your own ladder, start with the short term. Let's say you take out a ten-year term life policy for $250,000. You want this short-term policy to cover a period when you might have a lot of ongoing expenses, such as a mortgage or childcare costs, that others are depending on you to pay—so if you die and your income dies with you, you need a backup plan.

Next, move to the medium term: a twenty-year policy, again for $250,000. This rung on the ladder represents expenses in the near future that are likely to crop up but aren't immediate obligations, such as a child's education.

Finally, move to the long term: a thirty-year policy, again for $250,000, for things further down the line, such as supporting a spouse in retirement. (Note: I'm saying thirty years for simplicity's sake, but the *length* of your long-term coverage will vary depending on how old you are, because you want that last policy to be in effect when you die. So if you think you'll make it thirty years or longer from the day you buy the policies, adjust your ladder accordingly.)

With this "ladder" in place, you'll have staggered amounts of coverage ready to go. If (tragically) you were to die during the next three years, all three policies would pay out a death benefit. If you die between ten and twenty years from now, two of them

> would pay out. And if you survive the first two gauntlets, but pass on between twenty and thirty years from now, only the last policy would pay out.
>
> Why does this make more sense than getting one big ol' thirty-year, $750,000 policy? Because shorter-term policies generally have lower premiums than longer-term ones do—and by the time you're older (and, in this example, no longer raising kids or paying off a mortgage), you will probably have fewer expenses to cover and won't need as big a payout or the premiums that come with it. By laddering, you can achieve the same *total* coverage when it counts at a reduced cost.

That said, buying a life insurance policy is a little more involved than buying other kinds of insurance. Shopping for life insurance isn't like going to the store and shopping for a pair of jeans, where you pay the same price for a small size or a large. Because life insurance is basically a wager on when you will die, your life insurance costs are directly related to your current health status and your potential future health status, meaning that your prospective insurer is going to get *all* up in your business before it gives you a quote, let alone agrees to cover you. At minimum, they'll ask you a ton of questions about your lifestyle and hobbies, including whether you scuba dive or base jump, and contact your doctor for your medical records. At max, it's going to *examine* you (in my case, the company sent a nurse to my house to check my blood pressure, give me an EKG, and do a full blood panel, among many other fun things).

Sadly, even if you are perfectly healthy, the insurer will do its absolute best to find something to either disqualify you as "high risk" or increase your premiums significantly. And while I do not advocate for lying and I'm all for reducing the stigma around health conditions, what I *am* saying is that these questionnaires might not be the best place to pour out every detail of your anxiety issues.

On a similar note, because younger people are, statistically speaking, less likely to keel over and die, life insurance premiums will be lower the younger you are, so even if you're not actively supporting a family or are otherwise an irreplaceable source of financial support for someone else, it might be worth locking in a longer-term policy earlier so that when you *do* have beneficiaries, it's all set and ready to go.

> ### Survivor Benefits:
> ### Life Insurance from the Government (Kinda)
>
> Earlier, I expressed my skepticism that Social Security will still be in good working order by the time my peers and I reach retirement age—and rest assured, I am still not holding my breath. However, that doesn't mean that the Social Security Administration (SSA) is useless for us youngerish people, *especially* if we have kiddos to support.
>
> That's thanks to something called *survivor benefits*, a lesser known but valuable part of the SSA. If you're working and paying into Social Security with every paycheck, it's not going just to retirement benefits but also to benefits that could be awarded to your spouse and/or children in the event that you die while supporting them. Survivor benefits can be granted to surviving spouses supporting kids (even ex-spouses, if you were married for ten years or more), minor children or disabled adult children, and in some cases dependent parents, grandchildren, or stepfamily members. The amount of the benefit varies depending on the situation, but it can be as much as 75 percent of your (the deceased's) earned benefit for your children until they turn eighteen.
>
> In order to claim benefits, your surviving family members will need to call or visit a local SSA office and be prepared to supply

various documentation, but the hassle is very much worth it—and because survivor benefits are not typically awarded retroactively, it's important to make sure that your family members know to apply for them ASAP in the event that you die. (I know, it's grim to consider, but there's no point in leaving free money on the table.) You (the deceased) will also need to be eligible at the time of death, but generally speaking, you are if you've worked and paid into Social Security for at least ten years. You can check your progress to eligibility, as well as potential benefit amounts, at SSA.gov.

That said, survivor benefits are unquestionably helpful, but in my opinion, they can't fully replace the sense of security that a well-rounded life insurance policy brings. It's really a belt-or-suspenders situation in which having both is the best option.

Pet Insurance

Part of responsible pet ownership is taking care of your pet's medical needs. As I said before, the quality of your pet's life is pretty directly tied to how much money you spend on them—and pet insurance seems like the obvious solution. But while pets are like family, it doesn't mean that you can add them to your health care coverage, and it definitely doesn't mean that pet insurance is just "human insurance, but for dogs." In fact, pet insurance is easy to misunderstand precisely because it's kind of similar to human health coverage, but not exactly, and it is definitely not as regulated. To be sure, taking out pet insurance can be a good financial move, and lots of pet owners appreciate the peace of mind it brings, but it's important to understand the whole landscape before signing your little furball up.

Pet insurance, although it does cover health care costs, is technically classified as property and casualty insurance (rude!). There's no Affordable Care Act for pets, either; in fact, only four states have passed laws regulating pet insurance,[2] and the laws that do exist are less about ensuring that all dogs go to vet care and more that all disclosures should be made clear to the consumer.

In practice, this means that pet policies are free and clear to dictate things such as waiting periods, exclusions, premium hikes, and claim denials. For example, some pet insurance policies have deductibles not only per pet per year but per individual condition—so if your pet has an infection and then eats an entire metal grill brush, the medical expenses might count toward two different buckets. Most pet insurance also won't cover preexisting conditions, and it can have a decent amount of leeway in determining what those conditions are (like, a fever when you adopt your kitten might disqualify her for antibiotics coverage six months later). It may or may not cover routine and preventive care. The premiums might also go up as your pet ages *or* for other reasons (such as that the company's decided that vet care in your area has gotten more expensive, so now you have to pay more up front). That said, every insurer (and every pet) is different, so here's how to examine the fine print and weigh your options. Ask yourself:

- **Coverage type:** Does the plan cover accidents only or accidents *and* illnesses?
- **Deductible:** How much will I need to pay out of pocket before expenses are covered? Does this apply across the board or per category of medical expense?
- **Coverage limits:** Is there a yearly or lifetime coverage limit? Are limits determined per condition or all together?
- **Exclusions:** What *doesn't* the plan cover? How does the company determine what a preexisting condition is, and does my pet (by its criteria) have one?
- **Effective date and waiting period:** Does the policy start as soon as I sign up, or is the effective date later? Will I have to wait a

few weeks (or months) before I can put in a claim to cover a medical expense?
- **Renewal clause:** Does the insurance company reserve the right to cut my pet off if it gets too old or too sick?
- **Prescriptions:** Will the plan cover short-term prescriptions (such as pain medicine for an injury), long-term prescriptions (for an allergy or other chronic condition), both, or neither? What about prescription foods? (Yes, that's a thing.)
- **Premiums:** How much will these cost you per month?

If you *don't* opt for pet insurance, that doesn't mean you should just rawdog pet ownership and hope that no big bills come up. I recommend that you set up a sinking fund dedicated to potential vet expenses and make it a priority to contribute to it regularly.

How to Get the Best Insurance No Matter What

Clickbait title: There's no such thing as the "best insurance," and here's why.

Insurance is what's known as a *commoditized product*, which is a product where every single provider is selling the exact same thing. Think of gas stations: BP, Sunoco, Shell, they're all selling the same fuel. With insurance, if the policies are identical (meaning the same coverage and terms), one company isn't going to provide "better" insurance than another one is. They're both selling the same financial product. Incidentally, this is why insurance companies go all out in their ad campaigns: Because they're all selling more or less the same thing, the only way they can stand out is by being extra wacky, memorable, or annoying. Then, once they have you as a customer, you're much less likely to go through the hassle of switching companies, even if another one might be cheaper.

With that in mind, here's how to shop smart for insurance.

Compare apples to apples. When shopping around, make sure you're comparing the exact same policies; look at deductibles, coverage limits, terms, and exclusions. If you're not sure if the coverage is identical, get an agent on the phone and ask questions.

Don't get distracted by bells and whistles. Companies try to differentiate themselves with things such as great mobile apps, easy claim-filing systems, or various customer service promises—which are all well and good but not the point. Remember, they're all selling you the same coverage, so paying a higher premium just because you like the website is kind of a waste of money. As long as you're confident that the insurance company will remain solvent (that is, continue to have the money to be able to pay out your claims), if you have two identical policy offers in hand, go with the cheaper one.

Make companies compete. When there are two girls who want to take you to the dance, what do you do? Hold a dance-off, obviously. Get quotes from several providers and use them as leverage. This might involve making an actual phone call, but it can save you money in the long run if the agent really wants your business (they do have quotas to meet, after all). Say, "I'd be happy to go with you, ABC Insurance, but XYZ Insurance is offering me the same coverage for $200 less. Can you beat that?"

Ask about discounts. Many insurance companies offer discounts to members of certain organizations—and no, I don't mean fancy country clubs, I mean, like, Costco.

(Literally.) Professional associations, alumni groups, even AARP (Fun fact: You can join at age eighteen!) have deals with certain insurers, so it's definitely worth looking into them.

Take reviews with a grain of salt. Doing your due diligence is great, but online reviews tend to have a *heavy* bias toward people who are extremely pissed off. By all means, research a company on Trustpilot or the BBB (aka old-person Yelp), but bear in mind that the only people who are writing reviews are the ones who have been screwed—and every insurance company out there today has probably screwed *somebody*.

Don't be afraid to switch providers. Again, since insurance is a commoditized product, there's no real benefit to loyalty. If your insurer jacks your rates up when renewal time comes around, get a few quotes and be willing to switch. Insurance companies intentionally make the comparison process complex to discourage shopping around, but don't let that stop you; they're counting on your *not* taking the time to do so.

Money Management To-Dos for Chapter 10

- Review your existing homeowner's or renter's insurance policy (you should have one already): Does it cover all the things you want or need it to? If not, request quotes from your insurer to add those coverages.
- Ditto for your car: If you have one, review your policy and make sure it covers everything you want it to—and nothing you don't.
- If you have one-of-a-kind, irreplaceable valuables (such as an

engagement ring) and want to insure them, get an appraisal done and request quotes from insurers for a valuable articles policy.
- Check whether you have life insurance through your employer. If so, how much? Who is the beneficiary? If not, can you sign up during the next open enrollment period?
- Get life insurance quotes from several insurers based on a term that makes sense for you and your family situation.
- If you have pets, look into insuring them as well, weighing whether it makes sense given their general health, their age, and your ability to pay regular premiums as opposed to surprise bills.
- Check to see whether you're eligible for any discounts or promotions on any policies: maybe through your employer, your union, a membership program such as AAA, AARP, or Costco, or through bundling policies with your existing insurer.

Chapter Eleven

Estate Planning

In college, I dated a guy who came from big-time familial wealth, and it opened my eyes to a bunch of things that my family did not do—especially regarding estate planning.

Way back when, my then-boyfriend's grandfather had bought an industrial manufacturing company in Chicago. It was a fairly small-time operation, and they lived a comfortable but middle-class life. But his sons—my BF's dad and uncle—turned that company from a mom-and-pop business into a truly lucrative nationwide and global business, thus creating a huge amount of wealth for both their generation and the generation that followed, the kids.

Every year, the dad and uncle held a meeting to discuss the state of the family business. All the family members sat down with the accountant, the attorney, and the estate planner, and went through the year, discussing how much the business had made and what everyone was realistically entitled to. They'd be direct about how the estate would be divided upon the parental generation's death; there were ground rules for what the kids would have to do to stay in the will (such as be gainfully employed—no freeloading—and have a prenup if they got married), and there were provisions for the siblings with disabilities and how their medical expenses would continue to be taken care of. Since none of the kids really wanted to take over the industrial factory (one kid went into fashion, one was in finance, and so on), there were also meaningful conversations around whether (and how) they should sell the family company when the time came.

Long story short: It was very clear who would be getting what and what the succession plan was. The estate plan was *planned*. And to me, coming from middle-class suburban Maryland, that was entirely unheard of. I didn't know anyone with an "estate," and if I saw anyone making some kind of plan before they died, it was probably a bucket list of fun trips and experiences to knock out before their expiration date.

But I also remember that when my then-boyfriend told me about the whole setup, he made a really interesting observation: "Yeah, it's kind of annoying for all of us to get together for a board meeting, but generational wealth usually doesn't live past the third generation, so I get it. They're trying to protect us from ourselves."

That put things into perspective. Yes, there were lots of complex technicalities involved, since there was an actual family business to consider (as in *Succession*, but with way less backstabbing), but the core principle—ensuring that all the parents' and grandparents' hard work could continue to take care of their kids and legacy *even after they died*? That made perfect sense.

So while bucket lists with items such as "Go on an African safari" or "Eat at a Michelin-starred restaurant" are all very nice and good, you know what should really be on your bucket list? Creating an advance health care directive. Giving your kids power of attorney so that they can make decisions if you become incapacitated. Writing a damn last will and testament. That's the *real* bucket list.

In my opinion, there are three main reasons that people avoid making this kind of bucket list.

One, they assume that wills and estates are only for rich people. "I barely have any assets, so what do I need a will for?" False. (Why? Spoiler alert: There's a little thing called probate.) You don't have to have a full-on catered board meeting every year to figure out who'll take over your multinational business, but if you own any assets whatsoever, you *do* have an estate, and it's worth taking care of.

Two, they assume that estate planning is incredibly complicated and expensive. And sure, if you hire someone to create a bespoke plan, that will be pricey. But, as my doctor friend always answers when I text to say, "omg I have a slight itch on my left boob and Google says it's an obscure cancer, am I dying???": "You're not that special." In the same way that it's very, *very* unlikely that I have that one-in-a-quadrillion genetic mutation that means I have boob-itch cancer, it's very, very unlikely that your particular will-and-testament situation is going to be outstandingly complex. Realistically, if you have a normalish life, normalish job setup, and normalish assets, the odds are good that somebody else in a very similar position to you has already done this. Regardless, I can almost guarantee that you are neither the poorest nor the richest person an estate-planning attorney has ever spoken to.

And three: We don't like to admit that we're going to die. I get it; this conversation sucks. "What's going to happen after I die?" is much less sexy to contemplate than "What flowers should we have at the wedding?" or "What color should we paint the baby's room?" or even "Which target-date fund should I pick for my IRA?" So no, this is not a fun conversation to be having, but it's more important. No one will remember what flowers you had at your wedding. No one will remember the color you painted your nursery, least of all your baby. (And if you don't like it, you can always repaint it.) But how you set up your estate? That has long-lasting effects *on the people you love the most*. And when push comes to shove, isn't that where you want to put your efforts and energy? You'd let your phone drop to the ground and smash into a million tiny pieces before you'd let your kid fall, after all. You would use your own skull as a shield to make sure that your baby doesn't get hurt by a random projectile. So why aren't you willing to take a couple of hours to protect them in one of the biggest ways possible?

As my mom likes to remind me, you don't get to have a happily ever after and ride off into the sunset if you don't have a road map to get there—so make a plan. It's fine if you go in with the attitude "I have no intention of dying before I'm a hundred and thirty, *but* in case something happens, I want to make it as easy as possible on the people I love the most." Because the reality is that something *will* happen to you; it's just a matter of when.

The Legalese: Trusts, Powers of Attorney, and Wills

Trust funds, powers of attorney, and wills (both living and regular), aka estate plans, may sound fancy, but they're truly necessities. Nailing down the specifics of what will happen to your stuff (or yourself) in writing can help prevent a world of headache and heartache for your loved ones. Plus, if you die intestate—without a will—your family will not only just have to guess at what to do with everything you leave behind, they'll also be stuck in a lengthy court process, called *probate*, to do it. It doesn't matter if you leave behind six bucks and a pack of gum and your only surviving family member is an only child: The law's the law, and probate court is a bitch—an expensive, inefficient, stressful bitch.

Creating an estate plan is essentially writing out a bunch of instructions: If X occurs, Y is what you want to have happen. And while you will need a lawyer to make these things official, including filing documents with your county government, don't let that scare you off.

First, you can save a lot of time and hourly fees by planning out, in layman's terms, what you want and going in prepared with that when you do sit down with an attorney—instead of having them hand-hold you through question after question for $175 every fifteen minutes. (I'll cover that below.)

Second, while "finding a lawyer" as a to-do item has big "Where do I even *start*?" energy, it's actually not that much of a pain. The easiest way? Ask around: work mentors, rich friends, anyone who's had a brush with the legal system and come out relatively unscathed. Failing that, you ask if your employer offers legal services through an employee assistance program and try out what's on offer there. You can also just go the old-fashioned way and look up your local bar association, visit a few websites, and contact whoever seems to be competent and have good vibes.

Your first consultation with a lawyer should be free, and you should feel free to ask any and all questions you have, including "How much is this going to cost, all in?" I'd advise interviewing at least two lawyers just so you know you're not literally going with the first one you pick. Last, keep in mind that documents such as wills should be updated periodically (when you have kids, buy property, get married or divorced, or just have more stuff to divide), so you'll want someone you feel good about working with long term.

Trust Funds

Ah, the infamous trust fund. The hallmark of the spoiled rich kid. Practically a punch line in itself. Not for us normies, right?

Wrong. Yes, rich people set up their families with trust funds, but regular people can, too; they're not even that complicated, you just haven't been taught about them. That changes now.

A trust fund is a legal entity set up by a person called a *grantor* (that's you), so that they can leave assets such as real estate, investments, life insurance policies, and so on to someone else (the *beneficiary*). The "trust" part comes because you assign a *trustee*, usually a law firm, accountant, or close family member, to enact your wishes about *how* those assets are used. In other words, you get to dictate what, when, how, and why people will get what they do *from beyond the grave*.

This obviously comes in handy if you know that your potential beneficiaries are, let's just say, not very responsible—you don't want your whole net worth to be pissed away, after all—but it can also potentially keep assets away from creditors and reduce taxes.

That said, for most people with minor children, a UTMA or UGMA (see page 147) is a solid option for avoiding legal hassle while still ensuring that your kid will get their due. However, once your kid hits the age of majority, that UTMA or UGMA is theirs free and clear, no more strings attached. A trust fund, by contrast, is much more flexible, expansive, and *expensive*—you'll have to hire a lawyer, for starters—but it allows you to stipulate a lot more specifically what can and can't be spent, no matter the age of the beneficiary. Do you want your kid to use the money only for education? Can do. Don't want to release the funds unless they're married—*and* have a prenup? Fine, you do you. Want your heirs to take over your sports franchise if they have an MBA and five years of senior management experience? Oddly specific, but okay, Pat Bowlen, former owner of the Denver Broncos! (Kind of a genius move by Pat, if I'm being honest.)

Quickie Trust Q&As

Q: Is there anything I *can't* put into a trust?
A: Yes. Among other things, you can't directly transfer certain retirement accounts (such as IRAs and 401(k)s) into a trust while you're alive. What you *can* do is name the trust as the *beneficiary* of the retirement account. That way, the funds will be transferred to the trust after you die, and the trust can then distribute them according to your wishes.

Q: Does a trust give my assets any kind of special protection?
A: Hashtag #notalltrusts, but yes. Some trusts (usually irrevoca-

ble; see below) are protected from creditors and other legal claims in a way that assets held outside the trust are not.

Q: What's the deal with different types of trusts—revocable versus irrevocable, for example?

A: Trust me (heh), there are a *lot* of different types of trusts—but these are good to know. A *revocable* trust, as the name implies, can be revoked (and/or changed) during your lifetime (meaning that you can add or remove assets fairly easily). You also retain control over a revocable trust because you are the one acting as its trustee; this means that the assets inside it are still considered part of your estate, so they will be taxable when you die and are *not* protected from creditors (generally speaking). An *irrevocable* trust isn't, um, revocable; modifications to the trust usually require either all beneficiaries to sign off on them or a court order. You'll hand over the reins to a trustee you appoint rather than control it yourself, and the assets won't be considered part of your taxable estate or be gettable by creditors.

Another important distinction to note when it comes to trusts for kids is that while a revocable trust is usually counted as a parental asset for need-based financial aid purposes (assuming that you, the parent, are the grantor and trustee), an irrevocable trust for which the student (your kid) is the beneficiary and can use the funds for education will be counted as a *student* asset and factored in at a higher rate (see sidebar, page 248).

Bottom line: If flexibility and ease of transfer (from you to your beneficiaries) are your top priorities, a revocable trust might be one to decide on. But if you want those assets protected and/or want to reduce estate taxes when they're passed on, an irrevocable trust might make more sense.

> Q: I've heard that trusts have a lookback period. What is that? Do I need to worry about it?
>
> A: You might have heard about lookback periods as they pertain to qualified income trusts and asset protection trusts, aka Medicaid trusts. In a nutshell: Because Medicaid eligibility is income based, rich people sometimes open a qualified income trust and deposit their income there, making the trust the owner of the funds and making the funds no longer count against their Medicaid eligibility. An asset protection trust works similarly, by pulling assets away from your estate and into the trust's ownership, with the same basic idea, as well as protecting your assets from other potential creditors. The "lookback period" refers to the five years prior to applying for Medicaid that the government can factor in when assessing your assets, including trusts. So if you're setting up trusts with the intent of minimizing your "on paper" income and net worth, you'd want to do so at least five years prior to your application date.
>
> That said, this is different and separate from a trust you set up for your child, which would take effect as soon as the paperwork is filed, so a lookback period isn't an issue.

To be sure, trust funds aren't for everybody, but they're not only for rich folks, either. Maybe you want to leave all your money to your niece but you don't want her mom grabbing it to pay off her credit card debt. A trust fund can solve that and many other problems as well.

Power of Attorney

You know when you hand over your phone to your BFF to draft a reply to a cutie on Hinge because you are too anxious to think straight? You're basically saying, "Bestie, I trust you to act in my best interest and do exactly what I would do but better, because I am in *no state* to handle this right now." A power of attorney is essentially the same thing, but legally binding.

A power of attorney is a legal document that allows someone else to make decisions on your behalf, usually if you become incapacitated or otherwise unable to make those decisions for yourself. As the name suggests, it is quite *power*ful and not something to be given lightly—but when you need it, it can be crucial.

Most people think of *medical* power of attorney, and that's probably the one that makes the most sense across the board (we all have the capacity to get badly hurt, after all), but POAs do come in different flavors. You can delegate powers through everything from a general POA, which gives another person free rein to do pretty much anything in your name—obviously a good idea only in very limited circumstances, to a medical POA, which allows them to make medical decisions for you, but not, say, financial ones. A *durable* POA is one that will still apply if you become incapacitated, but all POAs expire when *you* expire (because a person can't act on behalf of someone else who's dead).

Speaking of medical power of attorney, it doesn't supersede things such as a living will or health care directive but rather takes care of the loopholes. For example, I could have a nice little flowchart for my care team saying, "If Vivian needs a feeding tube, give her a feeding tube" in my living will (which I'll cover in a bit), but I can't anticipate *every* freak edge case. So if my doctor says, "I suggest we amputate her arm. What should we do?," I've deputized my husband to make that call for me.

Your POA doesn't *have* to be a spouse, however, although many people do choose their husband or wife. Sometimes it's a parent or sibling; sometimes, especially as you get older, a child; and if you're doing this as a singleton, I would even ask your true best friend. The key is choosing someone you trust deeply *and* who's willing to do the job, which means having detailed conversations with them about your wishes *before* anything happens.

When establishing a power of attorney, you can use online legal services to create initial drafts of the appropriate documents for a few hundred dollars, but I highly recommend having a flesh-and-blood attorney review them afterward to ensure that everything's correct. Like all such documents, this isn't a set-it-and-forget-it situation; make sure you periodically review how your POA is set up and whether it still reflects what you want to happen and who you want to decide.

Wills, Wills, Wills

Most of us are at least vaguely familiar with what a will is—we've all seen *Knives Out*, right?—but just in case: A will is a legal document that specifies how you want your assets to be distributed after your death. That said, it's about more than just who gets what; it's also a place to express your last wishes, including things such as who will take care of your kids (or pets), and to map out a variety of scenarios, such as if you and your spouse die at the same time or if you die before your parents do. Specifically, a will can stipulate direct asset transfers to specific people (such as money to a spouse or kids), donations to organizations, educational bequests, guardianship designations for children or dependents, and even your desires for what will happen to your earthly remains, whether that's donating your body to science or being cremated instead of buried.

Do you need a will now, even though you have no intention of dying soon? Yes. That said, you know what's just as likely (if not more) than you straight-up dying, assuming you're young and relatively healthy? A bad accident that takes you out of commission. That's where a *living will*, also known as a health care or advance care directive, comes in.

This is a document that spells out, in no uncertain terms, what kind of medical care you want if you are unable to speak for yourself. If you're in a coma, you're not talking, but you're still *there*, a health care directive essentially preprograms what will happen to you until you (hopefully) recuperate. No one else has to guess or stress about it (more than needed, anyway).

Which brings me to my final point: Both of these documents are *about* you, but they're not *for* you. Wills and living wills are gifts to the people you love, and I don't mean because they involve bequeathing dollars and stuff; you're saving them the pain and strife of making huge, complicated decisions at what will likely be one of the lowest emotional points of their life. So if you do it for anything, do it for *them*.

What your will *(estate plan) should cover:*

- Who will get what: property, assets, bank and investment accounts
- Who will be in charge: who will be the executor in charge of managing your estate (carrying out the provisions of the will)
- Who will take care of the kids (and pets): designation of guardians for any minor children and/or instructions on caring for animals
- Any plans for charitable donations (more on this in a sec)
- Optional but helpful: a "letter of instruction" about your funeral preferences

---

What your living will *should cover:*

- Your wishes about various medical interventions (life support, yea or nay?)
- Your thoughts on pain management: How much do you want, and when?
- The family member (or friend) to call the shots if you can't
- Who will take care of your children/pets if you are temporarily incapacitated

- Your wishes for organ donation
- Any other things you do (or very much *don't*) want in the event you're in a bad way indefinitely, from the music you want played in your bedroom to any religious counseling you want (or don't want) to receive to specific photos of friends and family to have on hand for you to see
- Any other preferences about your medical care

Who Gets What? Planning Your Estate

Back in grade school, my teacher used to say, "You get what you get, and you don't get upset." That's fine when distributing colored pencils, but when it comes to how much cold, hard cash and assets you dole out to loved ones, people can and will get upset. (Again, we've all seen *Knives Out*.)

More than that, though, it's not that intuitive to work out what should go where. Even "leave it all to my kids" can get tricky when there are physical assets, such as a house, involved (what are they going to do, paint a sitcom-style red line down the middle?).

Don't worry: I've got you covered. Here's a step-by-step process for figuring out how you'll bequeath your hard-earned dollars (and stuff).

Step 1: Pick your beneficiaries.

Which kid do you love most? I'm joking—but in all seriousness, think hard about who you want to get your money. It's *your* money, after all. You worked your ass off for it, and you can decide exactly who will get it. Your kids, if you have them, are the obvious choice, but you might also want to consider your parents (in the event that you die before them), your siblings, your nieces and nephews, your life partner, and even causes and organizations (more on that in the next section).

Step 2: Carve up your monetary asset pie.

You've put together your guest list for the pizza party; now it's time to figure out how big a slice everyone will get. The simplest solution, as you might have guessed, is to divide everything into equal chunks, but that's not the *only* way. I recommend that you look at each beneficiary's financial capabilities and needs and weigh out what makes sense for each. For example, you might want to leave the lion's share of your assets to your kids but still leave something for your aging parents, so something like a 75 percent to offspring, 25 percent to parents split might make sense.

You can also divide up your estate by accounts: Bank accounts will go to your spouse, for example, while investment accounts will go to both your spouse and kids. For investment accounts with multiple beneficiaries, you'll likely want to designate a percentage for each rather than a dollar amount; because investment accounts can fluctuate in value, it will eliminate the headache of having a surplus or coming up short. You'll also want to consider tax strategy, sorry to say, because not all assets are treated equally.

> Estate planning is another part of your financial life where it's good to know the basics so you can make well-informed decisions, but the *specific* specifics of your needs and solutions are going to be nuanced—because everyone's family and asset mix is different (sometimes wildly). To prep for meeting with a pro, you can use my Ask Dolly app to go through the options and how each might make sense in your situation, then hammer out the details with a real-life attorney. Check it out at AskDolly.com.

The Gifting That Keeps On Giving

If you want to get superstrategic (and help your beneficiaries on the tax side), you can do what rich people do and dole out chunks of your estate *before you're dead*. You can give someone else a certain amount of money tax exempt every year: $19,000 as of 2025 (and if you're a couple, that's good for each of you, so $38,000 annually[1]). Of course, whether you can do that depends on your having that cash free and clear (i.e., not in a retirement account or anywhere else where you can't immediately access it), but making annual gifts like this will reduce your taxable estate *and* let you get to see your kids (or whoever your beneficiaries are) enjoy it. That said, when it comes to putting money into your kids' names, there are definitely some potential downsides, especially regarding financial aid and your control over those funds.

For one thing, assets held in a child's name are assessed at a much higher rate when calculating the Expected Family Contribution (EFC) for college financial aid. Specifically, 20 percent of the value of these assets is considered to be available for college expenses, compared to only 5.64 percent for assets held in a parent's name. This can significantly reduce your child's eligibility for need-based financial aid. 😳

For another, once your child reaches the age of majority (usually eighteen or twenty-one, depending on where you live), they will gain full control of the custodial account. This means that they will be able to use the funds however they wish, which might not align with your original intentions for the money. If maintaining control of the funds is important to you, other savings vehicles may be better options.

Finally, custodial accounts are subject to the "kiddie tax," which taxes unearned income above a certain threshold at the parent's marginal tax rate. For 2025, the first $1,350 of unearned income is exempt, but anything over $2,700 could be taxed at your higher rate, which might not be ideal.

Step 3: Account for your nonmonetary assets, too.

Whether it's your great-grandmother's engagement ring or your home sweet home, the *stuff* you pass down is likely going to have an emotional value that's more than its cash equivalent, and that—combined with the fact that you can't split a ring neatly in half like a chocolate chip cookie—can be the cause of some serious squabbles. If that's your case, think through whether or not you'll need to spell things out more specifically; some things can be fairly easily designated as jointly inherited (such as a house, if you expect all your heirs to sell it and split the proceeds), but some (such as that diamond ring) are easier to give to a single heir.

Step 4: Play out various scenarios.

This isn't that Justin Timberlake movie where we all know exactly when we're going to die; life's not that predictable, and you'll want to think through some contingencies. If you're married, what will happen if both of you die at the same time as opposed to one going first? What if you have a life partner but you are not legally married? (See page 118 for other things to consider in that scenario.) What if your parents are still living but your spouse's aren't or vice versa?

Step 5: If you have dependents, create a guardianship plan.

Who do you want to raise your kids—your sister, your bestie, your parents, Count Olaf? Think about it, and then talk to the potential guardian: Make your ask, and make it clear that you'll proceed only with their consent (you don't want someone who's unsure about it to take on this big duty, after all). You can also let them know, as part of that conversation, how you plan for your kid's needs to be provided for (a UTMA, a trust fund, etc.) so that they're clear about how they'd keep the little rascal fed and clothed.

Step 6: Bring in the pros.

With a plan sketched out, now's the time to talk to your estate-planning attorney (yes, you're getting fancy now) and get it down on paper. And yes, it's a good idea to have a physical copy of your will somewhere safe (as in a safe or safe deposit box). Depending on where you live, you may or may not need to have your will notarized, but a notarized (aka self-proving) will can make executing your estate that much faster, and your attorney can hook you up with a notary. You might also want to consult with a tax specialist to minimize the tax burden on your beneficiaries.

Step 7: Tell everyone.

You don't have to hard launch this on Instagram or go all "hear ye, hear ye," but it is important to let key players know where your will is, who prepared it (e.g., the lawyer), and the broad strokes of your intentions. This isn't to say that you're opening the floor for debate (you're not) or using your estate as a bargaining chip to pit family members against one another (for the last time, this is not *Knives Out*), but you are letting them know that there *is* a plan, should that fateful day arrive.

Step 8: Regularly review and update your estate plan as your life circumstances change.

You know how you can change your medical insurance plan whenever you have a "qualifying event" such as a new job, a new kid, a divorce, or a new spouse? Think of your will the same way: Any significant change to your financial circumstances should merit a check-in with your plans to make sure they still account for everything (and everyone) in your life.

Leaving a Legacy Behind: Giving to a Cause

We've seen the headlines: "Warren Buffett and Bill Gates promise to give away virtually all of their billions through the Giving Pledge."

While there are many reasons to give to charity and leave behind a philanthropic legacy, you don't need to have billions of dollars to make an impact. Regular people with regular wealth can still honor their favorite causes after they pass. You might not have a building named after you, but that doesn't mean your money won't make a difference to something you care about.

Cash donations: The simplest and most straightforward way is to give the charities of your choice a chunk of change. Name the nonprofits in your will or trust, and specify how much each will get.

Asset donations: The same idea as above, but for stuff: properties, valuables, anything that's not dollars and cents. This makes the most sense if you know the organization in question will actually use the thing itself (as opposed to selling it for cash): That Picasso you own could go to an art museum, or (more realistically) some family heirlooms or archives could go to a local historical society.

Account beneficiaries: Bank accounts will allow you to name a beneficiary as "transfer on death," which means exactly what it sounds like: When you die, the account is all theirs. You can also name a nonprofit as the beneficiary of a retirement account—your IRA or 401(k)—and donate to it that way, which has a neat little tax benefit: Retirement accounts are taxed pretty heavily if they're left to any other *person* besides your spouse, but they're *not* taxed if they're left to a nonprofit, maxing out your donation (and ensuring that less of your money is sucked up by the government).

Donor-advised funds: Ever wanted to have your own charity but don't want the hassle of setting up a foundation? A donor-advised fund could be for *you*. Such a fund is basically your own personal endowment fund: You put money into the fund, get an immediate tax deduction, buy investments within the fund, then advise the fund on which charities to support over time. You don't have to decide right away where your money will go, but you will get that tax deduction up front—*and* the money can grow with time, like any other investment. You can set one up with most major brokerages.

No matter which method you choose, it's always helpful to include an address and tax ID number for each charity in your will (you should be able to find those on their websites) since lots of organizations have similar names. And no matter how much you donate, know that your money is going to make the world a better place, even if you're no longer *in* the world—and that is one of the greatest gifts in and of itself.

Money Management To-Dos for Chapter 11

- Write out the basics you want your will and living will to cover, using the steps on page 246 (or my downloadable version at yourrichbff.com/wellclub).
- Take a look at your assets, and make a plan for how to distribute them in the event of your death. Consider your dependents and other family members, but also charitable giving. Write out that plan as well, including all your desired stipulations.
- Decide whether you want to grant someone medical (or any other) power of attorney, and write out exactly what decision-making powers you do or don't want them to have.
- Research local estate-planning pros for the documents you want to have prepared (e.g., a will, living will, and trust).

Epilogue

Happily Ever After

For nearly two years of my life, my Sunday routine looked like this: I would wake up at the crack of noon. I would walk my ass over to the bagel spot; get a bacon, egg, and cheese and a large Diet Coke; and I would pray to whatever holy being is out there to take my hangover away. Then I would suck down a blue Pedialyte (the best flavor), take a nap, and wake back up at around 3:45 p.m. with a feeling of dread.

Why was that my Sunday routine? Because I'd gone out on Friday night and I'd gone out on Saturday night, and I'd figured I'd "catch up" on Sunday. Except then Sunday turned into eating like crap and feeling like crap and staring down the barrel of a five-day workweek, wishing I had spent the precious limited time of my weekend a *little* more thoughtfully. Sunday Vivian was looking back at Friday Vivian and being like, "Why did you do this to me? Why didn't you make better decisions? Why didn't you have at least one glass of water the entire night?"

I feel as though, in a lot of ways, this is the perfect metaphor for life.

The mission of this book is to keep you from getting the Sunday scaries in the weekend that is your life. You know how easy it is for Friday You to make decisions based solely on the fact that *it's the freakin' weekend, baby* and there's "plenty of time" to recover from questionable decisions, take care of your responsibilities, and generally settle back into life. Now you just need to extend that thinking to the entire span of your human existence. The same way that the hangovers and regrets and chores that you swore you were going to get to before going out are going to be waiting for you when you pry open your eyes on Sunday morning, the consequences of how you spend your time *and* money in the first two-thirds of your life are going to be waiting for you when you wake up in your sixties.

I share this not to be a bummer, because there's actually good news here. Friday You and Saturday You and Sunday You? They're all the same person. And they can look out for each other. Maybe if Friday You has three drinks instead of seven, Saturday You can still wake up and be functional, and Sunday You can have a fun, chill day with friends, kick back with a li'l hobby, or just go out to touch some grass. Or maybe Friday You still wants to go hard but decides to buy some Pedialyte for the fridge *before* going out, so that Saturday or Sunday You doesn't have to do a sweatpants walk of shame to CVS. Or maybe Friday You is like, "Actually, I do not really care for the clerb at all and I'm maybe just going so I can have something to post about," and decides to scrap it and join a book club instead.

Whatever. The point is, Present You gets to determine what Future You's life will look like. And if you make strategic choices, spend your money wisely, and do what you can to get the greatest value out of your time and money now, you will get to live a life with much more ease down the road. Personally, I am well into my Saturday Vivian era now. And while I don't know *exactly* what kind of life Sunday Vivian—aka Retirement Vivian—will have, I do have a little preview in the form of my mom. Recently, my mom told me that she and my dad are thinking of spending an entire half of the year in Shanghai, where, thanks to being frugal their entire lives and working *super* hard, they now own an apartment in addition to their place in Maryland. Everything about the city is easier for them: It's more walkable, they have more social interactions, they speak the language at a native level, they have an easier time getting exactly what they want at the store, they see friends regularly—they really live the dream.

As my mom and I were chatting, she made a comment about how she used to look at her peers—her peers who are now still working, while she's retired. They had bigger homes, fancier cars, and just generally more stuff back then. "In the moment, I used to think, 'Am I doing it all wrong?'" she told me. "But now I think I did it right."

In the introduction, I clowned on the title of this book being a dick joke. (Which, again: It is.) But do you know what it is to actually be well endowed? Like, in the literal sense? An endowment is an investment fund that helps a nonprofit institution (a university, a charity, a hospital, etc.) sustain itself—indefinitely. It's what keeps the lights on, the staff paid, and the mission going no matter what happens. It is a foundation of security and stability so that more good stuff can keep on happening. Basically, when you're well endowed, you're set for life—and then some.

Now, I don't know what life will look like for Future You. Your priorities may be wildly different from mine, from my mom's, or plenty of other people's (the same way there are people who still want to party hard on Friday and people who'd rather chill with their dog and a book)—and that's fine. But I do know that you can—we *all* can—avoid the Sunday scaries of life if you go about leveraging your money thoughtfully and strategically.

My hope for you is that you will develop that same sense of *ease* that I see in my mom: so much free time, so many more options, and no pressure to have to do anything—just to get to do the things she wants to. That is the happy ending. That is living the dream. That, my friends, is being well endowed.

Acknowledgments

When I wrote my first book, I thought I had it all figured out. Joke's on me—that's not how life works. Nothing could have prepared me for what came next. I got married, froze embryos with my husband, set up a trust, helped to retire my parents, and even started a second company! That's the beauty of life: Change is inevitable and constant.

This second book exists because of that growth. It's born from the lessons I've learned, the mistakes I've made, and the wisdom I've gained from listening to thousands of you who reached out to me after reading my first book. The success of *Rich AF*, the feedback from readers, and the incredible opportunities that followed have fundamentally changed me—as a writer, as a teacher, and as a person. If there's any one piece of wisdom you take away from this book, let it be this: Growth never stops, and the people who support that growth are everything.

I am so incredibly lucky because my entire journey has been shaped by people who believed in my potential even when I couldn't see it myself. This book is a testament to their continued faith and to how much I've evolved since I first put pen to paper.

Thank you to Alyssa Reuben, my literary agent, for continuing to be my champion and believing in my vision once again. Your faith in my growth as an author and your ability to guide me through this second journey with even more confidence have been invaluable.

Thanks to Diana Baroni, my brilliant editor at Harper Wave, for your editorial insight and thoughtful comments. Your ability to help me refine not just my words but my evolved perspective has made this book infinitely better.

I'd also like to thank the HarperCollins team for seeing my vision and supporting this next chapter of my author journey. Your belief in my growth as an author and person means everything. A special shout-out goes out to Lynn Anderson and Lisa Glover for your precision and care in turning this manuscript into a real book.

Thank you once again to Blair Thornburgh and Meghan Stevenson for shepherding me through the book-writing process. Your continued support and coaching have made an immeasurable impact on me as an author, and I genuinely couldn't have done this without you. Our weekly meetings continue to be the highlight of my journey.

To my incredible Your Rich BFF team, you've watched me grow and supported every step of this evolution. Thank you to Grace Rittenhouse for collaborating with me on all of my harebrained schemes and half-baked ideas. Thank you to Alex Devlin at WME for continuing to manage the beautiful chaos that is my career and helping me navigate this next phase with grace. Thank you to Lauren Schwartz, my attorney extraordinaire, for your unwavering protection and guidance as I've stepped into this new version of myself as an author. Thank you to Bianca Bianconi, Devin Wolf, Amanda Toral, and Alexis Hoernschemeyer at 42West for your expertise in sharing my story and this book with the world.

Finally, last but not least, as always: This book couldn't exist without the BFFs, so thank you to all of the friends I've made, both online and offline, along the way. I love you.

Glossary

529 plan: A tax-advantaged investment account specifically for education expenses. The money grows tax free and stays that way when withdrawn for qualified expenses such as college tuition, K-12 private school tuition, or even student loan repayment. Funds can also be rolled over into an IRA account if not used for education.

Adjustable-rate mortgage (ARM): A mortgage that starts with a fixed interest rate for a set period (such as five, seven, or ten years), then adjusts periodically based on market conditions. For example, a 5/1 ARM at 5% will charge a 5% interest rate for the first five years and then adjust every year thereafter.

Amortization: The process of paying off a loan over time through regular, fixed payments that cover a chunk of both the amount you borrowed (aka the principal) and the interest (aka the fee you pay for the privilege of borrowing the money). With amortization, the proportion of each payment that goes to interest vs. principal shifts over time: payments you make at the beginning of the loan term will pay more toward interest and less toward the principal, but as time goes on, that flips. By the end of the loan term, your payment dollars are mostly knocking out the loan balance.

Amortization period: The fancy way of saying "loan term," aka the length of time you'll be paying back your mortgage. Most common in the United States is thirty years, but there are also ten-, fifteen-, and twenty-five-year options. The shorter the period, the higher your monthly payments but the less you'll pay in interest overall.

Beneficiary: The person or organization you're leaving your stuff to—whether money from your life insurance, investments from your retirement accounts, or assets in your will or trust.

Catch-up contributions: Basically what they sound like, for retirement accounts! If you're fifty or older, the government allows you to contribute extra money to your individual or employer-sponsored retirement accounts beyond the standard limits.

Collision coverage: The part of your car insurance that pays for damage to your own car after an accident, regardless of who was at fault. If you're financing or leasing, you'll probably be required to have this.

Comprehensive coverage: The part of your car insurance that covers damage that isn't from a crash, such as if your car gets stolen, a tree falls on it, or your local youths egg it on Mischief Night. It's not legally required but it could be a good idea if your car is worth anything.

Custodial Roth IRA: A retirement account for kids who earn income, even if it's just from babysitting or a lemonade stand. An adult manages it until the kid hits adulthood, but all the tax benefits and money go to the kid.

Delta: The difference between two rates of change—specifically, between how much money you're bringing in and how much you're spending. A positive delta means you're coming out ahead (wooo); a negative one means you're spending more than you're earning (booo).

Estate plan: The package of legal documents that spell out what will happen to your stuff after you die, as well as directives such as who will take care of your kids (or pets).

Executor: The person you designate in your will to carry out your final wishes. Your executor (or executrix if it's a lady, heyyy) is in charge of distributing your assets, paying off your debts, and making sure that everything goes where you want it to.

FU number: My term for the amount of money you need to live off of without bringing in additional income—basically, your "I can tell my boss to F off" number. Calculate it by dividing your annual expenses by 0.04 (which assumes a 4 percent withdrawal rate). So if you need $40,000 a year to live, your FU number is $1 million.

Grantor: The person who creates and funds a trust (that's you). The grantor decides what assets go into the trust, who will get those assets, and under what conditions they will get them.

Health savings account (HSA): A triple-tax-advantaged account you can use with a high-deductible medical plan. Money goes in tax free, grows tax free, and comes out tax free when used for qualified medical expenses.

Irrevocable trust: A trust that, once created, generally can't be changed or revoked without the beneficiaries' permission. The assets in it aren't considered part of your estate anymore, which means they're protected from creditors and estate taxes.

Joint tenants with rights of survivorship: A way of owning property where, if one owner dies, their share automatically transfers to the surviving owner(s) without having to go through probate.

Landlord policy: Insurance that covers a property you own but don't live in. Unlike regular homeowner's insurance, it can cover things such as lost rental income if your tenant has to move out due to damage and liability if someone gets hurt on your rental property.

Liability coverage: The part of insurance that protects you when you mess up and someone gets hurt or their property is damaged—i.e., you're "liable" for something. It's in your homeowner's, renter's, and auto policies.

Living will/advanced health care directive: A document that spells out what medical treatments you want (or don't want) if you can't speak for yourself.

Mortgage: The loan you take out to buy a house because almost nobody has hundreds of thousands of dollars in cash lying around. You make monthly payments that cover both the principal (the amount you borrowed) and the interest (the bank's fee for lending you the money) over a set time period.

Net new expense: A completely new category of spending that you've never had to budget for before, such as childcare (because you didn't have kids) or pet insurance (because you didn't have a pet).

Personal injury/medical payments coverage: The part of your car insurance that covers medical costs for you and your passengers after an accident, regardless of who was at fault. It can also cover lost wages if your injuries mean you can't work.

Power of attorney (POA): A legal document that gives someone else the authority to make decisions on your behalf. You can limit it to just finances or just medical care or give them complete decision-making power. A regular power of attorney ends if and when you become incapacitated, but a durable power of attorney will, as the name suggests, endure beyond that point, meaning that your POA designee can make those decisions if you've been severely hurt or disabled.

Preexisting conditions: Health issues you (or your pet) had before your insurance coverage started. For pets, treatments for these conditions are often excluded from coverage, so be sure to read the fine print of the policy.

Prenuptial agreement (prenup): A contract signed before marriage that spells out how your assets will be divided if you divorce. If you get divorced without a prenup, your assets will be divided according to state law, which may not be ideal.

Principal: The amount you borrowed when taking out a loan, not including any interest. With a mortgage, your monthly payment goes toward both the principal and interest, with more going to interest in the early years and more to the principal later on.

Probate: The legal process of validating a will and distributing assets after someone dies. It's public, can be slow and expensive, and is basically a huge pain in the ass—avoid it if possible by doing some estate planning.

Replacement cost: What it would cost to rebuild your home from scratch if it was completely destroyed. This is what your homeowner's insurance should cover (and it's *not* the same as the home's market value; it's about construction costs, not what a buyer would pay).

Revocable trust: A trust that can be changed or canceled during your lifetime. You maintain control of the assets, but they'll still go through probate when you die. It's the more flexible, less protective cousin of the irrevocable trust.

Target-date fund: An investment fund (such as a mutual fund) that automatically adjusts its asset mix as you get closer to your "target date" (usually retirement). It starts more aggressive with lots of stocks when you're young, then gets more conservative with more bonds as you age.

Tenants in common: A way of owning property where each owner has a specific percentage and can leave their share to whomever they want when they die (unlike joint tenants with rights of survivorship). If you're buying property with someone you're not married to, this gives you more control over how your share will be handled after your death.

Term life insurance: Life insurance that covers you for a specific period (such as ten, twenty, or thirty years). If you die during that term, your beneficiaries will be paid. (If you outlive the term, they get nothing, but hey—you're still alive.) It's much cheaper than whole life insurance.

Trustee: The person or institution who manages a trust. They're legally obligated to follow the trust's terms and act in the best interest of the beneficiaries.

Trust fund: A legal entity where someone (the grantor) transfers assets to benefit someone else (the beneficiary), with a third party (the trustee) managing the assets.

UGMA and UTMA accounts: Custodial investment accounts for minors. A Uniform Gifts to Minors Act (UGMA) account can hold cash and investments; a Uniform Transfers to Minors Act (UTMA) account can hold those plus other assets such as real estate. The money is controlled by an adult until the kid reaches the age of majority.

Underwriting: The process where insurance companies assess how risky you are to insure. For life insurance, they'll look at your health history (and maybe even send someone to check your blood pressure); for home insurance, they'll look at things such as the age of your roof, where you live, and whether you have safety measures in place such as security systems and carbon monoxide detectors.

Uninsured/Underinsured motorist coverage: The part of your car insurance that protects you if you're in an accident with someone who either has no insurance or doesn't have enough to cover your damages. It's legally required in many states and a good idea everywhere else.

Valuable articles insurance: Special coverage for your extrafancy possessions, such as engagement rings, art, or collectibles. It usually covers more scenarios than regular homeowner's insurance does and often doesn't have a deductible.

Whole life insurance: Life insurance that covers you for your entire life, with a death benefit plus a cash value component that grows over time. It's much more expensive than term life insurance and is usually pitched as an "investment"—but it's not really a good investment for almost all regular schmegular people, at least, compared to other, more traditional investment vehicles.

Notes

Chapter One: Deinfluencing Your Brain

1. Vanessa Friedman, "How Many Clothes Do I Really Need?," *New York Times*, October 10, 2022, https://www.nytimes.com/2022/10/10/style/clothes-wardrobe-need.html.
2. Naomi Subotnick, "Retail Encyclopedias: The Materials and Making of Sears Roebuck Catalogs," Material Matters, February 13, 2022, https://sites.udel.edu/materialmatters/2022/02/13/retail-encyclopedias-the-materials-and-making-of-sears-roebuck-catalogs.
3. Jan Whitaker, "The History of Department Stores," Department Store History, accessed May 15, 2025, https://www.departmentstorehistory.net.
4. Lydia Saad, "Gallup Vault: Americans Living Beyond Their Means," Gallup, December 15, 2016, https://news.gallup.com/vault/199631/thursday-midday-vault.aspx.
5. Bill Osgerby, "Understanding the 'Jackpot Market': Media, Marketing, and the Rise of the American Teenager," in *The Changing Portrayal of Adolescents in the Media Since 1950* (New York, 2008; online edition, Oxford Academic, April 1, 2010), accessed September 15, 2025, https://doi.org/10.1093/acprof:oso/9780195342956.003.0002.
6. Steve Allen and Robert J. Thompson, "The Late Golden Age," Britannica, https://www.britannica.com/art/television-in-the-United-States/The-late-Golden-Age.

7. Luc Gueriane, "A History of Payments: The Evolution of Credit Cards," Moorwand, March 30, 2021, https://www.moorwand.com/a-history-of-payments-the-evolution-of-credit-cards.
8. Jake Calhoun, "Through the Years: The 1990's and Y2K," Chain Store Guide, October 26, 2023, https://chainstoreguide.com/offthechain/2023/10/years-1990s-y2k.
9. Gaurav Menon, "Starbucks: Gamifying the Coffee Buying Experience," Medium, September 20, 2020, https://medium.com/design-bootcamp/starbucks-gamifying-the-coffee-buying-experience-212acc6b40eb.

Chapter Two: Investing in Yourself

1. Daniel Hamermesh, "Beauty Impacts Hiring, Salaries and Profits, Economist Finds," UT News, August 15, 2011, https://news.utexas.edu/2011/08/15/beauty-impacts-hiring-salaries-and-profits-economist-finds.
2. John Karl Scholz and Kamil Sicinski, "Facial Attractiveness and Lifetime Earnings: Evidence from a Cohort Study," *Review of Economics and Statistics* 97, no. 1 (2015): 14–28, https://doi.org/10.1162/REST_a_00435.
3. Daniel J. Gurney et al., "Dressing Up Posture: The Interactive Effects of Posture and Clothing on Competency Judgements," *British Journal of Psychology* 108, no. 2 (2016): 436–51, https://doi.org/10.1111/bjop.12209.

Chapter Three: Buying a Car

1. Mimi Sheller, "Automotive Emotions: Feeling the Car," Department of Sociology, Lancaster University, May 19, 2003, https://www.lancaster.ac.uk/fass/resources/sociology-online-papers/papers/sheller-automotive-emotions.pdf.
2. Birgitta Gatersleben, "Social-Symbolic and Affective Aspects of Car Ownership and Use," in *International Encyclopedia of Transportation*,

ed. Roger Vickerman (Oxford: Elsevier, 2021), 81–86, https://doi.org/10.1016/B978-0-08-102671-7.10661-X.
3. Katherine Schaeffer, "1 in 10 Americans Rarely or Never Drive a Car," Pew Research Center, November 14, 2024, https://www.pewresearch.org/short-reads/2024/11/14/1-in-10-americans-rarely-or-never-drive-a-car.
4. Sean Tucker, "New Car Prices Started to Inch Up in April," Kelley Blue Book, May 14, 2025, https://www.kbb.com/car-news/new-car-prices-started-to-inch-up-in-april.

Chapter Four: Buying a Home

1. "FHFA Announces Conforming Loan Limit Values for 2025," Federal Housing Finance Agency, November 26, 2024, https://www.fhfa.gov/news/news-release/fhfa-announces-conforming-loan-limit-values-for-2025.

Chapter Five: Marriage and Partnership

1. Wendy D. Manning and Lisa Carlson, "Trends in Cohabitation Prior to Marriage," National Center for Family & Marriage Research, 2021, https://doi.org/10.25035/ncfmr/fp-21-04.

Chapter Six: Kids

1. Aimee Picchi, "Almost 1 in 4 Millennials and Gen Z-ers Say They Won't Have Kids Due to Finances," CBS News, September 10, 2024, https://www.cbsnews.com/news/millennials-gen-z-childless-money-finances-massmutual.
2. Elizabeth Renter, "Study: Would-Be Parents Unprepared for Potential Cost of Raising a Baby," NerdWallet, accessed May 15, 2025, https://www.nerdwallet.com/article/insurance/cost-of-raising-baby.
3. "Interactive: The Hidden Cost of a Failing Child Care System,"

Center for American Progress, June 21, 2016, https://www.americanprogress.org/article/interactive-the-hidden-cost-of-a-failing-child-care-system.
4. Clare Coffey et al., "Time to Care: Unpaid and Underpaid Care Work and the Global Inequality Crisis," Oxfam International, January 2020, https://oxfamilibrary.openrepository.com/bitstream/handle/10546/620928/bp-time-to-care-inequality-200120-en.pdf.
5. "Fertility Statistics by Age," Extend Fertility, accessed May 15, 2025, https://extendfertility.com/your-fertility/fertility-statistics-by-age.
6. Isabel Goddard and Carolina Aragão, "A Growing Share of Americans Say They've Had Fertility Treatments or Know Someone Who Has," Pew Research Center, September 14, 2023, https://www.pewresearch.org/short-reads/2023/09/14/a-growing-share-of-americans-say-theyve-had-fertility-treatments-or-know-someone-who-has.
7. Kristen Cramer, "How Much Does It Cost to Adopt a Child?," TrustedCare, April 8, 2024, https://trustedcare.com/costs/cost-to-adopt-a-child.
8. Juliana Kaplan, "Millennial and Gen Z Parents Are Struggling," Business Insider, November 19, 2023, https://www.businessinsider.com/millennial-gen-z-parents-struggle-lonely-childcare-costs-money-friends-2023-11.
9. Georgia Poyatzis and Gretchen Livingston, "New Data: Childcare Costs Remain an Almost Prohibitive Expense," U.S. Department of Labor, November 19, 2024, https://blog.dol.gov/2024/11/19/new-data-childcare-costs-remain-an-almost-prohibitive-expense.

Chapter Seven: Family and Friends

1. Bill Rainaldi, "New Study Confirms: 20 Percent of Americans over Age 50 Have No Retirement Savings at All," Security Mutual Life, July 9, 2024, https://smlny.com/new-study-confirms-20-percent-of-americans-over-age-50-haveno-retirement-savings-at-all.
2. "How Many Americans Have a Will?," Gallup, June 23, 2021, https://news.gallup.com/poll/351500/how-many-americans-have-will.aspx.
3. "Millennial Pet Owners: Trends and Preferences," Doghop, accessed

May 15, 2025, https://web.archive.org/web/20250421211513/https://doghop.co.uk/millennial-pet-owners.
4. Anna Claire Vollers, "Vets Fret as Private Equity Snaps Up Clinics, Pet Care Companies," Stateline, March 29, 2024, https://stateline.org/2024/03/29/vets-fret-as-private-equity-snaps-up-clinics-pet-care-companies.
5. Michelle Andrews, "How Veterinarians Help Predatory Lenders," WUNC, August 31, 2010, https://www.wunc.org/2010-08-31/how-veterinarians-help-predatory-lenders.

Chapter Eight: Retirement

1. FINRA Investor Education Foundation and CFA Institute, "Gen Z and Investing: Social Media, Crypto, FOMO, and Family," May 2023, https://www.finrafoundation.org/sites/finrafoundation/files/2024-10/Gen-Z-and-Investing.pdf.
2. FINRA Investor Education Foundation and CFA Institute, "7 Myths About Millennials and Investing," 2018, https://www.finrafoundation.org/sites/finrafoundation/files/2024-10/Infographic-7-Myths-About-Millenials-and-Investing_1_0.pdf.
3. Anthony J. Porcelli and Mauricio R. Delgado, "Stress and Decision Making: Effects on Valuation, Learning, and Risk-Taking," *Current Opinion in Behavioral Sciences* 14 (2017): 33–39, https://www.ncbi.nlm.nih.gov/pmc/articles/PMC5201132.
4. Kerry Hannon, "Millennials Likely to Feel Biggest Burden of Fixing Social Security, Report Finds," Yahoo Finance, November 14, 2023, https://finance.yahoo.com/news/millennials-likely-to-feel-biggest-burden-of-fixing-social-security-report-finds-090039636.html.
5. "Fidelity Investments Releases 2024 Retiree Health Care Cost Estimate as Americans Seek Clarity Around Medicare Selection," Fidelity Investments, August 8, 2024, https://newsroom.fidelity.com/pressreleases/fidelity-investments--releases-2024-retiree-health-care-cost-estimate-as-americans-seek-clarity-arou/s/7322cc17-0b90-46c4-ba49-38d6e91c3961.
6. Joseph Coughlin. "Most Boomers Missed This Retirement Strategy

but Millennials Still Have Time," *Forbes*, October 17, 2023, https://www.forbes.com/sites/josephcoughlin/2023/10/17/most-boomers-missed-this-retirement-strategy-but-millennials-still-have-time.

7. Todd Schlanger, "The Global 60/40 Portfolio: Steady as It Goes," Vanguard, October 22, 2024, https://corporate.vanguard.com/content/corporatesite/us/en/corp/articles/global-60-40-portfolio-steady-as-it-goes.html.

8. "Federal, Private Sector Benefits Don't Compare Well Directly, Says Report," FEDweek, June 12, 2024, https://www.fedweek.com/retirement-financial-planning/federal-private-sector-benefits-dont-compare-well-directly-says-report.

9. David Zook, "How Do Retirement Plans for Private Industry and State and Local Government Workers Compare?," *Beyond the Numbers* 12, no. 1 (January 2023), https://www.bls.gov/opub/btn/volume-12/how-do-retirement-plans-for-private-industry-and-state-and-local-government-workers-compare.htm.

Chapter Ten: Insurance

1. Lindsay Bishop, "Average Cost of Renters Insurance," ValuePenguin, accessed July 22, 2025, https://www.valuepenguin.com/average-cost-renters-insurance.

2. Edie Lau, "More States Legislate Pet Insurance," Veterinary Information Network, July 11, 2023, https://news.vin.com/doc/?id=11590030.

Chapter Eleven: Estate Planning

1. "IRS Releases Tax Inflation Adjustments for Tax Year 2025," Internal Revenue Service, October 22, 2024, https://www.irs.gov/newsroom/irs-releases-tax-inflation-adjustments-for-tax-year-2025.

Index

Page numbers in *italics* refer to tables.

A

accessory dwelling units (ADUs), 215–16
accountants, finding, 201
accrued personal time off, using, 135–36
Achieving a Better Life Experience (ABLE), 166
actuaries, 211–12
adjustable-rate mortgage (ARM)
  defined, 259
  financing terms, 91
adoption, 141
advanced care directives (living wills)
  defined, 261
  setting up, 244–46
advertising
  anchoring bias in, 21–22
  beauty standards, gender norms, and, 19–20
  decoy effect in, 22
  diversity and, 24–25
  early television and use of, 15
  emotional appeal by, 18–19
  gamification in, 23–24
  psychological effect of, overview, 17–18
  reciprocity in, 22–23
  social media use of, 27–30
  social proof and, 21
  targeting by, 25–27
advisors, roboadvisors as, 194, 209
aesthetics, spending money on, 50–51
Affordable Care Act, 37
African countries/United Nations psychological experiment, 21

age issues
   aging parents, finances of, 158–62, *161*
   aging parents as beneficiaries, 247
   generational wealth transfer, 197–98 (*see also* estate planning)
   home buying and average buying age, 80 (*see also* home buying)
   intergenerational values differences and, 36
   retirement saving and, 177–79, 185 (*see also* retirement)
aggregator websites, for car buying, 60
amortization
   amortization period, defined, 259–60
   defined, 84, 259
   for refinancing, 92–93
anchoring bias, 21–22
Andre (windfall example), 156–57
anonymity, windfalls and, 201–2
appraisal
   home buying and, 84, 96
   valuable articles insurance and, 224
Ask Dolly app, 206, 247
assets
   asset mix for retirement planning, 194–95
   asset protection trusts, 242
   bequeathing, with estate planning, 246–50
   donating, 251
   estate planning for, 247 (*see also* estate planning)
   homes as illiquid assets, 86–87
   noncash assets as windfalls, 205
assisted living expenses, 182
attorneys
   for estate planning, 237, 239, 244, 250
   windfalls, consulting about, 200, 201
automobiles. *See* car buying; car insurance

B

bandwagon effect, 28–29
banking accounts
   estate planning and bank accounts, 247
   for romantic partners, 111–12, 115–17, 119
   transfer on death provisions, 251
beauty standards, advertising and, 19–20
beneficiaries
   defined, 239, 260
   estate planning and, 239–40, 246–50
   for 529 plans, 146
   for life insurance, 225
big-box stores, 16
Black Friday, 16

bodily injury liability (car insurance), 220
bonuses as compensation, 196–98, 202–5, 206–7
boundaries, for providing monetary help, 160–62, *161*, 163–67
breadwinner role, 138. *See also* homemaking
browser cookies, clearing, 27
budgeting
  helping parents with, 160
  retirement planning and, 186–87
  for weddings, 121
Buffett, Warren, 251
buffet restaurant example, 11–13
building codes, 215
businesses
  homeowner's insurance and, 215–16
  succession planning, 235–36
buyers' remorse, 51–52, 61
buying behavior, understanding, 30–33. *See also* consumerism
buying of cars. *See* car buying
buying of homes. *See* home buying
BuzzFeed, 17, 25, 30, 196, 202

C

cache, clearing, 27
calculators and spreadsheets
  Ask Dolly app for, 206, 247
  for childcare, 138
  Your Rich BFF resources for, 67, 76, 77, 93, 100, 184, 190, 195

California, homeowner's insurance in, 212
capital gains tax, 206
car buying, 57–77
  buying vs. financing vs. leasing, 63–69
  comparison shopping importance, 69–72
  comparison shopping with decision matrix, 72–76, *74, 75, 76*
  consumerism and, 14–15
  home buying and need for car, 94
  lifestyle inflation and, 200
  lifestyle quality and, 55–56, 57–59
  money management to-dos for, 77
  researching, 59–63
  used cars, age of, 72
  used cars, cash for, 64
car insurance
  collision coverage, 220, 260
  comprehensive coverage, 221
  liability coverage, 219–220
  need for, 219
  personal injury/medical payments coverage, 221–22
  uninsured/underinsured motorist coverage, 222, 263–64
cash
  for car buying, 64–65
  cash gifts as problematic, 163–64, *165*

cash (*cont.*)
  donating, 251
  "favors economy" vs. payment, 167–68
  forms of, 64
  loans vs., 165
CASH (Calculate, Account for taxes, Secure it, Hold it), 205–7
cashier's checks, 64
catch-up contributions
  defined, 260
  helping parents with, 160–62, 161
causes, legacy giving to, 251–52
Center for American Progress, 138
certified checks, 64
certified financial planners (CFPs), finding, 206
children, 131–55
  babies and young children, expenses associated with, 133–39
  childcare costs, 132, 142–45
  conversations about, with potential partners, 110
  financial impact of having children, 131–32
  future financial security and stability of, 132–33
  guardianship of, 249
  importance of planning for, 101–2
  investing for, 145–50
  money management to-dos for, 154–55
  reproductive assistance costs, 139–42
  Social Security survivor benefits for, 228–29
  teaching children about money, 151–54
Chinese buffet example, 11–13
CJ the DJ (money education example), 151–52
closing, defined, 85
closing costs
  defined, 85
  financing a home and, 84–85
  for refinancing, 92–93
clothing
  consumerism example, 13–14
  investing in, 44
codependence (financial), dangers of, 111–12
Cofertility, 141–42
collaboration, divorce and, 128
collision coverage
  buying, 220
  defined, 260
commoditized products, insurance as, 231
communicating about money
  about your parents' finances, 158–60
  boundary setting for providing monetary help, 160–62, *161*, 163–67
  with potential life partner, 105–7

with potential life partner, about plans for children, 110
with romantic partner on ongoing basis, 117–18
comparison shopping for cars. *See also* car buying
   with decision matrix, 72–76, 74, 75, 76
   importance of, 69–72
   researching, 59–63
compensation for work. *See* income
comprehensive coverage (car insurance)
   buying, 221
   defined, 260
consumerism. *See also* advertising
   advertising and its psychological effect, 17–27
   advertising and social media, 27–30
   buying according to your values and, 48–53
   deinfluencing your brain about, 11–13, 36
   history of, 13–16
   money management to-dos for, 33–34
   profit as goal of, 16–17
   understanding, for maximizing value, 11–13
   understanding why you buy, 30–33
   windfall precautions about, 197 (*see also* inheritance and windfalls)

contents of home, insurance for, 214, 218–19
convenience, comfort, or consumerism (three C's), 164
convenience, spending money for, 35–36, 45–48
conventional 97 loans, 97–98
co-payments (co-pays), defined, 38
cosigning, 166
Costco, 22–23, 232–33
cost vs. worth, 5, 47
credit
   credit cards, for car buying, 64
   credit cards, for minor children, 150
   credit cards, history of, 15
   credit score, for refinancing, 93
   credit score, levels, 89
   credit score, mortgage application, 95
   debt-to-income (DTI) ratio, 88
   installment plans, 14
cultural values, investing in yourself and, 43
custodial investment accounts
   custodial Roth IRAs, 148–49
   estate planning for, 248
   UGMAs, 147–48, 240, 263
   UTMAs, 147–48, 149, 240, 263
custodial Roth IRA, defined, 260

D

data, advertising industry's use of, 25–27

dating, casual, 107–8
day care. *See* children
De Beers, 20
debt
   car buying and avoiding debt, 57–59 (*see also* car buying)
   debt-to-income (DTI) ratio, 88
   paying down, 207–8
decision-making. *See also* optimizing for value
   about pets and lifestyle, 172
   anchoring bias and, 21–22
   bad decisions by family members, 166–67
   decision matrix, for car buying, 72–76, 74, 75, 76
   decision matrix, for home buying, 94
   decision matrix, spreadsheet, 76
   decoy effect and, 22
   leveraging decisions for growth, 6–7
   power of attorney (POA) for, 242–44
   windfall decision tree, 205–9
decoy effect, 22
deductible
   for car insurance, 220
   defined, 37–38
   strategic planning and, 41
defining the relationship (DTR), for romantic relationships, 108–110. *See also* marriage and partnership

deinfluencing your brain, 11–13, 36. *See also* advertising; consumerism
delta
   defined, 260
   figuring, 46–47
demographics, targeting of, 25–27
dental health and insurance, 40–41
Department of Agriculture (USDA), 98
Department of Labor, US, 142
Department of Veterans Affairs, US, 99
department stores, 14
Dependent Care FSA, 144
depreciation of cars, 65, 66
diamond engagement rings
   consumerism and, 20
   valuable articles insurance for, 222–24, 264
Difference in Conditions (DIC) insurance, 217
direct loans, by government, 98
disability. *See also* estate planning
   Achieving a Better Life Experience (ABLE), 166
   childbirth and, 135, 136
discounts
   for insurance, 232–33
   for mortgage interest rates, 96
District of Columbia (DC), uninsured/underinsured coverage in, 222
diversity, advertising and, 24–25

divorce
　financial expectations for, 124–25, 127–29
　prenuptial agreements and, 124–27
domestic partners, registration for, 120
domestic violence, 111–12
donation programs, egg-freezing treatment, 141–42
donor-advised funds, 252
down payment
　defined, 84
　home buying and options for, 97–99
　saving for, 89–90
downsizing, helping parents with, 162
Downton Abbey (television show), 13
dream vacation question, for potential partners, 108
dressing for success, 44
driving habits, considering, 68
durable power of attorney (POA), 242
dwelling coverage, insurance for, 213–14, 218–19

E

edge cases
　homeowner's insurance and, 217–18
　power of attorney (POA) for, 243

education
　estate planning and financial aid, 248
　home buying and school districts, 94
　mobility through, 58–59
　trusts for, 241
egg-freezing (fertility) treatment, 140, 141–42
ego depletion, 203
email, unsubscribing from marketing emails, 33–34
emergencies
　medical, 40
　pets and, 173
　saving for, 109, 116, 207
emotional appeal
　advertising tactic, 18–19
　emotional purchases and, 60
employment
　accrued personal time off, using, 135–36
　company benefits, Dependent Care FSA, 144
　company benefits, for IVF, 141
　company benefits, for retirement planning, 193
　health insurance through, 37, 39
　paying family members for work, 162
　windfalls and quitting your job, 199–200

employment (*cont.*)
   work from home (WFH) and childcare, 143
   working during retirement, 179–81, 182 (*see also* retirement)
endowment, 4, 255
escrow account
   defined, 85
   mortgage and, 213
estate planning, 235–54
   avoidance of, 236–38
   bequeathing assets with, 246–50
   estate plans, defined, 238, 260
   finding a lawyer for, 237, 239, 244, 250
   futurecasting for, 215
   helping parents with, 158
   legacy giving to causes, 251–52
   living wills/advanced health care directives, 244–46, 261
   money management to-dos for, 252
   power of attorney (POA), 242–44
   protecting generational wealth with, 235–36
   reviewing as life circumstances change, 250
   trust funds, 239–42
   wills (last will and testament), helping parents with, 158
   wills (last will and testament), writing, 244–46
estate tax, 206

executors
   choosing, 245
   defined, 260
Expected Family Contribution (EFC), 248
expenditures, cost vs. worth, 5, 47. *See also* investing in yourself
expenses, reducing, 191–192

F

family/friends, providing financial help to, 156–74
   aging parents' finances, 158–62, *161*
   boundaries around monetary help, 160–62, *161*, 163–67
   favors to friends and, 167–71
   finding balance for, 156–57
   money management to-dos for, 174
   pets and expenses, 171–74
Family Medical Leave Act (FMLA), 136
family members and friends. *See* children; estate planning; family/friends, providing financial help to; marriage and partnership; relationships and finances
Family Opportunity Mortgage (FOM), 162
family planning and reproductive assistance, 139–42
"favors economy," 167–71

278   Index

FDIC, 207
Federal Adoption Tax Credit, 142
Federal Emergency Management
    Agency (FEMA), 216
Federal Housing Authority (FHA),
    97
Fidelity Investments, 188
finances and growing your family.
    See relationships and
    finances
financial aid, applying for, 248. *See
    also* student debt
financial codependence, dangers
    of, 111–12
financial education, for children,
    151–54. *See also* Tu, Vivian
financial house, building,
    55–100
    car buying, 57–77 (*see also* car
        buying)
    home buying, 78–100 (*see also*
        home buying)
    quality of life and impact of,
        55–56
financing and loans. *See also*
    credit
    for cars, 66–67 (*see also* car
        buying)
    cosigning, 166
    financing, defined, 65
    for home buying, financing
        definitions (*see* home buying)
    installment plans, inception of,
        14
    for IVF, 141

making loans to family members,
    163–64, 165
for veterinary bills, 173
529 plans
    defined, 259
    for extended family, 165–66
    investing in, 146–47
Flexible Spending Accounts (FSA)
    defined, 41–42
    for Dependent Care, 144
    HSAs vs., 142
flood damage, insurance for, 216
Florida, retirement and taxes in,
    182
fostering of pets, 173–74
401(k) plans, 185
fuel efficiency, of cars, 75
"fun" spending (splurges), with
    windfalls, 202, 204
FU number
    defined, 260–61
    formula for, 183–84 (*see also*
        retirement)
future financial situation. *See also*
    optimizing for value
    car buying and, 68
    hot and cold cognition, 61–63,
        199
    importance of, 199, 252–55
    legacy and futurecasting, 175
        (*see also* legacy)
    planning and "put your own
        mask on before helping
        others" analogy, 101–2, 198
    planning and windfalls, 209

Index   279

future financial situation (*cont.*)
   retirement planning and, 187–89
   sinking funds and, 88, 89, 116, 172, 174, 204
   of your children, 132–33 (*see also* children)

G

gamification in advertising, 23–24
Gates, Bill, 21, 153–54
gender norms, advertising and, 19–20
generational wealth transfer, 197–98, 235–36. See also estate planning; inheritance and windfalls
"getting financially naked" (conversing about money with potential partner), 105–7. *See also* communicating about money
gifting, as part of estate planning, 248
Giving Pledge, 251
glossary, 259–64
Google, 60, 71
government agencies. *See also* taxes
   Department of Agriculture (USDA), 98

Department of Labor, US, 142
Department of Veterans Affairs, US, 99
FDIC, 207
Federal Emergency Management Agency (FEMA), 216
Federal Housing Authority (FHA), 97
Public Service Loan Forgiveness program and, 193
for Social Security, 184, 185, 228–29
working for, 193
grantors, defined, 239, 261
grants, from US Department of Agriculture (USDA), 98
guardianship, 249

H

health and wellness
   health insurance, for unmarried partners, 120
   health insurance, types of, 37–42, 39–40
   health of pets, 172
   life insurance and, 227–28
   medical expenses in retirement, 185, 187–88
   medical payments coverage (car insurance), 221–22
   mental/emotional health, 45, 128–29, 136, 142

physical wellness as "buying time," 35
spending money to invest in yourself for, 44–45
health care directive. *See* living wills/advanced health care directives
health maintenance organizations (HMOs), defined, 38
Health Savings Accounts (HSAs)
defined, 38, 41, 261
for fertility treatment, 142
retirement and, 185
high-deductible health plans (HDHP), defined, 38
highlight reels, social media and, 29
high-yield savings accounts (HYSAs), 199, 207
home buying, 78–100. *See also* homeowner's insurance
down payment options for, 97–99
expectations and mindset for, 79–83
financing definitions for, 83–85
financing research for, 95–96
financing timeline for, 88–92
helping parents with, 162
house equity and calculating retirement needs, 189
lifestyle quality and, 55–56, 78–79
location of home, 93–94
for married vs. unmarried partners, 119
money management to-dos for, 99–100
motivation for, 85–88
quality of life and impact of, 55–56
readiness for, 87
refinancing and, 92–93
retirement and location choice, 182
security and stability, evaluating for, 78–79
homemaking
economic value of, 138–39
homemaker and breadwinner roles, 138
homeowner's insurance, 213–18
accessory dwelling units (ADUs), 215–16
contents, 214
dwelling coverage, 213–14
flood damage, 216
liability, 214–15
natural disasters, 213, 216–17
renter's insurance and, 218–19
replacement cost, defined, 214
riders for edge cases (water, sewer), 217–18
rising costs of, 211–12
valuable articles insurance and, 223–24
Honey (shopping extension), 60

hot and cold cognition, 61–63, 199
"house poor" status, 88

I

illiquid assets, 86–87
income
    adjusting, for retirement, 192–93
    bonuses as compensation, 196–98, 202–5 (*see also* inheritance and windfalls)
    children and impact on, 134
    children and parental leave, 134–36
    children and taking career hiatus, 136–39
    income tax, 206–7
    from pet services, 173
    proof of, 93
    retirement financial planning and adjusting, 192–93
    35 percent of, car buying rule for, 68
    working as survival mode, 1–3
Industrial Revolution, 14
infertility interventions, 139–42
influencers, social media, 28
inheritance and windfalls, 196–209
    bonuses as compensation, 196–98, 202–5
    decision tree for, 205–9
    inheritance for unmarried partners, 120
    inheritance tax, 206
    limiting inheritance to children, 153–54
    lottery wins, 198, 201
    money management to-dos for, 209
    pitfalls of, 198–202
    retirement planning and, 192–93
    roboadvisors for, 194, 209
    security and stability with, 196–98
    windfall question for potential partners, 108
in-home day cares, 144
insecurity, understanding, 32–33
installment plans, inception of, 14
"instrument," body as, 44–45
insurance, 210–34
    car, 219–22, 260, 263–64
    futurecasting for, 175
    health insurance, 37–42, 39–40
    homeowner's, 213–18
    landlord insurance policies, 215, 218
    life, 224–29
    money management to-dos for, 53–54, 233–34
    as necessary protection, 210–13
    pet, 173, 229–31
    private mortgage insurance (PMI), 97
    renter's, 218–19
    shopping for, 227, 230–33
    short-term disability insurance and childbirth, 135

Social Security survivor benefits and, 228–29
title insurance, 85
valuable articles, 222–24
interest rates
    financing a home and, 84–85
    locking in, 96
    refinancing and, 92–93
    7% rule for paying down debt, 208
    types of, 90–92
internet. *See also* social media
    consumerism and internet inception, 16
    data tracking and advertising, 25–27
intestate, 238
intrauterine insemination (IUI), 140
investing
    childcare as investment, 145
    for children, 145–50
    custodial investment accounts, 147–48
    estate planning and investment accounts, 247
    life insurance vs., 224
    potential future growth, calculating, 187–89
    S&P 500 and, 68
    with windfalls, 208–9
investing in yourself, 35–54
    buying according to your values, 48–53
    money management to-dos for, 53–54
    outsourcing tasks to save time, 35–36, 45–49
    for perception of others and self-perception, 43–45
    understanding health insurance for, 37–42, 39–40
in vitro fertilization (IVF), 140, 141
irrevocable trusts, defined, 241, 261

J

jewelry, valuable articles insurance for, 222–24, 264
Jobs, Steve, 203
Joint Tenants with Right of Survivorship, defined, 119, 261

K

Kelley Blue Book, 72
"kiddie tax," 248

L

laddering, for life insurance, 226–27
landlord (insurance) policies
    defined, 261
    renter's insurance vs., 215, 218

last will and testament (wills). *See also* living wills/advanced health care directives
  helping parents with, 158
  writing, 244–46
lawn care example, 35–36, 46, 47
lawyers
  for estate planning, 237, 239, 244, 250
  windfalls, consulting about, 200, 201
leasing of cars. *See* car buying
legacy, 175–252
  estate planning, 235–54 (*see also* estate planning)
  futurecasting for, 175
  inheritance and windfalls, 196–209 (*see also* inheritance and windfalls)
  insurance and, 210–34 (*see also* insurance)
  retirement and, 177–95 (*see also* retirement)
legal issues. *See also* estate planning; marriage and partnership
  custodial accounts for children, 147–49
  of financial planning for unmarried partners, 118–20
liability coverage
  car insurance, 219–20
  defined, 261

homeowner's insurance, 214–15
renter's insurance, 218–19
life insurance, 224–29
lifestyle
  car buying and quality of, 55–56, 57–59
  decision-making about pets and, 172
  home buying and quality of, 55–56, 78–79
  inflation of, 200
  life stage and home buying decision, 86
  maximizing, 3–6
lifetime earning potential, 137
living wills/advanced health care directives
  defined, 261
  setting up, 244–46
Lizzie McGuire (television show), 13
loans. *See* credit; financing
local government workers, benefits for, 193
location of home, 93–94. *See also* home buying
lock-in rate, 96
lookback periods, 242
lottery wins, 198, 201
lower-down-payment mortgages, 97–99
luxury products/services, motivation and, 49–50

M

mail-order catalogs, 14
marketing. *See* advertising
marketing emails, unsubscribing from, 33–34
marketplace health plans, 37
marriage and partnership, 103–130
   childcare as family expense, 144–45
   choosing partner as most importance financial decision, 103–5
   dating casually, 107–8
   defining the relationship (DTR), 108–10
   divorce and, 124–25, 127–29
   estate planning scenarios of, 249
   financial codependence, dangers of, 111–12
   "getting financially naked" (early conversations about money), 105–7
   importance of planning for, 101–2
   money management to-dos for, 129–30
   moving in together (financially cohabitating), 110–20 (*see also* unmarried romantic partners)
   prenuptial agreements in, 124–27
   relationship cost of career hiatus for childrearing, 138–39
   retirement planning with partner, 182
   Social Security survivor benefits and, 228–29
   wedding planning, 120–23
   windfalls and conversations with, 202
"marry the house but date the rate," 92–93
media literacy, importance of, 17
Medicaid trusts, 242
medical costs. *See* health and wellness
medical power of attorney (POA), 242
mental/emotional health
   fertility treatment and, 142
   investing in, 45
   postpartum depression, 136
   therapy and, 128–29
mileage, of cars, 75
mindset, for home buying. *See* myths of home ownership
minimum viable product (MVP), 52–53
money management to-dos
   car buying, 77
   children, 154–55
   consumerism and, 33–34
   estate planning, 252

money management to-dos (*cont.*)
  helping family and friends, 174
  home buying, 99–100
  inheritance and windfalls, 209
  insurance, 233–34
  for investing in yourself, 53–54
  marriage and partnership, 129–30
  retirement, 195
money-planning strategy. *See* value of money
Monte Carlo simulation, 188
mortgage
  adjustable-rate mortgage (ARM), 91, 259
  defined, 84, 261
  homeowner's insurance required for, 213
  lower-down-payment mortgages, 97–99
  mortgage guarantee, US Department of Agriculture (USDA), 98
  rent as ceiling of cost vs. mortgage as floor, 88–89
  research for, 95–96
motivation. *See also* perception
  for car buying, 67–68
  for home buying, 85–88
myths of home ownership
  average buying age, 80
  home ownership as given, 82
  negative expectations for ownership, 81
  perfection of home and expectations, 80–81

N

nannies and nanny shares, 144
National Flood Insurance Program (NFIP), 216
natural disasters, homeowner's insurance for, 213, 216–17
NerdWallet, 132
net new expense
  childcare as, 143
  defined, 261
  pets as, 173
  retirement and, 181–82, 187
New Hampshire, car insurance and, 219–20
"no-fault" states (car insurance), 221

O

opportunity cost, defined, 68
optimizing for value, 9–54
  consumerism and influence on your spending, 11–34 (*see also* consumerism)
  investing in yourself, 35–54 (*see also* investing in yourself)
  optimization, defined, 11–13
  optimization equilibrium, car buying, 59, 70–72

optimization equilibrium, defined, 71
prioritizing yourself for, 9
organization of financial documents, divorce and, 127–28
"other structures coverage" (insurance), 215
outsourcing tasks, to save time, 35–36, 45–49
Ozempic, 18

P
paid family leave, 135
parental leave, 134–36
payment methods, for cars, 63–69, 75. *See also* car buying
Pedialyte, 18
pension plans, 193
perception
    car buying decisions and, 60–61
    investing in yourself for perception of others and self-perception, 43–45
    motivation for car buying, 67–68
    motivation for home buying, 85–88
    understanding motivation of your spending, 49–50
personal goals, understanding, 32
personal injury/medical payments coverage
    car insurance, 221–22
    defined, 262
pets
    expense and responsibility of, 171–74
    pet insurance, 173, 229–31
philanthropic legacy, 251
physical appearance, investing in yourself for, 43–45
pixels, tracking, 26
planning. *See* financial house, building; future financial situation; legacy; marriage and partnership
portfolio balancing, 194–95
postpartum depression, as disability, 136
power of attorney (POA)
    defined, 262
    setting up, 242–44
    for unmarried partners, 120
preexisting conditions, defined, 262
preferred provider organizations (PPOs), defined, 38
premiums, defined, 37
prenuptial agreements (prenups)
    defined, 262
    using, 124–27
preventive health care, importance of, 40
price, of cars, 75
principal, defined, 84, 262
private mortgage insurance (PMI), 97

private schools (K–12), 146
probate
  defined, 262
  estate planning importance and, 238
professionals, consulting. *See also* estate planning; inheritance and windfalls
  accountants, 201
  certified financial planners (CFPs), 206
  lawyers, 200, 201, 237, 239, 244, 250
profit, as consumerism goal, 16–17
property injury liability (car insurance), 220
protection, insurance for, 210–13. *See also* insurance
psychology of spending. *See also* consumerism
  advertising and, 17–27
  psychology of value and, 30–33
  social media and, 27–30
Public Service Loan Forgiveness program, 193
Puerto Rico, as "no-fault" (car insurance), 221
"put your own mask on before helping others" analogy, 101–2, 198

R

razors, gender norms and, 20
Realtor.com, 93
reciprocation, "favors economy" and, 167–71
refinancing, of homes, 92–93
registries, wedding, 26–27, 123
relationships and finances, 101–74. *See also* legacy
  children, 131–55 (*see also* children)
  family members as childcare providers, 144–45
  family support for reproductive assistance costs, 142
  helping family members and friends (*see* family/friends, providing financial help to)
  importance of planning for, 101–2
  marriage and partnership, 103–30 (*see also* marriage and partnership)
  planning for, 101–2
  power of attorney (POA), choosing, 243 (*see also* estate planning)
  teaching children about money, 151–54
  windfalls and maintaining privacy, 202
renting of home
  buying vs., 78–79, 82–83 (*see also* home buying)
  rent as ceiling of cost vs. mortgage as floor, 88–89
  renter's insurance and, 218–19
replacement cost, defined, 214, 262

research
- for car buying, 59–63 (*see also* car buying)
- of childcare options, 144
- for financing of homes, 95–96
- finding professional consultants, 200, 201, 206, 237, 239, 244, 250
- helping parents with, for assistance programs, 161
- for home location, 93–94
- for mortgage, 95–96 (*see also* home buying)
- shopping for insurance, 227, 230–33

restaurant buffet example, 11–13
retirement, 177–95
- financial need, adjusting, 190–93
- financial need, estimating, 183–90
- futurecasting (planning) for, 175, 254–55
- location choice for, 182
- major expenses, anticipating, 181–82
- money management to-dos for, 195
- partners in, 182
- portfolio balancing and, 194–95
- priorities for, 182–83
- retirement accounts, bequeathing to charities, 240
- retirement accounts and trusts, 240
- retirement account withdrawals, 184–85
- saving early for, 177–79
- Social Security and, 184, 185
- spending time as you like during, 179–81
- windfalls and, 208
- working during, 182

revocable trusts, defined, 241, 262
REVOLVE (website), 60
Rich AF (Tu)
- on budgeting, 186, 192
- on figuring your delta (to net you money), 46–47
- on financial literacy, 17
- goal of, 3
- on health insurance, 38
- on paying down debt, 207–8

"rich," defined, 112
riders, insurance, 217–18
ripped jeans example, 30–31
roboadvisors, 194, 209
Roth IRA
- qualified withdrawals from, 149
- rolling 529 plans into, 146

S

salary, bonuses vs., 196–98, 202–5
saving. *See also* banking accounts; investing
- for childcare, 143–44
- for down payment, 89–90
- for emergencies, 109, 116, 207

saving (*cont.*)
  parents' retirement savings, 158–62, *161*
  for pet expenses, 172
scams, avoiding, 161
security and stability. *See also* lifestyle
  home buying and evaluation of, 78–79
  insurance for, 212–13 (*see also* insurance)
  "rich," defined, 112
  securing windfalls, 207
  with windfalls, 196–98 (*see also* inheritance and windfalls)
self-control, 203
7% rule for paying down debt, 208
sewer damage, homeowner's insurance and, 217–18
shopping. *See* consumerism
short-term disability insurance, 135
sick time, using, 135–36
sinking funds, 88, 89, 116, 172, 174, 204
snail example, 55–56
social media
  account setting, checking, 33
  advertising and, 27–30
  bandwagon effect and, 28–29
  data tracking and, 25–27
  highlight reels of, 29
  influencers, 28
  as money-making entity, 29–30
social proof, 21

Social Security
  retirement planning and, 184, 185
  survivor benefits, 228–29
South Carolina, UTMAs unavailable in, 148
S&P 500, 68
splurges ("fun" spending), with windfalls, 202, 204
Starbucks, 23–24
state benefits, for parental leave, 135
state government workers, benefits for, 193
stay-at-home parents, 136–39
Strategist, 30
STRIP (Savings, Total debt, Retirement, Investments, and Planning), 207–9
student debt
  disclosing to potential partner, 109–10
  Public Service Loan Forgiveness program, 193
subscription services, 16
succession planning, 235–36
surrogacy, 140
survivor benefits, Social Security, 228–29

T

target-date funds
  defined, 263
  using, 194

targeting by advertising, 25–27
tattoo example, 51–52
taxes
  on bonus income, 204–5
  estate planning and, 247, 248
  fertility treatment and, 142
  529 plans and, 146–47
  "kiddie tax," 248
  for married vs. unmarried partners, 119
  retirement and, 182
  windfalls and accounting for, 206–7
teaser rates, 91
Tenants in Common, defined, 119, 263
term life insurance
  buying, 224–29
  defined, 263
35, car buying rule for, 68
three C's (convenience, comfort, or consumerism), 164
time issues. *See also* age issues; future financial situation; retirement
  buyers' remorse and, 51–52
  home buying and financing timeline, 88–92
  outsourcing tasks to save time, 35–36, 45–49
  psychology of value and, 32–33
  retirement and spending time as you like, 179–81
  retirement financial planning and, 190–91
  retirement saving and, 177–79, 185
  valuing your time, 7–8
title insurance, 85
total addressable market (TAM), 18
tracking pixels, 26
transfer on death provisions, 251
trustees, defined, 239, 263
trust funds. *See also* Uniform Gifts to Minors Act (UGMA); Uniform Transfers to Minors Act (UTMA) accounts
  custodial accounts vs., 147
  defined, 263
  types of, 239–42
Tu, Vivian. See also *Rich AF* (Tu)
  Ask Dolly app, 206, 247
  early career of, 17, 25, 30
  early life of, 1–3
  Well Endowed, 3–4, 255
20/4/10, car buying rule for, 68

U

underwriting, defined, 84, 263
Uniform Gifts to Minors Act (UGMA)
  defined, 263
  estate planning and, 240
  UTMAs and, 147–48

Uniform Transfers to Minors Act (UTMA) accounts
  defined, 263
  estate planning and, 240
  flexibility of, 149
  UGMAs and, 147–48
uninsured/underinsured motorist coverage
  buying, 222
  defined, 263–64
unmarried romantic partners
  avoiding financial codependence with, 111–12
  estate planning scenarios of, 249
  home ownership with, 115
  sharing expenses with, 110–17
US Department of Agriculture (USDA) loan, 98
US Department of Labor, 142
US Department of Veterans Affairs, 99
Utah, assisted living expenses in, 182

V

vacation time, using, 135–36
valuable articles
  estate planning for nonmonetary assets, 249
  insurance, buying, 222–24
  insurance, defined, 264

value of money
  maximizing, by understanding consumerism, 11–13 (*see also* consumerism)
  maximizing lifestyle and, 3–6
  money-planning strategy and, 6–8, 48–53
  psychology of, 30–33
  working as survival mode and, 1–3
values (ethics)
  casual dating and conversations about, 107–8
  intergenerational ideas about, 36
Vanguard, 177
Vermont
  assisted living expenses in, 182
  UTMAs unavailable in, 148
veterinarians, choosing, 172–73
vision health insurance, 41

W

water line damage, homeowner's insurance and, 217–18
weddings
  budgeting for, 121
  hidden costs of, 122–23
  planning for, 120–21
  wedding registries, 26–27, 123
  "wedding tax" (markups), 122
Well Endowed (Tu), 3–4, 255
whole life insurance, 224–29, 264

"Why do you buy?" questions, 32–34
wills
  helping parents with, 158
  living wills/advanced health care directives, 244–46, 261
  writing, 244–46
windfall question, for potential partners, 108
windfalls, handling. *See* inheritance and windfalls
Wirecutter, 30
withdrawal, from retirement accounts, 184–85
work from home (WFH), childcare and, 143
working, as survival mode, 1–3. *See also* employment; income
worth vs. cost, 5, 47

Y
Your Rich BFF (Tu)
  for car buying, 67, 76, 77
  goal of, 3
  for home buying/renting/refinancing, 93, 100
  for retirement planning, 184, 190, 195

Z
Zillow, 93